DISCOVERY OF HIDDEN CRIME

Self-Report Delinquency Surveys in
Criminal Policy Context

CLARENDON STUDIES IN CRIMINOLOGY

Published under the auspices of the Institute of Criminology, University of Cambridge; the Mannheim Centre, London School of Economics; and the Centre for Criminological Research, University of Oxford.

General Editor: Lucia Zedner
(*University of Oxford*)

Editors: Manuel Eisner, Alison Liebling, and Per-Olof Wikström
(*University of Cambridge*)

Robert Reiner, Jill Peay, and Tim Newburn
(*London School of Economics*)

Ian Loader and Julian Roberts
(*University of Oxford*)

RECENT TITLES IN THIS SERIES:

Serious Offenders: A Historical Study of Habitual Criminals
Godfrey, Cox, and Farrall

Penal Abolitionism
Ruggiero

Life after Life Imprisonment
Appleton

The Eternal Recurrence of Crime and Control: Essays in Honour of Paul Rock
Downes, Hobbs, and Newburn

Policing the Caribbean: Transnational Security Cooperation in Practice
Bowling

General Editor's Introduction

Clarendon Studies in Criminology aims to provide a forum for outstanding empirical and theoretical work in all aspects of criminology and criminal justice, broadly understood. The Editors welcome submissions from established scholars, as well as excellent PhD work. The *Series* was inaugurated in 1994, with Roger Hood as its first General Editor, following discussions between Oxford University Press and three criminology centres. It is edited under the auspices of these three centres: the Cambridge Institute of Criminology, the Mannheim Centre for Criminology at the London School of Economics, and the Centre for Criminology at the University of Oxford. Each supplies members of the Editorial Board and, in turn, the Series Editor.

Today the crime survey is accepted as an essential empirical instrument in the criminological toolkit—so much so that we rarely consider its origins or evolution. In *Discovery of Hidden Crime* Janne Kivivuori makes good this deficit by charting an absorbing history of the crime survey, its moral and scientific origins, and its development as a means of transcending the limits of official statistics to reveal the field of hidden crime.

A central theme, developed throughout the book, is that the historical promoters of the crime survey were motivated to reveal the relative normality of crime by providing evidence that in some real sense 'we are all criminals'. In their inception the self-report survey was, therefore, no mere data-gathering instrument but a normative tool. It provided the means by which to challenge the dominant metaphor of crime as disease or pathology and, by establishing the normality of crime, to transform the moral matrix in which criminal policy was determined. As Kivivuori observes 'the Nordic pioneers of the hidden crime research were driven by strong moral motives and ideals. Their urge to redescribe (some types of) crime as normal was linked to the goal of humanizing the treatment and sanctioning of offenders and deviants.' By demonstrating the prevalence of petty and occasional offending, the crime survey furnished the data with which to displace the abnormality paradigm, to promote tolerance and to counter punitive tendencies. The early hidden crime survey can thus be understood as an exercise in public criminology, aimed at influencing public understanding of a major social problem.

And yet, as Kivivuori makes clear, this moral imperative had to contend with the social reality of crime, which the survey itself revealed, not least findings of persistent offending by a minority of delinquents and strong links between social class and crime. Moreover, although the intentions of its initiators were humane, the crime survey produced data that came later to contribute to an altogether more punitive turn, fostered by the fact that the ubiquity of crime cast doubt on the possibility of treatment and reform. While depicting these twists and turns, *Discovery of Hidden Crime* charts a fascinating interdisciplinary battle between sociology, criminology, psychiatry and psychology. The hidden crime survey emerged out of interdisciplinary strife and became a major tool in the battle for disciplinary hegemony, not least in skirmishes over the key concepts of abnormality and normality. As such it played a decisive role in the larger history of sociological enquiry.

Long after its birth in the early years of the twentieth century, the hidden crime survey really took off in the middle decades, through the 1930s–1960s. This development also coincided with the detachment of the crime survey from its moral roots in the 'normalization' of crime to become a more neutral tool of empirical scientific enquiry and data gathering. Out of it grew the tools of the trade—the self-report crime survey and, later, the victim survey—which are so central to modern criminological enquiry. By tracing its scientific, intellectual, moral, policy, and political genealogy, *Discovery of Hidden Crime* reveals the modern crime survey to be an altogether more complex and less pre-determined instrument than we might otherwise imagine. Criminology is still too young a discipline to care as much about its past as it should; this book makes a major contribution to rectifying that indifference.

For all these reasons, the Editors welcome this important addition to the *Series*.

Lucia Zedner
University of Oxford
May 2011

Acknowledgements

In contemporary scholarship, it is sometimes fashionable to critique the concept of *influence* in the explanation of scientific developments. In defiance of this, I acknowledge debt to several scholars who influenced this manuscript by offering critical and constructive comments. I am particularly grateful to Research Director Britta Kyvsgaard (Ministry of Justice, Denmark), Professor Petteri Pietikäinen (University of Oulu), Professor Joachim Savelsberg (University of Minnesota), Professor Jukka Savolainen (University of Nebraska), and three anonymous reviewers. Thanks also to Lucy Alexander, Lina Andersson, Petri Danielsson, Emma Hawes, Ilse Lehtimaja, and Julian Roberts for help in various phases and aspects of the project.

A decisive point in the final formation of this book was my stay as a visiting fellow at the Centre for Criminology, University of Oxford. There, I benefitted from the feedback of Professor Ian Loader and the participants of the 'Brown Bag' seminar. I wish to acknowledge the support of the Kone Foundation whose funding made my stay in Oxford possible.

This book is about the scientific, cultural and political origins of the self-report delinquency survey. One chapter of the book is devoted to the first generation of Nordic self-report researchers; from among their ranks, I gratefully acknowledge the kind help of Risto Jaakkola.

Influences additionally come from people who have not been involved in this study. In particular, Josine Junger-Tas (1929–2011), the founder of the *International Self-Report Delinquency Study*, and Kauko Aromaa, who 20 years ago invited me to the world of self-report surveys, influenced the way I see criminological surveys. Last but not least, I am in debt to the research community in which I have worked since then: the Criminological Unit of Finland's National Research Institute of Legal Policy. This book would not have been possible without the support of the NRILP staff and Director Tapio Lappi-Seppälä.

Janne Kivivuori
May 2011

Contents

1. Introduction	**1**
A tool and an idea	1
Confessing society	5
Myopic Panopticon	6
Satire in science	8
2. Key Concepts	**11**
Context of discovery and justification	11
Rhetorical redescription	13
The concept of normalization	15
Interpretive frames constrained but not determined by data	17
Neutralization theory: Offenders as innovating ideologists	18
Public criminology	19
Area and period focus	20
3. Contours of the Battlefield	**22**
The abnormality paradigm	24
The normality paradigm	28
4. Discovery of Hidden Crime	**39**
The view from within: Moral statistics and the official control barrier	40
Per scientiam ad justitiam	46
The white-collar offender as a prototype of the hidden criminal	55
The immediate foreground	62
Sophia Moses Robison	73
Sutherland experiments in the 1930s	78
Harnessing confession: Austin Larimore Porterfield	82
The law-abiding law-breaker	91
Cambridge-Somerville Youth Study	101

x Contents

    Normalization of sex: The Kinsey Report   103
    The Americanization of the hidden crime survey
        in the 1950s   108

5. He Who is Without Sin Among You Let Him Cast the First Stone: Deployment of Hidden Crime Studies in the Nordic Area   **126**
    Twelve-year hunt for the dark number   127
    Normality of crime as a policy frame   129
    Anomalous findings   139
    Additional sources of the normality frame   145
    Later developments in hidden crime data interpretation   150
    Effects of the hidden crime survey   155

6. Concluding Discussion   **160**
    Internal logic: The diffusion of the survey method
        to new topics   161
    Preconditions of survey penetration   163
    From abnormality to flexible normalization   164
    Sociological bid for disciplinary hegemony   166
    The populist soil   167
    Can self-report surveys increase crime?   169
    The changing political uses of crime survey   171
    The expanding circle   175

Bibliography   177
Index   197

The barriers which the criminal law has erected about that field [of criminology] must somehow be razed.
(Thorsten Sellin, 1938)

1
Introduction

In the year 811, Charlemagne, the emperor of the West, ordered a questionnaire to be prepared and sent to local magistrates and magnates. This incident is a candidate for the world's first ever structured survey (Petersen et al, 2004). Many design features of Charlemagne's survey are uncannily modern: the structured and standardized questionnaire with a written sequence of questions, the wish to collect direct information from local people, the 'national' coverage of the survey, and the interest to explore the causes of phenomena.

More astonishing still, it seems that Charlemagne's survey was actually a crime survey. The last years of his reign were affected by civil unrest and disorder (Petersen et al, 2004: 740–1). He was therefore interested to know why many people refused to do service in the border defences. The third question of his survey questionnaire stated that theft was widespread in the realm and asked what caused people to steal one another's property? These topics of inquiry are not far from the interests of modern crime surveys. Unfortunately, the results of Charlemagne's survey largely vanished during the subsequent millennium, save for one short summary that attributes theft causation to problems of authority, poverty and family structure (Petersen et al, 2004: 744). The inquiry additionally concluded that the peasants had become less obedient than they used to be.

A tool and an idea

Today, crime surveys are routinely conducted in most developed nations. Roughly divided, they come in two forms: the victimization survey and the self-report delinquency survey. In victimization surveys, people are asked whether they have been victims of crimes in a certain time period. In self-report crime surveys, people are asked whether they have committed crimes.

Introduction

During recent decades, the self-report crime survey has become extremely widespread in criminological research, especially as applied to juvenile populations. Today, it may be the most frequently used method in the study of crime and delinquency. It facilitated several important theoretical developments in criminology, such as the rise of labelling theory in the 1960s. Since the 1950s, it opened a new frontier for empirical research seeking to establish individual level causes of criminal behaviour. This path has culminated in many prospective longitudinal research programmes, such as the *National Youth Survey*, the *Pittsburgh Youth Study*, the *Rochester Youth Development Study*, and the British *Cambridge Study in Delinquent Development*, which use self-report delinquency methodology in following people's criminality over time (Krohn et al, 2010).

Apart from longitudinal studies exploring individual-level causation of crime, the self-report method has been used in repeated cross-sectional survey designs. These typically aim at describing changes in the prevalence and patterns of crime over time. Often, the goal is to create a statistical alternative to official statistics of recorded crime. Thus, in the US, the first nationally representative self-report delinquency survey, the *National Survey of Youth*, was conducted in 1967 (Williams and Gold, 1972; Krohn et al, 2010). Later on, many European countries launched national indicator systems based on self-report crime surveys (Zauberman, 2009). The Nordic countries were at the forefront of developments in the 1960s, but their current national systems mostly date from the 1990s. Finland and Sweden started national crime survey systems among youths in 1995. Denmark started an important research series in 1979, Norway in 1992.[1] In the UK, the method has been used in the *Offending, Crime and Justice Survey* (Roe and Ashe, 2008). It seems to be a natural phase in the deployment of social science methods that, at some point, international projects are initiated. In self-report delinquency research, such a step was particularly logical because the method allows international comparisons that by-pass problems caused by national differences in criminal law and recording practices. The first such project was the *Nordic Draftee Research Programme* of the Scandinavian countries, launched in 1962 (see Chapter 5). It took 30 years before the

---

[1] For a detailed summary of Nordic self-report indicator systems, see Kivivuori (2007) and Chapter 5. Norway was building a national survey system in the 1960s, but that was discontinued.

is associated with large-scale and macro-cultural transformations of social regulation in developed societies. The source of normative regulation has gradually shifted from pre-defined norms to beliefs about the factual prevalence of human behaviours, that is to statistical normality.

Today, the self-report delinquency survey is a neutral *tool* in the hands of criminologists. Traditionally, the first use of that method has been attributed to Austin L. Porterfield, a Texas-based sociologist who in 1940 conducted the first criminological self-report survey to be published (Porterfield, 1943). This fact will not be refuted here, but a more nuanced and entangled picture will emerge. Another sociologist, Edwin Sutherland, was experimenting with the method before Porterfield, trying to find a way out of the impasse created by criminal statistics and local fact-finding missions that relied on officially published statistics. And there were other anticipations, most notably in the field of sex research. But the history of how the modern sample survey was harnessed to solve the riddle of unrecorded crime is additionally a story of an *idea*. This idea is the idea of hidden crime as a source from which moral lessons can and should be drawn. The most important interpretive frame was the idea that because crime was prevalent, it was also normal. It was argued that since so many 'criminals' were not detected, it was unfair to punish harshly the few who were caught. The self-report or hidden crime survey was born and developed in close interaction with this kind of argumentation.

In the early nineteenth century, there was an explosion of published numbers (statistics). This historical moment has been described variously as a 'statistical movement' (Beirne, 1993: 72), an 'avalanche of numbers' (Hacking, 2002: 2), or a 'torrent of statistics' (Yeo, 2004: 86). Since the 1820s, this torrent was joined by so-called moral statistics, which dealt with morality related matters such as divorce, suicide and crime (von Mayr, 1917). Subsequently, moral statisticians became worried, if not obsessed, with the murky depths that remained outside the statistics. For a long time the main consolation was the 'constant ratio doctrine' stipulating that the ratio of unrecorded incidents to recorded incidents was a constant (Schneider, 1987: 183). But the worry lingered on and never disappeared. In the early twentieth century, pioneering researchers started to explore the survey as a means of asking people directly about crime. The moral and political context of this project went beyond purely scientific interest, and became closely intertwined crucial further step was taken in 1992, when the *International Self-Report Delinquency Survey* (ISRD) began on the initiative of Josine Junger-Tas. In the second ISRD sweep (2006), almost 30 nations participated (Enzmann et al, 2010).

There is a burgeoning literature on the methodology of the self-report crime survey. Extensive reviews of methodological research are available as well (Junger-Tas and Haen Marshall, 1999; Thornberry and Krohn, 2003: Kivivuori, 2007: 17–34; Aebi, 2009: 31–43; Krohn et al, 2010). By and large, this body of research indicates that self-report surveys are a reliable and fairly valid means of measuring the prevalence and incidence of crime especially in juvenile and young adult populations. As such, the self-report delinquency survey has become a standard technique of criminological research.

This book is a *history* of the self-report crime survey as a method of criminological inquiry. Thirty years ago, Hindelang, Hirschi and Weis (1981: 22) described the self-report method as 'dominant' in the study of the causes of crime. More recently, John Laub described the invention of the method as one of the turning points of twentieth century criminology (Laub, 2004: 9), while Krohn et al (2010) describe the rise of self-report surveys as one of the most important methodological developments over the past 100 years. To study why and how some criminologists broke through the official control barrier[2] in crime measurement is therefore warranted from the point of view of methods history and disciplinary self-reflection. However, I believe that the history of the self-report method transgresses the strict boundaries of methods history. First, the method was born in a moral framework, as a means of attacking punitive attitudes towards criminal offenders. Second, it was born of disciplinary tension between sociology and the psy-sciences, as part of sociology's bid for power in the study of crime. To examine the discovery of hidden crime as a measurable entity thus offers an interesting perspective to wider questions of how criminology developed in the tension field between facts and policy goals. Third, the rise of the self-report crime survey

---

[2] By official control barrier I refer to the fact that early criminologists had to rely on official statistics (police, prosecutor, and court statistics, or clinical data associated with such control institutions) in measuring and analysing crime. These statistics are a by-product of governmental control. That this was a problematic 'barrier' was sensed and discussed very early on during the nineteenth century (see Chapter 4).

with the rise of peculiarly modern identity politics and moral crusades against normative regulation.

Confessing society

In self-report delinquency surveys, people are asked about the crimes they have committed. Such surveys have become a regular operation in many Western nations. They represent the modern apogee of the hidden crime research tradition whose rise is charted in this book. To give an example from my own country, Finland: in 2008, 65,000 comprehensive school students, 28,633 high school students, and 19,436 vocational school students responded anonymously to questions about crime they had committed. In a country with a total population of five million, these figures are high, representing roughly 40 per cent of the targeted age cohorts. Much of this avalanche of questioning was related to school health surveys and some to specific delinquency surveys probing deeply into patterns of unrecorded offending. But the figures speak for themselves. You can speak of standardized mass confessions on an industrial scale.

In his history of sexuality, Foucault linked the nineteenth century rise of the *scientia sexualis* to a deep historical background in the Western religious practice of confession. In the high middle ages, confession became a central technique of establishing truth.

> We have since become a singularly confessing society. The confession has spread its effects far and wide. It plays a part in justice, medicine, education, family relationships, and love relations, in the most ordinary affairs of everyday life, and in the most solemn rites; one confesses one's crimes, one's sins, one's thoughts and desires, one's illnesses and troubles; one goes about telling with the greatest precision, whatever is most difficult to tell. [...] Western man has become a confessing animal. (Foucault, 1990 [1976]: 59.)

The huge prevalence of anonymous crime confessions solicited in the self-report surveys is consistent with Foucault's epochal theory. There is reason to search for religious traces and sediments in the history of hidden crime research agenda. One of the earliest pioneers of the method, the German sexologist Magnus Hirschfeld, was inspired by the sacrament of confession, which indicated that people were ready to confess their sins under conditions of anonymity. Initially, Hirschfeld decided to structure his clinical case interviews by using a questionnaire. Some years later he deployed an anonymous self-report crime survey in a non-clinical community sample. In the first years of the twentieth century, this decision resulted in prosecution for libel.

Foucault wrote his history of sexuality in the 1970s, which was the last decade of Freudian cultural hegemony in the West. When speaking about confession, he seems to be constantly and mostly implicitly thinking about the kind of intimate and personal intercourse that characterizes psychoanalytic treatment. The practice of secular confession takes place between the patient and the clinical listener whose presence is overwhelming; 'the one who listened was. . . the master of truth' (Foucault, 1990 [1976]: 66–7). The promise is to heal the confessing individual, and the practice is to specify the unique case history of the person (pp. 42–3). All this is in contrast with the self-report surveys where people are anonymously revealing facts about their sexuality and their crimes to a researcher whom they will never meet and whose name will probably remain unknown to them. Sometimes data are gathered by face-to-face interviews, but the interviewer is probably an assistant, not the researcher and interpreter. The rise of the medicalized confession during the nineteenth century was about creating a detailed case history for the specific individual. The modern anonymous self-report survey is different. As a historical formation, it may nevertheless be associated with the grand shift from repressive-juridical power formation to productive bio-power concerned with how people deviate from the norm of mean.

Myopic Panopticon

Foucault further argued that towards the end of the eighteenth century and at the beginning of the nineteenth century the way power worked shifted from juridical-repressive mode, symbolized by death, to productive mode, symbolized by life. The old juridical system was centred primarily on 'deduction and death', and it was 'utterly incongruous with the new methods of power whose operation is not ensured by right but by technique, not by law but by normalization, not by punishment but by control, methods [. . .] that go beyond the state and its apparatus'. (Foucault, 1990 [1976]: 89.) The rise of the prison during the nineteenth century symptomized this shift. The symbol of the new type of knowledge/power nexus was the 'Panopticon', Bentham's model prison where the guards could see everything. The function of the new carceral power was not to curtail crime but instead to produce a more controlled, differentiated and known type of delinquency (Foucault, 2009 [1976]: 18–23).

The vast reality of hidden crime contradicts the idea that power's ability to see constitutes delinquency. The high prevalence and incidence of offences that are not detected and processed by the police or other authorities of the state would seem to suggest *how blind, or at least seriously myopic, the Panopticon of the modern state is*. Hidden crimes are hidden from the view of the state. The massive prevalence of hidden crime, revealed by the first self-report surveys, must have been a serious embarrassment for the Panopticon. On the other hand, the effort to see hidden crime fits the Foucauldian paradigm. Hidden crime measurement is an attempt by the Panopticon to see better and more accurately. As noted by Yeo, vision is integral to the 'survey', a link revealed by the early synonym of survey, 'surview' (Yeo, 2004: 84). The hidden crime research programme can thus be seen as means of improving the state's capability to see citizen behaviour. Confession was harnessed to serve as the peephole through which power could see what the police, the statistician, and the physician could not see. The self-report method realized the elusive dream of the nineteenth century moral statisticians: To see beyond the official control barrier constituted by the activity of the criminal justice system.

The rise of hidden crime research, especially the self-report method, is undoubtedly connected to the development of state institutions. The early social survey movement, initiated by Charles Booth, relied on the testimony of school board visitors who visited the poorest neighbourhoods of London. They went there because the state had enacted a law on compulsory education. Early sex researchers used student self-report surveys to estimate the prevalence of sexually transmitted diseases. Similarly, the rise of self-report delinquency survey was connected with educational institutions, first universities and then increasingly schools. The gaze of the hidden crime research tradition could penetrate deeply into the social body because state institutions had already shaped and arranged social reality so as to make such capillary penetration possible. The Panopticon had created the institutional archipelago that made systematic hidden crime research possible.

Satire in science

An essential aspect of Foucault's work was a deep mistrust of supposedly emancipatory and humane reforms. For him, any relaxation of repressive-juridical power typically reflected a stratagem of power working productively, not repressively (Foucault, 2009 [1976]). In his power analysis, there seems to be little room for the notion that the efficacy of control is, as such, a variable, or that individual scholars or movements could successfully reduce the grip of power on people. While there is great merit to the power analytical approach, this study takes a different angle. Local battles for decriminalization and normalization of deviance are examined as genuine attempts to loosen the hold of power and as action by individuals in social and historical context. Using a concept borrowed from Skinner (2002), the main actors in these local battles are here described as innovating ideologists who sought to redescribe previously condemned behaviours as, first, highly prevalent, and second, therefore normal. They applied the tool of crime survey to reframe large chunks of the crime problem as statistically normal. This was a means of fighting against repressive legal and social norms. The key innovators were inspired and ignited by moral emotions and guided by rational tactics.

The idea of hidden crime as a measurable entity was born as a part of such local battles. The early discoverers wanted to show that (occasional) crime was extremely widespread and prevalent, and therefore normal. I will call this argument the *normal-because-prevalent argument*. The purpose of the argument was to influence criminal policy: to decriminalize specific offence types and/or to make punishments less severe. This is why the discovery of the hidden crime survey took place in an emotionally charged atmosphere. It was wrong to be harsh on the detected offender because many people committed the same offences but went scot-free. One of the most eloquent expressions of this was the famous 1910 Prison Vote speech of Winston Churchill:

> [Unnecessary imprisonment] is an evil which falls only on the sons of the working classes. The sons of other classes may commit many of the same kind of offences and in boisterous and exuberant moments, whether at Oxford or anywhere else, may do things for which the working classes are committed to prison, although injury may not be inflicted on anyone. (Churchill, 1910: 1347.)

Sentiments like this inspired the quest to measure the full extent of hidden crime. Not only the content, but the style in which Churchill spoke was to recur in the discovery of hidden crime through the decades to follow. Many of the early pioneers of this tradition used satire as their style. The sting in the idea of hidden crime was always that crime was not a specifically lowest class or underclass activity. The middle classes and the upper classes were criminal as well, albeit in a hidden, protected and camouflaged manner. The satire could be demanding in a mild and self-ironic manner, as in Churchill; it could be morose and vengeful, as in Edwin Sutherland's attack against the white-collar offender; or it could be almost hilarious, as in Austin Porterfield's exposure of hypocritical country club elites in rural America. On reading the first generation of hidden crime criminologists, one senses that many of them revelled in the chance to expose the hypocrisy of the middle and upper classes. The tradition of satire has deep roots in antiquity and streams through medieval times in the shape of anti-clerical verse against lusty and worldly prelates and bishops, the 'hidden criminals' of their own day.

The modern hidden crime survey was discovered in the context of this tradition of satirical critique of middle and upper classes. The questionnaire survey could be harnessed to such purposes, and this is why the earliest hidden crime survey studies were closely connected with, and interpreted as representing, studies on white-collar crime. The moral and satirical momentum was at its clearest during the initial discovery phase of the hidden crime survey lasting roughly from 1930 to 1960 (see Figure 4.1 in Chapter 4, p. 121). This 'moral' phase of the discovery reached its apogee with the 1947 publication of the article 'Our Law-Abiding Law-Breakers' by Wallerstein and Wyle. During the 1950s, the self-report method was made more scientific during the overall 'Americanization' of the social sciences. The early moral, carnevalistic spirit was suppressed, even though it lasted longer in the peripheries such as the Nordic countries.

The people who engaged in local moral combat did not have to invent their rhetoric from scratch, at least not all of it. Like radicals and innovators before them, they could resort to a pre-existing cultural lexicon. An important source of moral concepts was the cultural movement of Romanticism. Radical forms of that movement endorsed personal authenticity against social norms. An authentic and genuine person was defined as a nonconformist, an innovator in the face of tradition and law (Berlin, 2000; Taylor, 1991: 63–5). This lexicon was combined with an innovation of the nineteenth century, statistical thinking, producing the normal-because-prevalent argument. This in turn was capitalized by the first generation of sociologists who suggested that crime was socially normal. A related context of the hidden crime tradition was quasi-religious: after all, punitive condemners could be criticized by suggesting that they were sinners as well. While marginally influenced by the Catholic confession, the concept of the hidden crime survey was invented by people stemming from Protestant areas (north Germany, US midwest, Scandinavia).

Today, when conservative and punitivist policies appear to have an upper hand in many nations, it is of some interest to study the movement of crime normalization. Some of the ideas described and examined in this book may sound strange to us. The idea that we are all criminals is a case in point. These may have become 'outworn metaphysical notions' to our punitive minds. But following Skinner, the analysis of such notions is important precisely because they have become strange to us (Skinner, 2002: 88–9). To describe them is almost like encountering an alien culture. There really was a socio-cultural constellation where intellectuals saying such strange things were heard, and even places where their ideas influenced social policies.

2
Key Concepts

Moral statisticians and early criminologists had always been aware that there was such a thing as unrecorded crime or hidden crime, but they despaired that it could not be studied in a controlled and systematic manner. Their research activity was limited to observations based on statistics that were based on the control behaviour of criminal justice officials. They could not conceive how quantitative study could transgress the official control barrier. The story of how hidden crime was discovered is the story of how it was discovered to be a measurable entity: an entity that could be empirically studied by means of a standardized crime survey based on peoples' readiness to confess their crimes anonymously. Arguably, the core innovation was to use the survey as a means of reframing criminal behaviour, quite literally showing it in a new light. In a world that places great value on numbers and quantities, the choice of survey as a tool was a means of rhetorical influence.

Context of discovery and justification

From the purely 'internal' perspective of science, the discovery of hidden crime is an intellectual process in which researchers tackle the problem of unrecorded crime and suggest ways to study its extent by diverse means. This internal process refers to standard forms of documentation and validation in science. From an 'external' perspective, non-scientific cultural and political factors influenced the discovery of hidden crime as a measurable entity. The difference between internal and external factors roughly corresponds to the so-called context distinction in the explanation of scientific discovery.

The context distinction has several versions and I do not intend to discuss their difference. The original formulator of the distinction, the philosopher Hans Reichenbach, illuminated it as follows: *the context of discovery* is how the scientist really arrives at a discovery, and *the context of justification* is how he/she would, or ideally should, convey and justify the finding to other scholars (Schiemann, 2006: 25). Basically, context of discovery refers to the totality of the historical, social and psychological factors that led to the generation of a theory or an empirical description. Context of justification refers to the normative evaluation of the truth of a proposition in terms of coherence, correspondence and the standard criteria of proof.[1] The question, 'What historical, social and political factors led to this discovery?' refers to the context of discovery, while the question, 'Can the scientific statement be justified in accordance with the normal standards of evidence', refers to the context of justification (Hoyningen-Huene, 2006: 122–3).

The context distinction additionally relates to the problem of anachronism in explanation. When the context of validation is examined, the evidence marshalled by the historical discoverer can be judged from the point of view of what we know today about his/her subject matter (more on this, see Nickles, 2006: 160). It is for this reason that Skinner observes that in the historical analysis of scientific beliefs, 'the question of truth may perhaps be of some interest' (Skinner, 2002: 52). In contrast, when the context of discovery is analysed, we should not project our own concerns to the past. In other words, the context of discovery of a scientific statement is fixed and frozen in the historical moment of the discovery. We may never know all of the social, psychological and historical factors that led to the discovery, but they remain the same. In assessing the context of validation, we may judge by 'anachronistic' modern criteria.

Additionally, the context distinction reminds us that the moral factors that inspired the original discovery have no bearing on the truth of the discovery (Nickles, 2006: 176). The discoverer's social and political motives may be commendable or abject to us, but his/her claims about the empirical world, or the methods used to study that world, are not influenced by such motives. Analogously, political goodness or benevolent intentions do not contribute anything to the empirical assessment or verisimilitude of a statement.

---

[1] The concept of 'justification' may be misleading because it may be misunderstood to refer to moral philosophy. The context of *validation* might be a better concept, or the context of *verification*, as used by the US sociologist Charles Lundberg (Steinmetz, 2007: 318).

The context distinction thus controls our natural inclination to infer truth from benevolence, and error from malice.

Rhetorical redescription

One of the main points in this book is that the discovery of hidden crime as a measurable entity was not simply an 'internal' methodological solution to a riddle defined by the limitations of official statistics. The discovery of self-report delinquency survey as a means of quantitative analysis was deeply embedded in an 'external' context of discovery. In studying this context, certain concepts and principles used by Quentin Skinner appear to be useful. According to Skinner, the task of the history of ideas is 'to situate texts we study within such intellectual contexts as enable us to make sense of what their authors were doing in writing them'. The point is not to enter the thoughts of long-dead thinkers, but to 'grasp their concepts, to follow their distinctions, to appreciate their beliefs and, so far as possible, to see things their way' (Skinner, 2002: 3, 47). Skinner underscores the importance of language and concepts because we use rhetoric to claim authority and to arouse emotions (p. 5). Loader and Sparks (2004) have advocated the application of Skinner's principles in the historiography of criminal justice ideas and policies. The challenge of the historiographer is to grasp the styles of reasoning of the actors that comprise the field, to respect the motivations and intentions of agents, and to understand what people are morally doing by saying the things they say (Loader and Sparks, 2004: 11–2).

To use Skinner's concepts, the scholars who came up with the idea of self-report crime survey as a means of measuring hidden crime were *innovating ideologists*[2] using *evaluative-descriptive terms* in the *rhetorical redescription* of behavioural forms. According to Skinner, innovating ideologists typically seek to legitimize a form of social behaviour that is generally agreed to be questionable. They try to convince other people to adopt a novel point of view to some specific behaviour (Skinner, 2002: 148–9).

---

[2] Ideology is here used in a neutral sense; it is not meant to rhetorically redescribe a scientific innovation as dubious or erroneous.

14 Key Concepts

Skinner recommends that analysts of innovating ideologists should focus on evaluative-descriptive terms that are

[W]ords that perform an evaluative as well as descriptive function at the same time. They are used, that is, to describe individual actions and to characterise the motives for which they are performed. Whenever they are used to describe actions, however, they have the effect of evaluating them at the same time. (Skinner, 2002: 148.)

But let us look at the example Skinner used in elucidating the activities of innovating ideologists. He examined the role of ideas in historical causation by re-examining Max Weber's classic case of capitalism in early modern Europe. The early entrepreneurs of large-scale commerce were faced with a special problem. The social and religious standards of their age were such that their conduct appeared to be morally dubious (Skinner, 2002: 147). Moralists were constantly attacking these capitalist pioneers for their 'wicked' and usurious dealings. In this general context, the entrepreneurs had to engage in what Skinner calls rhetorical redescription of their activities in order to describe it as moral. In so doing, these innovating ideologists managed to describe commercial activity as religious. They applied a prevailing moral vocabulary to legitimize a condemned way of life. Societies establish, uphold and alter their moral identity by the rhetorical manipulation of evaluative-descriptive terms (Skinner, 2002: 149, 151).

There is an indirect substantial link between Skinner's core example of early capitalists on one hand and the discovery of hidden crime on the other. As will be shown below (Chapter 4), the first prototype of the hidden criminal was the white-collar offender. The history of the concept goes back to the progressive critique of the 'robber barons' and 'captains of industry' in late nineteenth century America. Some of the early critical impetus came from religious movements. In a way, the conceptual innovation of white-collar criminal is almost like a mirror image of the early modern process that was studied by Weber and Skinner. The early capitalists described their behaviour as moral and religious. The early US sociologists described contemporary capitalists as immoral and irreligious—'criminaloids', in the words of Edward Alsworth Ross.

But how can this kind of labelling be associated with the rhetorical redescription of crime as normal, if white-collar criminals were demonized as immoral monsters? The link to the normality frame was based on two factors. First, the existence of the white-collar offender was anomalous from the point of view of the biological abnormality view of crime. Second, the white-collar criminal showed that crime was not concentrated on the lowest classes. Instead, crime appeared to be more prevalent than hitherto believed and evenly distributed in various social strata. Recent studies suggest that the successful moralization of forms of behaviour may depend on the ability of innovating ideologists to define the behaviour as an underclass phenomenon.[3] Similarly, a successful redescription of previously moralized type of behaviour may depend on the fact that it is no longer seen as a typical lowest class activity. Thus, the discovery of the white-collar offender served the trajectory of crime normalization even though early sociologists vilified him as immoral and deviant.

The concept of normalization

The central evaluative-descriptive term whose deployment is explored in this study is *normal* when used as an attribute of criminal behaviour. The idea of surveying crime directly and quantitatively by means of self-reports was deeply related to the concept of normality in the beginning of the twentieth century (Chapters 4 and 5). Crime was revealed to be a prevalent type of activity in the sense that almost everybody had occasionally committed some crimes. Because of this, petty and occasional crime was redescribed as normal.

At this point it is important to clarify that when using the concept normalization, I am referring to scholarly attempt to redescribe previously condemned behaviours as normal. Thus, the concept of normalization does not here refer to a new modality of power (Foucault, 1990 [1976]: 89; Foucault, 2009 [1976]: 24; Garland, 1985: 239; Beirne, 1993: 68–9, 71; Link 1997). There is a tendency in modern power analysis to regard changes in control institutions as moves to make power ever more efficient. Thus, in discussing new prison policies that aimed at integrating inmates to society, such as paid work, family visitation rights, prison leave, and non-carceral sanctions like community service, Foucault famously described these not as the liberation of prisoners but as the liberation of carceral functions from the prison. Community sanctions

---

[3] Witness the case of smoking, increasingly defined as 'abnormal' behaviour with social locus in the lowest classes (Rozin, 1999; Parker, Williams and Judith, 2002).

'disseminated as far as possible all those forms of power that belonged to the prison, to spread them as a *cancerous growth* beyond the prison walls' (Foucault, 2009 [1976]: 16–17, emphasis added). Clearly, what we have here is a mode of analysis that relies on the cunning of power to make itself felt no matter what happens. Comparing non-custodial sanctions to cancer, Foucault also made it clear that he somehow preferred the older, more visible types of control.

In this study, 'normalization' refers to a project, undertaken by individual historical actors, that *aimed at genuine relaxation of both legal-juridical and therapeutic modalities of power*. The case of the normality paradigm in criminology is particularly interesting because its advocates attacked both repressive and therapeutic forms of power in the criminal justice system. They were against both the old legal-repressive and the new psychologically oriented forms of control. I do not deny that normalization and decriminalization could be profitably analysed as ultimately repressive pseudo-liberalization or as a manifestation of the cunning of power. The choice between 'genuine liberalization' and 'cunning of power' frameworks may be a relatively fundamental question of analytical point of departure, not something that could be decided *exclusively* on the basis of historical and archival data. This is so because there is a sense in which normative social regulation appears to be extremely diehard. The revelation that sexual deviance or minor criminality is very prevalent can liberate people if it results in decriminalization or reduction of official and/or informal control. Yet, at the same time it creates a new kind of normative beacon to which people are drawn: the actual prevalence of behaviours in the population. To put it bluntly, we want to be normal, and feel pressured to conform to majority behavioural patterns (Cialdini, 2005). To simply describe the prevalence of behaviours is therefore not completely devoid of normative content. Yet, cultural normalization of deviance clearly differs from legal-penal regulation and psychiatric and psychological treatment modalities in terms of coercive power. It therefore appears warranted to treat not only the quality but also the quantity of power as a social and historical variable.[4]

---

[4] For alternative discussions of the normalization concept from within the 'genuine liberalization' perspective, see, for example, Wolfensberger and Tullman (1982) and Parker, Williams and Judith (2002).

Interpretive frames constrained but not determined by data

The findings of the first-generation hidden crime survey researchers were not false or erroneous. The redescription of crime as prevalent emerged from the data. In the actual empirical process, the redescriptive potential was decided in several stages. First, the results were influenced by what kind of questions were posed to reality (=to survey respondents). The questions had to include at least something about relatively non-serious crimes in order to yield high prevalence figures. Second, the results were influenced by the analytical procedures that were adopted when the survey data was at hand. For example, the use of sum scales with multiple offence types[5] teased out the high prevalence finding. Third, the interpretation of findings was underdetermined by data in that certain findings were seen as more profound than others. For example, high lifetime prevalence of offending was underscored while the accumulation of offences to a minority of respondents was much less emphasized. The redescription of (certain types of) crime as normal was thus not somehow completely detached from the reality of human behaviour. Interpretation was constrained but not determined by external facts.

Thus, there are real differences in the actual prevalence of behavioural forms. An empirical example may be helpful to elucidate this. Since the 1990s, British drug researchers have used the concept of normalization to describe drugs use by youths in their country (Parker, Williams and Judith, 2002; Measham and Shiner, 2009). The normality concept is based on survey findings indicating the high prevalence of drugs use, being offered drugs, and accepting drugs use. However, since the normalization of deviant behavioural forms is always a 'two-way street', the behaviour could become abnormal again. Indeed, research on drugs normalization has defined that trend as 'a contingent process negotiated by distinct social groups operating in bounded situations' (Measham and Shiner, 2009: 502). One thing that binds the freedom of redescription is the actual prevalence of the behavioural form that is being redescribed as normal. Yet there is some leeway for interpretive work by distinct social groups such as researchers and offenders.

---

[5] Sum scales refer to the practice of survey researchers to ask multiple offending items separately and then summing them up to measure general delinquency.

Neutralization theory: Offenders as innovating ideologists

Criminology has developed its own theory that is concerned about the rhetorical redescription of crime. This is the neutralization theory as originally developed by Gresham Sykes and David Matza in their 1957 article on 'Techniques of Neutralization'. The logic of this theory is rather similar to Skinner's approach to history of ideas, even though the carriers of the ideas are very different: In neutralization theory, the 'innovating ideologists' are the offenders themselves. Neutralization refers to the rhetorical redescription of the offence in a manner that excuses or justifies the act. Sykes and Matza described five techniques of neutralization used by offenders in rhetorically redescribing their acts as not condemnable. These were: denial of responsibility, denial of injury, denial of victim, appeal to higher loyalties, and condemning the condemners. Subsequently, a host of other techniques of rhetorical redescription has been described.

The causal role of neutralizations in the explanation of delinquent behaviour has been a much debated topic in criminology. It is therefore of some interest to see what Skinner, an historian of ideas, has to say about this. He critiques the notion that the moral principles of historical actors are mere ex post facto rationalizations of behaviour that is ultimately or exclusively caused by material interests or forces. He writes: 'It does not follow from the fact that someone's professed principles may be ex post facto rationalisations that those principles play no role in explaining their behaviour.' Even though people may originally use rhetorical redescription or neutralization as an ex post facto justification or excuse, 'they will find themselves committed to behaving in such a way that their actions remain compatible' with the rhetorical constructs employed (Skinner, 2002: 155). It is true that what Skinner has in mind here are activities that are somehow assumed to be recursive, like business, but the general rationalization plus causation argument applies to neutralizing criminal activity as well. The criminologist Travis Hirschi also argued that rhetorical devices used *after* the offence can ease the perpetration of the *next* offence (Hirschi, 1969: 208).

Neutralization theory is not only about explanation of behaviour; it is also about double hermeneutics. Sykes and Matza observed that many delinquents know about sociological and psychological explanations of crime, thus establishing a link between the history of scientific ideas and everyday behaviour. Causal explanations depicting the offender as a pawn of greater social forces was a case in point; there was a clear similarity between delinquent 'denial of responsibility' and sociologically oriented 'humane jurisprudence' (Sykes and Matza, 1957: 667). Today, offenders may use the rhetoric of health or normality to construct their offence as understandable (Kivivuori, 2000). It thus seems that cultural movements can influence both social reactions to deviance and deviance as such. I will return to this observation in the final pages of this study, when the social and behavioural effects of criminological ideas are discussed. At this point, suffice it to say that public criminology has a potential to alter the way society sees its offenders, and how offenders see themselves.

Public criminology

Over the recent decade or so, the question of whether (and how) social scientists can influence the public understanding of social problems has preoccupied many scholars (Haney, 2009). Arguably, the problem is particularly relevant for criminologists whose topic is prone to evoke moral and other emotions (Loader and Sparks, 2011). I will argue in this book that the discovery of hidden crime as a measurable entity was, for the discoverers, an exercise in public criminology. The activity of rhetorically redescribing criminal activity is a form of *public criminology* that seeks to influence the way people see crime and criminals.

Scholars have used slightly varying concepts to catch how criminological theories shape the sensibilities toward crime and criminal policy. Matza (1969: 103) explained how the *commanding imagery* of crime shapes practices. According to Garland, *new ideational materials* are relevant in the explanation of how social regulation changes (Garland, 1985: 73). Skinner used the concept of *cultural lexicon* in a similar function, to describe how a social vocabulary helps to constitute the character of social practices and direct the behaviour of people (Skinner, 2002: 158–74). Loader and Sparks (2004: 13) have examined how theories provide *meanings-in-use* for policy actors. Especially the way hidden delinquency surveys were used in the Nordic countries (Chapter 5) exemplify the structure of feeling or sensibility of the criminological experts and their core beliefs about the proper conduct of government towards crime and crime control (Loader, 2006: 562).

Often crime-related ideational materials come in the shape of core *metaphors* that are used to describe crime. In metaphor, the topic domain (crime) is compared or equated with a vehicle domain (disease, health, normality). The framing of social problems 'depends upon metaphors underlying the stories which generate problem setting and set the direction of problem solving' (Schön, 1980: 255). Thus, the idea that crime could be likened to disease was a core nineteenth century metaphor that paved the way for new types of non-legal social regulation based on 'treatment' and ultimately to the so-called penal-welfare regime (Garland, 1985: 194–5). In contrast, the present study is largely about *a movement that aimed at destroying the disease metaphor of crime*. Instead, crime was likened to health, normality or innovation. The problem setting was radically transformed. Punitive regulation became the problem when contrasted with the massive prevalence of norm-breaking behaviour. The normality of crime is a powerful metaphor-in-use, which was meant to influence the moral matrix in which decisions about criminal policy are made. The success of this effort varied from failure to qualified success, as in the Nordic countries.

Area and period focus

In describing the discovery of hidden crime I will focus on a limited number of strategic and classical studies. Considerable attention is devoted to the early German and Dutch studies conducted by von Römer and Hirschfeld between 1901 and 1904 because the combination of prevalence measurement and normality argumentation was clearly present in them. The main discovery phase, taking place in the US roughly between 1930 and 1960, is described in detail, and again focussing on the moral and policy interpretation of the findings. In Chapter 5, the initial surge of Nordic self-report research during the 1960s is described in its policy context. What happened with the self-report surveys in the US and UK after 1960 is discussed briefly in Chapter 4 as a backdrop and contrast to the Nordic case.

After 1960, the use of the self-report method increased radically in the US and proliferated to other countries. In this study, I will focus on a single proliferation area, the Nordic countries. There are two justifications for this. First, the Nordic beginnings of the self-report delinquency survey repeated the morally embedded 'heroic' phase of the US hidden crime surveyors. Chapter 5 is therefore a case study, or a test, which confirms how the rise of the self-report method was intimately connected with the moral and policy platform of the crime normalization movement. The Nordic discovery phase took place roughly between 1959 and 1974; as such, it was a continuation of the US original discovery phase at a time when self-report surveys had become 'mere tools' in America. Second, after the US discovery of the self-report offender survey, the Nordics were generally identified as belonging to the cutting edge of the field. In the 1960s, when US and UK authors reviewed existing self-report research, practically *all* non-American contributions were Nordic (Sellin and Wolfgang, 1964; West, 1970 [1967]). As late as in 1982, the UK criminologist D. J. West could write that 'most studies of self-reported delinquency have been American or Scandinavian' (West, 1982: 20). Thus, in the 1960s the Nordic countries were one of the two global centres of gravity in the field of self-report delinquency studies.[6]

Already during the 1950s, the self-report method started to detach from its moral context, becoming what it is today: a technical resource in the toolkit of empirically minded criminologists. In this study, only the very beginnings of the 'Americanization' process are discussed as they mark the end of the discovery era that lasted roughly from 1930 to 1960. The concept of Americanization refers to positivism, empiricism, value neutrality and disengagement from politics (Haney, 2009); of course, in the geographical sense, the survey tradition that became 'Americanized' was already American. Thus, instead of being a total or global history of the self-report method, this study focuses on the discovery phase that was engaged in a liberal moral reading of the empirical results. It is possible that the post-1960 deployment of the method in countries outside Scandinavia was unrelated to the moral and policy tradition described in this study.

---

[6] There is a shortage of historical information about the initiation of self-report delinquency surveys in other European countries, but see Zaubermann 2009 where some of the national chapters contain historical references.

3
Contours of the Battlefield

When writing this study, I was struck by the fact that many historians of ideas appear to use metaphors of war and combat to make sense of intellectual activity. Thus, Schön wrote that conflicts about social policy are rarely solved by external facts; instead, they reflect 'stubborn conflicts of perspective, full of potential for violent contention' (Schön, 1980: 256). According to Collins (1998: 1) 'a small number of warring camps is the pattern of intellectual history'. Skinner wrote that the principles governing our moral and political life have generally been disputed in a manner 'more reminiscent of the battlefield than the seminar room' (Skinner, 2002: 7). Loader and Sparks speak of political combat and local struggles that shape the change of crime control (Loader and Sparks, 2006: 16–17). Language is a resource in this battlefield, a potent means of shaping the social world. It makes a difference whether offenders are seen as monsters, terrorists or normal.

In this chapter, I will briefly outline the intellectual context in which the quantitative hidden crime survey was discovered. Needless to say, there is no claim to exhaustive historical description. The purpose is to describe, in an ideal typical manner, the discursive field that constituted an important cultural context of discovery for the invention of the hidden crime survey. After all, the scholars who broke the official control barrier in crime measurement tended to be critics of the abnormality paradigm of criminology. Thus, the purpose of this chapter is much more limited than the goal of describing criminological thought as it is embedded in penal practices. For instance, scholars such as Foucault and Garland have studied effective concepts and social categories that became cemented in the institutional practices of society. Garland (2001: 25) uses the concept of 'working social category' when referring to parts of criminology that actually are 'sanctioned by social authorities and backed up by institutional power'. While penal and regulative practices are important, I delimit the scope of this chapter to the discursive environment in which the hidden crime survey was discovered, leaving aside the practical dimension. However, the concept of the penal-welfare complex needs to be briefly addressed because it can be seen, in an ideal typical sense, as the practical side of the criminological abnormality paradigm.

According to Garland, the penal-welfare complex replaced (in the UK) the preceding Victorian penal regime roughly between the years 1890 and 1914 (Garland, 1985). The Victorian model was more legal, overtly repressive and based on the classical notions of free will and rational capacity to avoid pain and seek pleasure (pp. 6–18). In contrast, the penal-welfare complex saw crime as resulting from social and individual causes: crime was seen as determined behaviour, not chosen action. When the Victorian penal regime was partially replaced by the new complex, emphasis shifted from the offence to the offender (p. 28). Forms of regulation moved from prohibition and retribution to normalization based on individually tailored treatment (p. 29). Thus, the penal regime that ruled from the early twentieth century to the 1980s was based on the notion that crime reflected individual and social pathology. It could therefore be combated by social reform and individual treatment (Garland, 2001: 34–40).

One of the core discursive features of the penal-welfare complex was the distinction between 'the normal' and 'the pathological', with focus upon the latter. Inspired by psychiatric medicine and individual psychology, the regime relied on the epistemic centrality of individual and social risk factors producing pathological behaviour (Garland, 2001: 42–3). According to Garland, the penal-welfare complex used three modes of operation: the normalizing, the corrective and the segregative sectors. By normalizing institutions Garland referred to probation, after-care and licensed supervision that aimed to inculcate norms and make people become 'good citizens'. Normalization 'specified more detailed normative requirements' (Garland, 1985: 239). Garland thus used the concept of normalization to refer to power techniques applied within the intellectual matrix of the abnormality paradigm of crime. The liberal normalization movement, which is the main topic of this study, had different goals: instead of making the individual conform to rules, it suggested that *the rules should conform* to the way individuals were empirically behaving.

The abnormality paradigm

Garland (1985) has identified the rise of criminology in the late nineteenth century as one of the factors buttressing the penal-welfare regime. This criminology was positivist and determinist: it described legal and classical concepts such as free will as outdated superstitions. Late nineteenth century criminology drew inspiration from the prestige of psychiatry and was based on the notions of differentiation and pathology. The differentiation between the individuals who offend and the ones who do not was at the core of criminology. Criminal behaviour was seen as a deviation from the normal as opposed to violation of conventional norms (Garland, 1985: 90–3). In what follows, I will briefly describe the basic ideas of the abnormality paradigm, while additionally observing how that paradigm was never fully stable. Instead, there appears to have taken place a gradual shift towards normalization of the offender.

The 'born criminal'

Lombroso's theory of the 'born criminal' is the paradigmatic exemplar of the abnormality paradigm. That theory consists of five core propositions. First, there are born criminals whose congenital features propel them to enjoy harming others. Second, these born criminals exist because of atavism: they are throwbacks to earlier stages of the evolution of humans. Third, the born criminals are a distinct sub-category of *homo sapiens*. Fourth, this subcategory of humans is recognizable because of several visible bodily and invisible psychological characteristics. Fifth, Lombroso maintained that the criminal man was very different from the normal man (Galassi, 2004: 141–3).

However, Lombroso did not claim that all criminal offenders were born criminals. As a response to his critics, he incorporated additional causal sources of crime to his theory. During his long career, he was continually giving lower estimates about how many of the convicted offenders could be regarded as born criminals (Galassi, 2004: 147). He introduced elements from the degeneration theory (see below) that claimed that environmental factors influenced biological propensities in a criminogenic manner (Gibson, 2006: 145). He also increasingly incorporated sociological factors into his overall theory of crime, ending up with a multiple factor theory of crime (Beirne, 1988: 335). In 1882, Lombroso suggested that crime ultimately reflected the interaction of natural and environmental factors. Education and penal deterrence suppressed natural instincts, while negative environmental factors triggered their full expression. The most important triggers were economic factors, imitation, alcohol consumption, and mental and other diseases (Lombroso, 1882: 113). Perhaps most importantly, Lombroso increasingly downplayed the role of physical stigmata as evidence of inborn criminal tendency and began to focus upon mental qualities. In so doing he began what has been described as the *psychologization of deviance* (Gibson, 2006: 144). Arguably, distance to the idea of outwardly visible stigmata was a step towards the 'normalization' of the criminal.

Lombroso's conception of the criminal offender was not completely ahistorical or non-cultural. While he thought that the born criminal's behaviour was maladaptive in modern society, such behaviour had been adaptive in earlier evolutionary epochs. This notion resembles the position of modern evolutionary criminology (Rafter, 2006: 31–2). The historicity of the born criminal was based on the super-long duration of the evolutionary time scale: The born criminal was abnormal in our time, but he had been normal in the environment of evolutionary adaptation. Indeed, Lombroso went so far as to describe crime as a *notwendige Naturerscheinung*, something necessary and natural (Lombroso, 1882: 113).

Because of Lombroso's receptivity to critical comments, his theoretical edifice became a synthesis of late nineteenth and early twentieth century criminological thought, a kind of multiple factor theory that underlined the importance of individual-level causation but did not neglect sociological causes. In spite of this internal development and his evolutionary normality conception, it cannot be said that Lombroso ended up with a normality conception of crime. The language used by him and his followers underscored the deep divide between the abnormal born criminal and the normal person. The criminal was contrasted with the 'normal man', and the bad with the good (Galassi, 2004: 164; Lombroso, 1882: 117). As a slogan, the 'born criminal' suppressed the underlying diversity of observations, just like the similar slogans of 'shades of grey' and 'crime is normal' did some hundred years later.

Degeneration

Nineteenth century criminology received an important boost from the various kinds of reactions to Lombroso's thought. In continental Europe, so-called degeneration theory of crime was supported by many prominent psychiatrists. They suggested that environmental conditions like the 'nervousness' of city life, and bad habits such as drinking, could cause degeneration in individuals, a propensity that could then run in families. This conception was rational in the context of beliefs that were held as true among many nineteenth century scientists. Degeneration theory was based on Lamarckism that stipulated that acquired characteristics could be inherited, so that degeneracy triggered by bad habits in one generation could pass into the next generation by direct inheritance. For example, a child sired by an alcoholic would have above-average risk of manifesting some type of degeneration simply because of genetic transmission of propensity (Rafter, 1997: 240; Galassi, 2004: 171, 174–5, 179). Environmental triggers implied a further step away from the conception of offender as essentially abnormal and pathological. Degeneration theorists rejected the Lombrosian conception of the born criminal. The difference between born criminals and normal people was seen as a continuum with innumerable variations (Galassi, 2004: 177). Moreover, families could move on this continuum from one generation to the next, in principle to both directions. The notion of continuum and transformation were based on the premise that criminals and normal people shared 'anthropological and typological identity' (Galassi, 2004: 177–8).[1]

Psychologization of abnormality

A third school of the nineteenth century German criminology rejected both the concept of the born criminal and the moral insanity concept of the degeneration theorists. The multi-factor theorists[2] argued that heredity and environment interacted to produce criminal behaviour. Some supporters of this approach deduced their descriptive and explanatory framework from the policy need to rehabilitate offenders. If offenders were to be reformed, they had to be malleable (Galassi, 2004: 189). Environmental factors were underscored from the point of view of criminal policy considerations. Such factors included climate, cultural patterns of

---

[1] The return of the continuum concept in the hidden crime survey tradition is discussed below in the section 'The Americanization of the hidden crime survey in the 1950s' and in Chapter 5.

[2] Galassi (2004) calls this group the combination theorists (*Vereinigungstheorie*), meaning that they saw individual and environmental factors as functioning in combination. I prefer the concept of multi-factor theory.

alcohol consumption, poverty, inequality and opportunity structure (Galassi, 2004: 189, 199–225).

The multi-factor school manifested a step away from the ideal typical abnormality paradigm. In the 1910s, two influential books were published that critiqued the born criminal concept: Charles Goring's *The English Convict* and William Healy's *The Individual Delinquent*. Based on his studies on UK prisoners, Goring concluded that the 'the anthropological monster', that is, the born criminal, 'has no existence in fact' (Goring, 1913: 370). However, Goring remained within the tradition of the abnormality paradigm, suggesting that criminals were born with inferior weight, stature and intellect, and that these features were hereditary (Beirne, 1988: 335–6). Healy, an American psychologist, went slightly further in the psychologization of abnormality. He argued that offenders labelled as born criminals were actually persistent offenders because of environmental influences: there was 'much reason for believing the environment to be a big factor'. Such persons were definitely not normal; instead, they belonged to the 'scientific categories of mental defect and mental aberration' (Healy, 1915: 781–2; see also Snodgrass, 1972: 9–10). Healy also observed that delinquency and abnormality were not a priori the same thing. He was clearly breaking away from the discursive space defined by the biological abnormality paradigm. Feeling the power of metaphor to guide perception, he explicitly noted that 'such statements as "crime is a disease" appear dubiously cheap in the light of our experience' (Healy, 1915: 4). As early as in 1891, the German criminologist Franz von Liszt had declared: 'In most cases, the offender is a human being, just like all of us who have been fortunate enough to be protected from environmental causes of crime' (Galassi, 2004: 231).

The abnormality paradigm was thus internally multi-faceted and pluralistic. At an early stage, it became a multiple factor theory. It contained elements that could have been (and to some extent were) used to argue for the normality of criminal behaviour. Within the abnormality paradigm, the most important change was from criminal anthropology to criminal psychology. Deviance was first conceptualized as something that is externally visible to bare eyes as deformations of the skull, atavistic facial bone structure and other stigmata. Towards the end of the nineteenth century and early twentieth century, deviance was psychologized: it became embedded in the inner qualities and propensities of a person. The change from visible deviance to mental concepts *normalized the criminal body*

(Rafter, 1997: 236) while *leaving the criminal 'soul' deviant*. The concept of psychopath was introduced in the US criminology during the first decades of the twentieth century as an alternative to constitutional and externally visible deviance: the psychopath occupied the grey area 'between normality and abnormality' (Rafter, 1997: 250). The uncoupling of deviance from physical stigmata was an important step in the long road towards crime normalization, because deviance became *physically normal* while remaining *psychologically abnormal*.

Recent scholarship and new translations of nineteenth century classic texts have changed the way we see nineteenth century and early twentieth century criminology today. The view of nineteenth century bio-criminologists as evil monsters has been replaced by a more nuanced view. Few of them were adherents of the simple 'born criminal' concept; perhaps not even Lombroso himself (Beirne, 1988: 335). The dichotomy of abnormality and normality paradigm might be replaced by a conception that sees a gradual shift from extreme abnormality to increasing recognition of normality. However, for heuristic purposes the dichotomy is useful. It is also useful in that the sociologists and criminologists who later attacked the abnormality paradigm wanted to underscore the difference. Thus, in comparative historical perspective it remains true that 'the early specialists in the causes of crime all assumed that criminals are biologically abnormal; that is, they generally subscribed to what is now called the "medical model" or view that criminals are in some sense sick' (Rafter, 2006: 39). Additionally, scholars and practitioners who worked from within the abnormality paradigm shared an important basic feature: they were strongly influenced by the institutions of criminal justice and the police and the normative definitions of crime and deviance such institutions applied in their practices (Becker and Wetzell, 2006: 8). It is probably not a coincidence that people who wanted to break the barrier created by official control-based data were also people who were prone to attack the abnormality paradigm.

The normality paradigm

The formative late nineteenth century debates of sociology and criminology revolved around the twin concepts of normality and abnormality. To some extent, this was a conflict of nations as well as ideas. Many Italians supported the abnormality concept, while the French rallied around the concept of normality. It has been suggested that the decision of Emile Durkheim to defect from abnormality to normality paradigm some time in 1893 was partially motivated by this kind of national rivalry (Hacking, 2002: 174, 176). Durkheim became one of the great advocates of the normality paradigm, and an important source of inspiration for twentieth century movements to normalize deviant behaviours. In what follows, I will first briefly describe some of the intellectual currents that preceded Durkheim, and then discuss some of his thoughts related to normality.

Building blocks of normality

As a description of the intellectual foreground of Durkheim's (and Merton's) normality doctrines, I will briefly discuss three sources: functionalist medicine, Romanticism and statistical fatalism.

(1) Functionalist theory of disease. Before the late nineteenth century breakthroughs in the germ theory of disease, there were two competing notions of disease: ontological and functional. Ontological conception of disease saw pathology as alien to the human body, just like the germ theory posits. The disease enters the human body, causing pathology, and exits the body when health is restored. There was thus a clear qualitative difference between health and pathology. In contrast, the functionalist conception of disease saw normality and pathology, health and disease, as differing poles on a single continuum. There was no fundamental or essential difference. In contrast, the functionalist theory of disease connected the normal and the abnormal, as here described by Canguilhem:

> pathological phenomena found in living organisms are nothing more than quantitative variations, greater of lesser according to corresponding physiological phenomena. Semantically, the pathological is designated as departing from the normal not so much by *a* or *dys* as by *hyper* or *hypo*. While retaining the ontological theory's soothing confidence in the possibility of technical conquest of disease, this approach is far from considering health and sickness as qualitatively opposed, or as forces joined in battle. The need to re-establish continuity in order to gain more knowledge for more effective action is such that the concept of disease would finally vanish. (Canguilhem, 1978 [1943]: 13.)

Deep down the functionalist theory of disease represented the conviction that evil has no independent reality. The functional theory spread from medicine to philosophy, psychology and sociology, where Auguste Comte endorsed it (Canguilhem, 1978 [1943]: 18, 54).

(2) Romanticism was an intellectual and artistic movement that attacked the rationalistic ideals of the Enlightenment between roughly 1760 and 1830 (Berlin, 2000). One of the central themes in Romantic literature and thought was the critique of the recurring and 'boring' aspects of everyday life. While the Romantics rarely used the word, they were fiercely suspicious of the normal features of social interaction. They sensed that the recurring features of everyday life had normative power on people's behaviour (Pikulik, 1979: 17). The prime example of repressive normative regulation was found in the eighteenth century court protocols that were redescribed by Romantics as inauthentic because they suppressed natural emotions. After the French revolution, the critique of inauthentic behaviour was redirected at egalitarian mass society and commercial business activities (Pikulik, 1977: 48–9). Irrespective of the vilified life form, *deviance from social norms was rhetorically redescribed as good*. The incarnations of the good deviant were many: the Romantic artist as a genius, the middle or upper class person who defied social customs in the face of familial opposition, the medieval fool, the madman, and, in many cases, the criminal offender (Berlin, 2000: 14, 18, 51). The celebration of the criminal finally evolved into the 'superhuman' transgressor, the 'great sinner' for whom everything was permitted. While the rationalism of the Enlightenment science was abhorrent to Romantics, the pioneer scientist revealing the secrets of nature could be praised as a positive deviant. In contrast, the negative aspects of normality coalesced in the extremely vilified character type of the philistine (pp. 13, 82–3). The philistine combined outward conformism with potential closet deviance, making him a hypocrite. Celebrating antinormative behaviours, the poet Baudelaire famously addressed his *Les Fleurs du mal* (1857) to the 'hypocrite reader'. Thus, the Romantic movement defined conformist behaviour as the most pressing problem of the age (Pikulik, 1979: 151). This was so because humans were seen to be much like hydraulic machines. There were authentic internal needs that were repressed by external conditions. The German poet Eichendorff argued that if fantasy were to be blocked (*in ihren natürlichen tiefen Lebensströmungen gehemmt*), its energies would find expression in socially disapproved and subversive actions (Pikulik, 1979: 51), a theory that would be later rekindled by Merton.

(3) Statistical fatalism. The French government started to publish crime statistics during the 1820s. This revolutionary change was brought about by Andre-Michel Guerry. Facing his own creation, he was struck by the fixity or stability of the annual number of crimes (Rafter, 2009: 269). Building on Guerry's work, the Belgian astronomer and statistician Adolphe Quetelet wondered whether this stability reflected some kind of mysterious law or determinism. His solution was to explain statistical stability as a property of society instead of individuals. It was possible to study collectives or aggregates without reducing the explanations to the level of individuals (Porter, 2004: 241). Like Guerry, Quetelet testified to his 'surprise at the constancy one finds in the results that present themselves, year after year, in the records of the administration of justice' (Quetelet, 2009 [1835]: 277). The doctrine of statistical law was interpreted as denying the existence of free will. Largely because of this, it retained its ability to shock contemporary observers for decades (Porter, 2004: 241; Beirne, 1993: 78–9).

It should be noted that the doctrine of statistical fatalism cannot be equated with the later prevalence-related normality argument. Nineteenth century statistical fatalism was a 'normal because regular' argument, referring to regularity of incidence. The 'normal because prevalent' argument, referring to high prevalence, was developed later. Aggregate criminality was regular and in that sense normal, but individual offenders were still seen as pathological (Beirne, 1993: 89–90). The idea that crime was inevitable was shocking to many but appealing to scholars who wanted to build a non-psychological science of society.

Durkheim: Crime as normal

The most important of such scholars was Emile Durkheim. He classified crime as among the phenomena of normal sociology. At the most basic level, he argued that crime is normal because it is so common. Moreover, the increase of reported crime testified to its fundamental normality in a given society (Link, 1997: 260). In developing this argument, Durkheim pioneered the basic prevalence-based normality rhetoric that would later form the moral core of the hidden delinquency research programme. But his conception of crime as normality had other elements as well. Crime was not only normal; it was positive. Crime 'is a factor of public health, an integrative element in any healthy society' (Durkheim, 1982

[1895]: 98). Crime was normal because 'it is completely impossible for any society entirely free of it to exist'. To illustrate this thesis, Durkheim offered a famous thought experiment. He asked his readers to imagine a community of saints. Crime would be unknown, but extremely minor transgressions would evoke 'the same scandal as does normal crime' (p. 100). Since there was behavioural variation in every society, there were also statistical deviations from the mean or collective type, and some of these deviations would inevitably be defined as crimes. In his famous words that would echo through the next century, he wrote: 'Thus crime is necessary'. Additionally, Durkheim argued that super-efficient social control might eradicate crime, but such a state would be pathological. Social control must not be too efficient so that 'individual originality' could manifest itself (p. 100). That was the indirect utility of crime. Additionally, some crimes could promote the development of society. As an example, Durkheim referred to Socrates' crimes in ancient Greece. This argument resembled the celebration of the norm-breaking 'genius' of Romanticism.

Durkheim understood his own role as an innovating ideologist trying to redescribe moralized phenomena as neutral or useful. He critiqued 'current ideas' according to which the criminal was 'an utterly unsociable creature, a sort of parasitic element, a foreign, unassimilable body introduced into the bosom of society'. Instead, the criminal 'plays a *normal* role in social life' (p. 102). In footnotes, he was careful to delimit this novel conception of normal crime. He maintained that crime can be a normal phenomenon even though individual offenders might be biologically or psychologically abnormal. Moreover, he disavowed any overt intention to demoralize the crime question. The conception of socially normal crime did not imply that 'we should not abhor' crime (pp. 106–7). Not surprisingly, these caveats did not prevent critics from attacking Durkheim's position. An important critic was Gabriel Tarde, who attacked him on the question of normality. Tarde claimed that Durkheim equated normality with statistical generality; instead, it should be equated with an ideal or perfect condition: 'The normal, then, for a society, is peace in justice and light, the complete extermination of crime, vice, ignorance, poverty, corruption.' (Tarde, 1983 [1895]: 90; on Durkheim's statistical normality, p. 82.) Durkheim responded by repeating his original notion stressing the empirical variation in human behaviour that inevitably resulted in some outliers being defined as criminal. The entire shape of the behavioural distribution was normal, not only the middle part of the continuum (Durkheim, 1983 [1895]: 99). He also repeated the argument that crime could be a source of moral innovation (for a full description of the Durkheim–Tarde debate, see Beirne, 1993: 164–70).

Durkheim's conception of normal crime was an alternative to the abnormality paradigm. He combined the Romantic notion of the norm-breaking innovator with Quetelet-style statistical fatalism to graft a new kind of dynamic idea of crime normality. But why did he do it? At least two related motives can be discerned. First, normalization of crime was part of what has been called Durkheim's 'messianic quest to develop an autonomous sociology' (Beirne, 1993: 164). An important part of this quest was his attack on all kinds of individual-level explanations of human behaviour. Like suicide, crime was a phenomenon that most people would intuitively explain individually and often morally, in the belief that external behaviour reflects inner character. In examining crime and suicide, Durkheim took the battle to the territory of the enemy, showing that the very heartland of individual motivation was moulded by social forces.[3] Secondly, Durkheim believed that true science would inevitably yield results that would shock the sensibilities of the common man. In the first pages of his *Rules of Sociological Method*, he wrote that the 'science of society should cause us *to see things in a different way from the ordinary man*, for the purpose of any science is to make discoveries, and *all such discoveries more or less upset accepted opinions*'. (Durkheim, 1982 [1895]: 31, emphasis added.) The claim that crime is a normal part of a healthy society was meant to evoke uproar, and so it did. It was regarded by contemporaries as offensive (Lukes, 1985: 308).

Merton: Crime as innovation

The idea that true findings are revealed by their capacity to shock the common man, has been a potent force in the history of social thought. Robert K. Merton followed in Durkheim's footsteps in this regard. Many of his important articles suggest that the good

---

[3] It is instructive to note that a century later another emerging criminology paradigm would do the same. Routine activity theorists Ron Clarke and Pat Mayhew (1988) used the 'British gas suicide story' to underscore the striking fact that removing an easy means of suicide reduced the incidence of suicide without any changes in individual motivation.

can produce the bad. The egalitarian principle of equal access to wealth creates criminal motivation; social action has unanticipated consequences; bad things like crime have latent functions for society at large. Merton's writings contain references and allusions to Freud. This may reveal something of his self-understanding as a scientist. He was out to reveal sociological truths that were repressed by the society, just like Freud had exposed truths hidden by individual repression.

The article 'Social Structure and Anomie', published by Merton in 1938, is probably one of the most influential texts ever written in criminology and sociology. The first sentence of that article reads:

There persists a notable tendency in sociological theory to attribute the malfunctioning of social structure primarily to those of man's imperious biological drives which are not adequately restrained by social control. (Merton, 1938: 672.)

This tendency, the abnormality paradigm of deviance causation, was the target of Merton's critique. In the last sentence of the first paragraph he states his mission in positive terms: 'In this paper, it will be suggested that certain phases of social structure generate the circumstances in which infringement of social codes constitutes a "normal" response.' (Merton, 1938: 672.) Merton thus sought to replace the abnormality paradigm by the normality paradigm. When speaking of normality, he did not (at least originally) think of the high prevalence of deviance. Instead, he was referring to causal mechanisms that generate deviance, including crime. In other words, the causal explanation of norm breaking does not require any reference to pathology at the level of individuals. His 1938 article was ambivalent from the point of view of prevalence-based crime normalization, because the main thesis of the article depended on the premise that the lower classes really were more criminal than others. However, in that article, Merton performed possibly the best known act of rhetorical redescription in criminology. He examined crime under the general label of *innovation*. People who wanted to become wealthy but did not have legal means to achieve that goal developed a social motive to innovate an adaptation to this situation. Crime and delinquency were subsumed under this adaptive behaviour, even though other solutions were also possible. Merton later argued that he used the concept of innovation because it was a neutral term that did not communicate any valuation (Merton, in Witmer and Kotinsky, 1955: 45).

Merton was a central figure in the intellectual movement that sought to normalize social deviance. Many of his core concepts are related to the normalization quest. For example, the concept of *latent function* had great potential to normalize activities that evoked condemnation. Merton used the example of political corruption, showing that rackets such as bribery had positive latent functions for society (Merton, 1996a [1949]: 94–5). He disavowed any intent of supporting political corruption, but maintained that any sociological explanation had to consider its latent positive functions. He also wrote that 'frequently the nonconforming minority in a society represents its ultimate values and interests more fully than the conforming majority', echoing Durkheim's prior use of the Socrates argument. While adding that 'this is not a moral judgement' (Merton, 1996b: 100), he was actually trying to demoralize and de-emotionalize social issues: 'Moral evaluations, generally based on [. . .] manifest consequences, tend to be polarized, *in terms of black and white*.[4] But the perception of further (latent) consequences often complicates the picture.' The concept of latent function was meant to combat 'naïve moral judgements' (Merton, 1996a [1949]: 94; see also Matza, 1969: 55–8). Clearly his use of concepts such as latent function and innovation in the analysis of crime are good examples of rhetorical redescription. Latent functionality belongs to the family of concepts that simultaneously describe and evaluate an activity. Thus, Merton was an innovating ideologist when he redescribed crime as *innovative* response to structural strain and sometimes *latently functional* for society at large.

It is another question to what extent he succeeded in changing the cultural lexicon of Western societies. Matza (1969: 58) claims that except among a few thousand sociologists, functionalism passed unnoticed. But Gouldner testified that when Merton published his groundbreaking work, it was a '*liberative* work for those who lived with it as part of a living culture' (Gouldner, 1973). Perhaps it is no small accomplishment to influence how a few thousand sociologists see the world. Be that as it may, Merton himself observed the success of the normalcy paradigm. The change can be noted by comparing the various versions of the 'Social structure

---

[4] Later hidden crime researchers attacked the 'black and white' conception and offered their new metaphors of 'shades of grey' and 'normality' to replace it (see Chapter 5).

and anomie' article. The original 1938 article began with the words, *'there persists* a notable tendency in sociological theory' to attribute social problems to man's biological drives. In later editions, he wrote that *'until recently, and all the more notably before then, one could speak of a marked tendency'* in both psychology and sociology to attribute social problems to man's biological drives (Merton, 1968 [1938]: 185, emphasis added). Clearly he had observed the success of the normality paradigm during the intervening years. The two or three decades immediately following the Second World War were the climax of the normalization quest.

Merton's decision to redescribe crime as innovation connected him to the Romantic tradition. He underscored the normality of crime causation by using the hydraulic notion of human motivation. When a motive, like the wish to be rich, was repressed by social conditions, its pressure sought alternative outlets, like innovation, including crime. Anomie could *'release energies* that led to repudiation of norms' (Merton, in Witmer and Kotinsky, 1955: 67, emphasis added). Recall how the Romantic poet Eichendorff saw subversion as an outlet for repressed needs. The two outlets mentioned by Eichendorff, zealotry (*Schwärmerei*) and political subversion, are also included in Merton's theory. They sprang from the similar malfunction of the hydraulic machine as crime did, but in them the deviant energy was differently expressed.[5]

In the 1980s, when interviewed by Francis Cullen and Steven Messner, Merton reflected on his relationship to abnormality paradigm. He denied ever having taken 'the polar position that if you're a sociologist, you dare not slip into considering questions of psychological process'. However, he admitted that 'there is a great tendency in the Durkheimian tradition to do just that, because Durkheim [. . .] was fighting entrenched groups of psychologists and social psychologists who were questioning the intellectual legitimacy of sociology' (Merton as cited in Cullen and Messner, 2007: 21). As it happens, back in the 1950s Merton himself had been guarding the frontiers of sociology against encroachments by psychiatrists. In this task, he had found self-report delinquency

---

[5] Merton was not the only sociologist who used the hydraulic framework. The civilization theory of Norbert Elias, often used in criminological research, was also based on the romantic-hydraulic notion of human motivation (Kivivuori, Savolainen and Danielsson, forthcoming).

surveys quite useful (see section 'The law-abiding law-breaker' below).

Attack against the social pathologists

Merton was not alone in mounting an attack against the pathology paradigm. In this respect, an equally important broadside was delivered by C. Wright Mills in his 1943 article 'The Professional Ideology of Social Pathologists'. In this classic piece of intellectual debunking, Mills analysed 24 sociology textbooks and tore them apart. According to Mills, one of the cardinal sins of the textbooks of the 'social pathologists' was that they took existing social norms as given. Norm-breaking behaviour was described as disorganization. The textbook authors were typically from rural origins and were inclined to describe urban phenomena as deviant. They explained deviance by biological impulses and 'paste-pot eclectic psychology'. A comprehensive problematization was 'blocked by biological theory of social deviation' (Mills, 1943: 169.) Thus, Mills' attack against the social pathologists was part of his general critique of biological conceptions of human nature, especially as applied by the philosopher John Dewey (Tilman, 1984: 155–8). The critique of biological causation was also related to a critique of the so-called multiple factor approach to crime. Mills wrote that multiple factor theory was dangerous because it diverted social attention from attempts to change the status quo by way of a 'total structural consideration' (Mills, 1943: 172; see also Sutherland, 1945). This argument did not address the *truth* of the multiple factor approach; instead, Mills suggested that the approach inspired the wrong kind of political mentality. Deep down, the critiques of psychology, biology, and multiple factor approach were all directed against the abnormality paradigm of deviant behaviour. The term 'social pathologists' referred to scholars who regarded deviance as pathology.

Two years later, in 1945, Edwin Sutherland joined in the attack against social pathologists in his article 'Social Pathology'. Like Mills, he underscored the relativity, and hence the social normality, of deviance, including crime. Sutherland pressed this point, often using a satirical style that puts the behaviour of the 'law-abiding people' into perspective. When a community was disorganized in terms of crime, some groups in the community were organized for crime while others were organized against crime; there was no immanent pathology in either of these groups (p. 431). Therefore, crime could be taken as a problem, but 'the problem may equally well be the behaviour of a crime commission' (p. 433). Sutherland further cited approvingly Lester Ward's dictum that criminals are the geniuses of the slums. The ultimate conclusion to be drawn from this was the need to redescribe specific behaviours: 'Because of the absolutistic connotations of the term "pathology", it is not an appropriate designation for these relativistic phenomena.' (Sutherland, 1945: 431.) Scholars like Mills and Sutherland were primed to see the relativity of social norms by the Boasian culturalist paradigm that had taken over sociology during the 1920s (Camic, 2007: 230). From this point of view, the 'social pathologist' was someone who did not appreciate that abnormality was socially and culturally constructed, and could therefore be deconstructed by cultural redescription as ideological innovation.

Interestingly, in arguing against the social pathologists, Mills referred to the prevalence of deviant behaviour in urban areas. He observed that many 'deviations' examined by social pathologists were so prevalent in the city that they were in fact statistically normal phenomena (Mills, 1943: 174). Moreover, he noted that some of the problems caused by norms might be solved by *changing the norms*, not people's behaviour. These thoughts were highly suggestive and even prescient of how self-report delinquency studies and sex survey studies were later motivated and used: if deviations were very prevalent, they were factually normal. The problem setting was thus radically transformed. Petty and occasional crime was not the problem; wasting time and money to suppress it was. In the next chapter, I describe how the discovery of hidden crime as a measurable entity was deeply embedded in local battles to abolish outdated social and legal regulation. Additionally, the discovery of hidden crime was embedded in the disciplinary battle of sociology to achieve hegemony over criminology.

4
Discovery of Hidden Crime

In 1941, the Texan sociologist Austin L. Porterfield published a book titled *Creative Factors in Scientific Research*. In the introduction, he wrote how the individual scientist, while influenced by history, imaginatively anticipates some aspects of the evolving future in his attempts at discovery (Porterfield, 1941: 6). In the book itself, there is very little about criminology, and nothing there suggests that Porterfield was struggling with his own attempts at discovery. However, at the same time he must have been finalizing *Creative Factors*, in 1940, he did something that secured him a lasting fame in the annals of criminology: he conducted the first criminological self-report delinquency survey. The findings were published in *American Journal of Sociology* as the article 'Delinquency and Its Outcome in Court and College' (1943), a characteristically satirical title for the discoverer of the hidden crime survey.

If someone were to ask me, when and by whom the self-report delinquency survey was invented, I would name Porterfield and the year 1940. Yet, perhaps like most discoveries, it appears that the self-report delinquency survey was invented more than once and by several scholars. The whole process of coming up with the idea of a confession-based but standardized survey was collective and complex. In his book *Creative Factors in Scientific Research*, Porterfield himself acknowledged and examined the cultural and social embeddedness of individual scholars and their work. True to this insight, in this chapter I will navigate towards Porterfield's discovery as if going through a series of concentric circles, from the broad cultural contexts of discovery to its immediate foreground, and then to the discovery itself. In following this trail, it is a good idea to look at Figure 4.1 below, p. 121, which schematically shows how the invention of the self-report survey reflected factors both internal and external to science.

The view from within: Moral statistics and the official control barrier

In the systematic study of crime, the problem of hidden crime was born exactly the same time as early moral statisticians started using crime statistics. France was the first nation to produce and publish official crime statistics during the 1820s. This development was a part of the great surge of officially published statistics, described as an 'avalanche of numbers' and a 'torrent of statistics' (Hacking, 2002; Yeo, 2004). The first moral statisticians, like Guerry and Quetelet, were aware of the problem of undetected and unrecorded offences. For decades, many scholars were satisfied to cite Quetelet's *constant ratio doctrine*, which stated that the ratio of hidden crime to known crime was stable (Schneider, 1987: 183; Beirne, 1993: 80). Therefore, official statistics were a valid proxy for total crime. From the internal perspective of scientific development, the critique of the constant ratio doctrine initiated the process that led to the discovery of hidden crime as a statistically measurable entity.

When he started to analyse the newly created French criminal statistics in the late 1820s, Adolphe Quetelet formulated the famous constant ratio doctrine. In his view, any scientific analysis of crime statistics must assume 'a relationship nearly invariable between offences known and judged and the unknown sum total of offences committed' (Beirne, 1993: 80). It is open to question how seriously the constant ratio doctrine was ever taken, or how long it was taken seriously. Indeed, Quetelet himself came up with an impressive list of auxiliary assumptions upon which the constant ratio rested: law enforcement integrity, offender capacity to avoid detection, reporting propensity, and knowledge about the law among victims.[1] The nineteenth century moral statisticians thus knew that criminal statistics of recorded crimes rested on a shaky foundation: the likelihood of a criminal offence becoming known to the police. This in turn depended on factors such as police competence and people's propensity to report an offence to authorities. This last mechanism was discussed by German-speaking criminologists as *kriminelle Reizbarkeit*, the 'crime-related irritability' of the people (Aschaffenburg, 1903: 7). The concept referred to how easily crimes irritated or aroused people to report them to

---

[1] This list is a 'modernized' version of factors listed by Quetelet (Beirne, 1993: 80).

the police. Indeed, Georg von Mayr explicitly stated that modern moral statisticians did not subscribe to Quetelet's constant ratio doctrine. They knew that there was geographic, temporal and social class related variation in people's propensity to report crimes to the police (von Mayr, 1917: 414, 418). In the US, the inadequacy of the official statistics of crime was similarly known and discussed at length (Sutherland, 1924: 31–61). In the late 1920s, the Nordic expatriate criminologist Thorsten Sellin denied the constant ratio doctrine, a statement he made nearly a hundred years after the birth of moral statistics on crime (Sellin, 1928: 53).

European moral statisticians thus knew the problem of unrecorded crimes and discussed it in some detail by using concepts like constant ratio and criminal irritability. On reading the writings of moral statisticians during the first decades of the twentieth century, one gets the feeling that they were themselves *irritated* by the fact that they could not by-pass official statistics as a measure of crime. I think it is warranted to speak of an *official control barrier* in crime measurement, a pervasive sense that the field of moral statistics could not bloom unless that barrier could be somehow broken. It may not be altogether wrong to compare that barrier with Heisenberg's uncertainty principle in physics: at least on the subjective level, the official control barrier must have seemed like an insurmountable limit to empirical observation. In any case, there was agreement on what constituted a central problem. Frustrated claims that the official control barrier could never be crossed were common. In Germany, von Mayr could not imagine any way to transcend the realm of official statistics. 'The inclusion of real criminality to statistics is out of the question', he wrote (von Mayr, 1917: 414). In the US, similar statements were made (Mayo-Smith, 1895: 261; Sellin, 1928: 53; Sutherland and Gehlke, 1933: 1123). Scandinavian scholars similarly commented on the 'momentous scientific debate' about the official control barrier (Verkko, 1930; Ekelund, 1932).

Shigema Oba and the dark figure of crime

In the moral statistics era from the 1820s to 1930s, the notion of unrecorded offences was discussed under multiple labels. It was sometimes labelled real, unpunished or even masked criminality (Sellin, 1937: 71–2). One of the most popular concepts was the dark figure (*Dunkelziffer*), coined by the Japanese prosecutor Shigema Oba in his 1908 dissertation in Germany (Oba, 1908: 27–8). Oba belongs to the tradition of German moral statistics. He won a permanent place in the footnotes of criminology because of his conceptual innovation, and sometimes his errors of translation from English to German are briefly discussed.

What was Oba doing when he raised the question of hidden crime? The general topic of his thesis was the so-called incorrigible offender. But the immediate context where Oba examines undetected offences, and introduces the concept of *Dunkelziffer*, is a discussion of general and special deterrence. He points out that because of the enormity of hidden crime, deterrence cannot function as effectively as is often believed (Oba, 1908: 27, 29). In other words, so many offenders 'get away with it', that they cannot entertain any illusions about the efficacy of the police and the courts. Oba also connects the discussion of undetected cases to cases that are known to the police but for some reason fail to reach the courts and the sentencing phase. Towards the end of his dissertation, he calls for strong measures in the fight against 'generally dangerous' offences such as theft, and refers to the vast extent of hidden thefts (Oba, 1908: 73–4).

Oba was attacking the reform movement of the German penal law that sought to replace the classical proportionality of punishment by individually tailored treatment and preventive incapacitation. In some sense, he was building a case against the introduction of the penal-welfare regime (Garland, 1985), which was just then being built on notions of individually tailored treatment and rehabilitation. He critiqued the idea that penal sanctions could be based on risk assessments concerning the convict's likely future behaviour (Oba, 1908: 33). He sided with the critics of the abnormality paradigm, denying the existence of the life-course persistent 'incurable' or 'incorrigible' offender. Instead, he underscored the importance of environmental causation of crime, pointing out that in dire circumstances *every person commits occasional crimes* (Oba, 1908: 34). Oba's dissertation is not a very coherent study, but there are uncanny resemblances to later developments. For example, many scholars who would later use the hidden crime survey were similarly opposed to 'treatment ideology' and the abnormality paradigm of crime.[2]

---

[2] See sections on Sutherland and James Wallerstein below, and Chapter 5 on Nordic developments in the 1960s.

Moving towards the offence

The discipline of moral statistics was thus never completely stable or retrograde. There was a more or less constant debate between the *institutionalists* and the *realists* (Biderman and Reiss, 1967). The institutionalists supported the use of court statistics because, in their view, police statistics of both ascertained and reported crimes included a huge number of non-crimes. The institutionalist position was thus juristic in nature: since people were innocent until proven guilty, police and prosecutor statistics were useless as indices of crime. In contrast, the realists advocated the use of police statistics because that source was believed to be more inclusive of all crimes. During the century spanning the 'avalanche of published numbers' in the 1820s and the creation of the US Uniform Crime Reports in 1929, the realist position gradually gained the upper hand in this schism over proper ways to measure crime. The shift from court statistics to police statistics meant that the approved measure of crime slowly migrated backwards in time, from the end of the judicial process (conviction) towards its ultimate source (the criminal offence). This migration of acceptable crime data source probably reflected the increasing prestige and professionalism of the police. But it additionally reflected the frustration felt by moral statisticians about the stubbornness of the official control barrier. They were drawn towards the offence as the ultimate data source of any quantitative analyst of crime.

Thorsten Sellin was a criminologist of Scandinavian origin[3] who made his career in the US. In the late 1920s and early 1930s, he critiqued the use of official statistics as a measure of criminal behaviour. In a way, he is a transitional figure between European moral statistics and the US criminological tradition that some years later broke the official control barrier in empirical criminology. In critiquing official criminal justice statistics as a measure of crime he built on the work of European scholars such as von Mayr, Tarde and Verkko who had critiqued the constant ratio doctrine (Sellin, 1931–32: 337–8; Sellin, 1937: 66–72). In the 1931 article 'The Basis of a Crime Index' he formulated the principle that is still called Sellin's law: 'Due to a number of variable elements represented by changes in administrative policies and efficiency, the value of a crime rate for index purposes decreases as the distance

---

[3] Born in Sweden in 1897, Sellin emigrated to Canada in 1913 but made his professional career in the US (Wolf, 1994).

from the crime itself in terms of procedure increases'. (Sellin, 1931–32: 346; Sellin, 1937: 74.) He then concluded that crimes known to the police were most likely to furnish a good basis of crime index. Sellin's law represents a movement down the institutional ladder: prison and court statistics were worse than prosecutor statistics, which in turn were worse than police statistics. Commenting on Sellin's paper, Edwin Sutherland had suggested that this should be taken to the logical conclusion of using arrest rates instead of police records of ascertained crimes (Sellin, 1931–32: 348–9; see also Sutherland, 1924: 35–7). Sutherland thus prompted his colleague to move further towards the criminal incident as a basis of a crime index. However, Sellin remained spellbound by official statistics while acutely sensing them as a constraint. His 1938 book *Culture Conflict and Crime* is an eloquent testimony of how criminologists experienced the official control barrier as an iron cage limiting their vision, and as a source of an internal crisis. Sellin variously described law-based measures as *shackles* forged by the criminal law, and as *barriers restraining*, *frustrating* and *handicapping* criminology as a science (Sellin, 1938: 23–4, 55, 57). At the time Sellin was writing these words, Sutherland had already reconnoitred beyond the official control barrier by experimenting with student self-reports (see section 'Sutherland experiments in the 1930s' below).

There were at least two contextual reasons why Sellin distrusted official crime statistics. *First*, he observed that the belief in the 'Negro's higher criminality' was based on the apparent instead of the real criminality of the African Americans. In his view, the differential treatment of African Americans by the criminal justice system was bound to create 'a profound distrust of official records in general' (Sellin, 1928: 54). Pending better data sources, racial theories of inferiority should be doubted (p. 64). *Second*, writing at the time of unprecedented legislative activity, Sellin observed the 'enormous increase of the scope of federal law' (Sellin, 1937: 15). More and more types of behaviour were being criminalized, and this was reflected in the official statistics of recorded crimes. Much of this legislative activity was related to the progressive era of US politics, including the 1920–33 prohibition of alcohol (Nugent, 2010).

As it happens, Finland also experimented with the prohibition of alcohol from 1919 to 1932. During that period, the Finnish criminologist Veli Verkko used the geographical variability of prohibition enforcement to underscore the problems of using official statistics as a basis of crime index. Prohibition was a piece of legislation to which people responded very differently in different parts of Finland, a case in point for a criminologist critiquing the constant ratio doctrine. Criminal justice statistics were about control and its administration, not about human behaviour. Legislative activism thus highlighted the problems involved in using official control-based statistics as measures of crime. In these analyses Verkko formulated principles that are close to what are today better remembered as 'Sellin's law' (see Verkko, 1930: 98).

Non-survey responses to the hidden crime riddle

Various methods of assessing the extent of unrecorded crimes were tried. At the most rudimentary level, these could be based on guesses by experienced police officers (Heindl, 1927: 220–1). Stories were told about detected offenders who proudly confessed a huge number of undetected offences. If multiplied by the number of detected offenders, an estimate on the total number offences resulted; the assumption was that all offenders, but not all offences, were detected (Meyer, 1941: 77–8). Additionally, information from philanthropic services, medical sources, insurance companies, banking associations and private firms were used to estimate unrecorded crimes (von Mayr, 1917: 414–5; Sutherland, 1924: 37–42; Meyer, 1941). This work continued surprisingly long and overlapped for at least two decades with the era of standardized self-report delinquency survey. It was sometimes characterized by anecdotal compilation of detached pieces of information from various sources, including police folklore (see, for example, von Hentig, 1964; also Sellin and Wolfgang, 1964: 37–9; Popitz, 1968).

The British tackled the problem of unrecorded crime by means of their national Mass Observation project which relied on direct observation, sometimes in combination with various proxy and self reports. Published in 1949, the *Report on Juvenile Delinquency* by H. D. Willcock relied on the standard Mass Observation method of collecting reports by various kinds of observers on the lives and exploits of juveniles. The third chapter of Willcock's report recounted anecdotal evidence that so-called respectable people frequently engaged in petty offending (Willcock, 1949: 31–6). Willcock was impressed about the small difference 'between them and us' but acknowledged the trivial nature of the crimes committed by the respectable people (pp. 34–5). The Mass Observation approach seems to have been a rather unsystematic and non-standardized means of data collection. Anecdotal observation could not provide a basis for representative and standardized surveying of hidden crime. Willcock's name will resurface in this narrative later on, as the pioneer of British self-report delinquency surveys in the 1960s.

Yet another attempt to by-pass the official control barrier of crime data was the reporting propensity approach. In contrast with police experience and direct observation, the reporting propensity method is more systematic, a clear improvement. The basic idea is that if we know what proportion of all offences known to somebody are reported to the police, the ratio of reported offences can be used to estimate the total number of crimes, *ceteris paribus*. Here the requirement is the presence and availability of that 'somebody'. For example, department stores can be used as informants in this respect. Thus, Sellin (1937: 69–70) reported that Philadelphia department stores mostly did not report thefts to the police (see also Mannheim, 1965).

Per scientiam ad justitiam
An age haunted by the facade normality

Above, the technical, scientifically 'internal' background of the hidden crime survey has been described. From that point of view, the standardized self-report survey was a solution to a problem that criminological science posed internally to itself. But there were additional, external cultural aspects that form a relevant context of discovery for the discovery of hidden crime as a statistically measurable entity. Just as science posed a question for itself to solve, the broader cultural environment made certain questions more salient than others.

The late nineteenth century has been described as obsessed with the potential and prevalence of degeneration, abnormality and deviance. When deviation was defined as abnormality, people had a strong motive to be 'closet deviants' for fear of being labelled as misfits and offenders. The nineteenth century bourgeoisie were obsessed with hypocrisy as the ubiquitous corollary of normative behaviour, and saw crime as a crack in the facade of conformity (Link, 1994; Pilarczyk, 1997). The age was preoccupied with facades, camouflage, mimicry and hypocrisy (Link, 1994: 78, 337;

Jazbinsek, 2005: 10). Naturalist novelists like Zola were particularly interested in tearing down facades of decency by exposing people's real behaviour. In the novels of Zola, the motifs of unveiling and disclosure were omnipresent (Baguley, 1990: 175). He wanted to strip life of its veils, illusions and pretensions, shams and hypocrisies, in its 'monstrous, demystifying nakedness'. The aim of exposure was to shock bourgeois opinion to scandalous effect. To do this, the naturalist novelist naturally turned to hidden crimes. In exposing hidden crime, naturalist fiction explored the frontier between the normal and the pathological. In terms of their unveiled frequency, transgressions became the norm, not the exception. The naturalist novelists saw themselves as engaged in scientific work.[4] Their method was satirical exposure that abolished differences by showing that all ranks of life were equally corrupt and criminal (Baguley, 1990: 175–8, 209–10, 218).

In contrast, other intellectuals objected to the naturalist exposure of people's hidden transgressions. One of their arguments was that unveiling the truth would further corrupt people's morality. In his book *Social Control*, published in 1901, the American sociologist Edward Alsworth Ross attacked French realists like Flaubert and Zola. Ross argued that 'with all their indignant pulling off of bourgeois masks', these novelists had not 'regenerated their people' (Ross, 2009 [1901]: 160). In fact, Ross suggested that the successful operation of social control called for 'the fig-leaf, the veil, the mask, the screen' (p. 159). Had someone suggested to him that the true prevalence of crime could and should be unveiled by a hidden crime survey, he would have pointed out the moral hazard involved. The belief that people did not break norms was one of the 'beneficent illusions' upon which social order depended (p. 156).

The idea of the facade normality and the related culture of suspicion and exposure were important cultural contexts that influenced the discovery of hidden crime. Irrespective of which side was taken, the distinction between a beneficent facade and exposed truth was a focal concern that shaped the formation of the hidden crime survey.[5] There were scholars who were looking for instruments

---

[4] Zola is known to have consulted Cesare Lombroso's *L'Uomo delinquente* when preparing his novel *La Bête humaine* (Baguley, 1990: 209).

[5] The fact that a few years after the publication of *Social Control*, Ross himself was exposing the hidden crimes of white-collar 'criminaloids' (a Lombrosian concept), exemplifies the persistence of this cultural perception.

that could be used in the scientific study of the facade normality of the middle and upper classes. In the genesis of the hidden crime survey, this motif was not associated with a need to suppress deviance once it had been detected. In contrast, the pioneers engaged in local battles to show that rigid normative regulation of deviance was misplaced or impossible because 'deviance' was in fact statistically normal. The quest to normalize behaviours defined as crimes was an important context of discovery that shaped the direction and interpretation of hidden delinquency research.

A case in point is the fight against the criminalization of homosexual behaviour that took place in Germany during the early years of the twentieth century. In the German Reich, homosexual behaviour was criminalized (1871) in paragraph 175 of the penal code. In 1897, a group of scholars and activists formed a committee whose purpose was to decriminalize homosexuality. The committee was named as the *Wissenschaftlich-humanitäres Komitee* (Scientific Humanitarian Committee or SHC, Lindemann, 1993: 99). The driving force behind the committee was Magnus Hirschfeld (1868–1935), one of the founders of the science of sexology.[6] His personal motto was *per scientiam ad justitiam*, 'Justice through Science'. In the midst of this political conflict, the circle of the Scientific Humanitarian Committee discovered the self-report survey as an instrument of moral and policy argumentation. Their innovation was to *combine* the quantitative survey with the normal-because-prevalent argument. Hirschfeld's personal influence and his groundbreaking surveys of 1903 and 1904 were pivotal in this process, but the story begins some years earlier in Amsterdam.

Von Römer's 1901 survey in Amsterdam

The Dutch physician Lucien von Römer (1873–1965) is a serious contender for the nomination as the first self-report delinquency survey researcher. In a letter to Freud, the famous psychoanalyst Carl Jung described von Römer as the 'Dutch Hirschfeld', and a champion of the homosexual cause (Lieshout, 1993: 145). von Römer was a member of Hirschfeld's Scientific Humanitarian Committee and he was centrally involved in establishing a similar pressure group in the Netherlands (Lieshout, 1993: 141–2).

---

[6] For Hirschfeld's life and role in sexology, see Bullough 2003.

In 1901, von Römer conducted an anonymous self-report survey of homosexuality in Amsterdam, targeting 600 students and receiving 308 completed questionnaires (von Römer, 1905: 39–41). Judging from anachronistic modern standards, von Römer's survey was rather sophisticated. Instead of a single question, he used a multiple-item scale of homosexuality that proceeded gradually from roundabout inquiries to a direct question of sexual orientation, thus comprising an early version of the Guttman-type scale. von Römer underscored the originality of his questionnaire, pointing out that the subsequent German surveys by Hirschfeld were based on his questionnaire (von Römer, 1905: 39). It is true that Hirschfeld's only question is the same as von Römer's fourth question, and Hirschfeld acknowledged von Römer's priority. Since it may be impossible to ascertain definite priority, it could be said that the hidden crime survey was invented as a moral instrument in the circles of the German and Dutch Scientific-Humanitarian Committee. The Skinnerian question, what these people where doing when they conducted the surveys, is easy to answer: they were engaged in a local criminal policy battle.

To be sure, the circle of the SHC was not alone in sending self-report questionnaires to students. About the same time, European sex researchers were launching similar projects. In 1904, a Russian physician named Tschlenoff organized a sexual survey among Moscow university students (Tschlenoff, 1908). With 2,150 respondents he reported that 92 per cent of the sample experienced 'early manifestation of the sexual instinct'. Similarly, 16 per cent reported liking pornographic literature, 67 per cent had experienced sexual intercourse before attending the university, 90 per cent had nocturnal emissions, 60 per cent masturbated, and 25 per cent had sexually transmitted diseases, and so on. While most of these behaviours and states may have been technically legal at the time and location of the survey, Tschlenoff's team was clearly engaged in the self-report survey of extremely sensitive behavioural topics. He did not however interpret his high prevalence findings from the moral standpoint of statistical normality and the consequent need to reduce repressive normative regulation. However, it is interesting that Tschelnoff observed a virtual avalanche of sensitive topics surveys in the first years of the twentieth century (p. 211) in various cities of the Russian empire and elsewhere.

Another tradition that may have influenced early European hidden crime research is the American educational research of the 1890s. Lucien von Römer was familiar with the researches of

W. S. Monroe whose work was translated to the Dutch language in 1904. He cited Monroe's student questionnaires before reporting his own findings of hidden homosexuality (von Römer, 1905: 38). Monroe had been conducting relatively large-scale survey research in American schools. For example, the book cited by von Römer contained an article by Monroe on school discipline. In this article, which originally appeared in 1897, Monroe surveyed student attitudes towards informing on rule-breakers, using a Massachusetts school sample with 2,972 respondents. The survey was not self-report delinquency research, but it was certainly self-report research on a sensitive topic related to norm-breaking. Importantly, Monroe expressed the opinion that the *adults who create school rules and enforce them should know the real codes of behaviour among children*. 'The best results in school discipline cannot be attained if [the child] is forced to obey regulations opposed to what he considers a just code of ethics.' (Monroe, 1897: 456; Monroe, 1904: 99–100.) Monroe thus clearly suggested that the empirical reality of norm-breaking and attitudes toward norms should influence the creation and enforcement of rules. The argumentation of both Monroe and von Römer points towards a flexible normalization of behaviours that were previously defined as deviant.

Hirschfeld's 1903 and 1904 surveys

Trained in medicine, Magnus Hirschfeld saw sexual orientation as biologically based, as opposed to socially constructed or learned inclination. In his writings, he often equated heterosexuality with normality and homosexuality with abnormality. However, his methodological approach departed from the typical approach of scholars representing the abnormality paradigm. He pointed out that the full extent and reality of homosexual behaviour could not be ascertained by using clinical samples or court-based samples (Hirschfeld, 1914: vii). His attempts to break out from the restricting boundaries of the clinical gaze and the legal process secured his position in the history of science (Lindemann, 1993: 97). Furthermore, he believed that the creation and validity of official norms should rest on empirical information on people's real behaviour. His overarching goal was the decriminalization of homosexuality in the German Reich. To accomplish this, he devised a pincer movement. Using the method of anonymous self-report delinquency research, he would show the high prevalence and hence normality of homosexuality. Using multiple literary sources, he would expose the high prevalence of homosexuality in the higher echelons of society.[7]

A primary step towards transgressing clinical and court-based data was Hirschfeld's psychobiological questionnaire, which he published in 1899. It was a self-administered survey with open-ended questions, targeted at his patients, a clinical sample (Hirschfeld, 1914: 240). In 1903 he went further and conducted a community sample based self-report survey of homosexual orientation. He sent anonymous self-report survey questionnaires to students and metalworkers to measure the true prevalence of homosexuality, which at that time was a criminal offence in Germany. While today homosexuality is not a crime in democratic societies, a hundred years ago it was criminalized in most nations. Therefore, Hirschfeld's studies can be seen as precursors of later hidden crime surveys.

Hirschfeld's questionnaire was a postcard that could be anonymously sent back. The sole independent variable included in this questionnaire was the age of the respondent. The gross samples he used were relatively large, 2,897 students and 4,597 metalworkers, yielding net samples of 1,696 (59 per cent response rate) and 1,912 (42 per cent response rate) (Hirschfeld, 1914: 480, 490). Among the student population, 1.5 per cent said they were exclusively homosexual and 4.5 per cent bisexual. In the metalworker sample, the corresponding figures were 1.2 and 3.2 per cent. Based on more detailed classification of people reporting bisexual orientation, he concluded that the percentage of homosexuals in the population was 2.3 (Hirschfeld, 1914: 492–3). Hirschfeld's prevalence figures were extremely consistent with the above described Dutch study (von Römer, 1905: 39–41; Hirschfeld, 1914: 485–6). While these figures may sound low, to contemporaries they were shockingly high, especially when they were used to estimate the absolute number of homosexuals and bisexuals in the German Reich. The estimate was about 1.5 million homosexuals (Hirschfeld, 1914: 493). Hirschfeld himself did not describe

---

[7] This two-pronged attack on the abnormality paradigm of crime would later be repeated by the core American innovator of hidden crime research, Edwin Sutherland. It is also probable that the normal-because-prevalent argument had been used in European discussions on criminal policy before 1903 (see Hirschfeld, 1914: 466).

homosexuality as normal, but he was using the high prevalence finding to influence societal reactions toward a mode of behaviour that was then defined as criminal. Like the hidden delinquency scholars who would later follow his path, he found out that deviance was equally prevalent in various social strata (Hirschfeld, 1914: 521).

Hirschfeld thus wanted to show two things. First, homosexuality was very prevalent, and, second, that it was evenly distributed across social stratification. This latter point was a means of uncoupling the phenomenon from lowest class associations. He accomplished it by charting the prevalence of homosexuality in various highly respected professions, such as law, medicine, military, and the police (Hirschfeld, 1914: 475, 515–9). This strategy of social exposure should be seen in the context of Wilhelmine Germany's cultural scene and its countercultural currents. Turn-of-the-century Germany witnessed a surge of liberal social satire targeted at the conservative and authoritarian political culture. The vanguard of liberal satire extended its critique of hypocrisy to sexual questions like prostitution (Allen, 1984: 144–55). The aim was to 'expose the discrepancy between pious principle and cynical practice' (p. 151). The liberal satirists attacked the excessively punitive attitudes of the conservative clergy by citing from the Bible: who is to cast the first stone? Hirschfeld's rhetorical strategy was similar. He represented liberal satire that exposed the hypocrisy of the highest classes, citing satirical literature as evidence for his argument (Hirschfeld, 1914: 506). Hirschfeld even went so far as to name high officials whom he knew or believed to be homosexuals, a decision that tarnished his reputation. His strategies were not very far from 'muckraking' journalism, which also sought to expose corruption and vice in high society.

What made Hirschfeld trust the confessions he was soliciting by mail and on an industrial scale? Probably his medical practice had shown that people were ready to discuss private and sensitive matters if they felt safe to do so. Additionally and interestingly, his decision to use anonymous self-reports was inspired by the catholic practice of strictly anonymous confession of sins. Several Catholic priests had confided to him that they had a habit of directly asking about sins such as homosexuality during confessions, and that people responded frankly (Hirschfeld, 1914: 472–3). Hirschfeld drew the conclusion that people were ready to self-report offences under conditions of guaranteed anonymity. The importance of religious practices and thought should not be underestimated as contexts of criminological discovery.

The Römer-Hirschfeld paradigm did not lead to proliferation of similar or other self-report surveys in Germany, or to the application of the method to other criminalized behaviours. This is hardly surprising considering the public reaction to their research. Like Socrates in ancient Athens, Hirschfeld was accused of corrupting the morals of youth because he was asking too many questions. Libel charges were brought against him because six persons who received his questionnaire claimed that the mere question about homosexuality defamed their honour. In the resulting trial, Hirschfeld proudly defended his research, concluding his final statement with the defiant exclamation: *per scientiam ad justitiam!* In spite of his spirited defence, he was convicted and ordered to pay fines (Hirschfeld, 1914: 481–2).[8] Hirschfeld's libel charges underscore an easily overlooked fact. Asking people point blank whether they have committed crimes presupposes that they *may have* committed crimes. This can be offensive to people's honour. Germany's honour culture during the pre-1945 era possibly explains why hidden crime surveys were not further developed there.

Writing in 1939, during the Nazi period, the German criminologist Kurt Meyer charted the extent of hidden crime systematically in multiple offence categories. Crimes against sexual morals (*Sittlichkeitsdelikte*) were the only crime type where he was able to refer to self-report findings, and these were Hirschfeld's pioneering studies. Meyer was correct when he stated that Hirschfeld's *context of discovery* was his spirited fight against paragraph 175 of the German penal code. Meyer observed that the abolitionists had a stake in coming up with high prevalence figures of homosexuality (Meyer, 1941: 25). On the other hand, he was unable to mount a good challenge against the validity of Hirschfeld's innovative method. Instead, he vacuously referred to 'multiple sources of error' and pointed out that Hirschfeld was a Jew, as if that was somehow relevant. And yet, in spite of such blunders, Meyer's detailed treatment betrays a certain fascination with the idea that the official control barrier of crime measurement could be by-passed by means

---

[8] Hirschfeld's political cause, the decriminalization of homosexual behaviour, did not fare much better. Repeated initiatives from the SHC to the German Reichstag failed. The early twentieth century was so dominated by strictly moral-normative argumentation that the idea to let the empirical facts of behaviour influence moral regulation did not gain ground (Lindemann, 1993: 102).

of a survey.[9] A much more balanced assessment was provided a few years later by Kinsey, Pomeroy, and Martin (1948: 618–20). The Kinsey team concluded that Hirschfeld deserves 'considerable credit for having tried on a larger scale than anyone had before to ascertain the facts on a matter that has always been difficult to survey' (p. 620).

Von Römer and Hirschfeld invested their science-based figures with moral meaning, trying to influence society's norms by disclosing the empirical factuality of human behaviour. Their use of survey-generated prevalence figures makes them the closest 'predecessors' of the later criminological hunt for the dark number of crime. This invites comparison to later crime normalizers. Some three decades later, the American criminologist Edwin H. Sutherland initiated a more general attack on the abnormality paradigm of crime. He utilized many of the same tactics as Hirschfeld. He exposed the criminality of the highest social classes, like corporate executives. He started to develop the method of hidden crime survey in order to reveal the extremely high prevalence (and therefore psychological normality) of crime. He even used the proxy survey method, asking people from various trades, 'what crooked practices exist in your profession?', much like Hirschfeld had charted the true prevalence of sexual deviance. What we have here is the paradigmatic strategy of redescribing deviance as normal: first, show that it is prevalent, and, second, show that all social strata are doing it. This similarity does not mean that Sutherland was directly influenced by Hirschfeld's example. There is no evidence of such a link, even though the early American Chicago-based sociologists were well informed about the German research scene during the imperial and Weimar eras (Jazbinsek, Joerges, and Thies, 2001). On the other hand, influence is not needed to explain similarity. The contours of the battlefield and the positions of the enemy forces—the abnormality paradigm and the repressive punitivists—in that battlefield suggested similar operations for scholars who did not otherwise know one another's work.

---

[9] In contrast, it is noteworthy that Wolfgang and Sellin do not mention Hirschfeld's survey in their relatively detailed commentary of Meyer's work (Wolfgang and Sellin, 1964: 37–8).

The white-collar offender as a prototype of the hidden criminal

The idea that the privileged classes are criminal is probably as old as critical social commentary. Witness the following rhyme from *The Beggar's Opera*, first published in 1728. Tyburn was the traditional hanging place of old London:

But gold from the law can take out the sting;
And if rich men like us were to swing,
'Twould thin the land, such numbers to string
Upon Tyburn Tree!

In effect, the speaker says that crime is highly prevalent in the upper echelons of society, but the law fails to prosecute rich men. Andrea McKenzie (2006) has recently analysed the cultural context from which *The Beggar's Opera* sprang. At least in the English-speaking world, the early eighteenth century culture was fascinated with the 'gentleman highwayman' whose figure blurred the traditional divide between the criminal underclass and supposedly non-criminal higher classes. The literate public was eager to read about the exploits of such criminals, many of whom published autobiographies, confessing their true and unrecorded crimes for all to read about. The gentleman robber became a social critic who used the discourse of *satire* to expose the corruption of the middle and upper classes. Attacking lawyers, moneylenders, physicians, courtiers, crooked tradesmen, South Sea directors, and other upper class figures for their crimes and machinations, the robbers claimed that all men and women were rogues, but only lowest class offenders were prosecuted and punished (pp. 584–7). They contrasted the trivial nature of conventional crimes with the much greater societal harm resulting from upper class crime: 'common rogueries' were petty by comparison with 'public calamities' (p. 589). They exposed the hypocrisy and pretensions of the middle and upper classes, ridiculing upper class people committing economic crimes with 'supercilious faces' (p. 594).

While this kind of popular commentary has always existed,[10] it penetrated social science in the late nineteenth century. In this section, I will further describe the cultural context in which hidden

---

[10] In earlier historical periods, it probably existed in the form of popular critique and satire of corrupt clerics.

crime became an object of quantitative inquiry by tracing the genealogy of the concept of white-collar crime.

Progressive and religious impact on early American sociology

The concept of the white-collar criminal goes back to the populist and progressive critique of robber barons and capitalists during the late nineteenth and early twentieth centuries. In his classic treatment of the subject, Hofstadter (1977 [1955]) saw populism and Progressivism as different yet closely interrelated movements climaxing in the period from the 1890s to the First World War. He wrote that a too sharp distinction between the two movements would distort reality. Both accelerated during a rapid and turbulent transition from an agrarian society to urban society. Progressivism[11] critiqued 'big business' and 'robber barons', which were seen as having destroyed the honest and largely rural cultural base of America. Corruption, money power and 'plutocrats' were intensely critiqued. The progressive view of history was conspiratorial: Reality was seen to lay behind facades (Hofstadter, 1977 [1955]: 4–7, 65, 71, 133). The progressives prided in being *realists*, that is they wanted to expose the sordid reality behind supercilious and hypocritical facades. They exposed reality in its fullness and subjected it to moral exhortation (Hofstadter, 1977 [1955]: 199). At the same time the new mass journalism partook in this 'realist' drive to disclose the massive prevalence of corruption. Evil-doing among respectable people was seen as the 'real' character of American life; corruption was found on every side, and mischief was interpreted as 'widespread breaking of the law' (Hofstadter, 1977 [1955]: 202). In its fight against corporate 'interests' and corrupt powers, progressives were joined by religious movements and the young science of sociology.

Progressivism reflected the moral traditions of rural evangelical Protestantism (Hofstadter, 1977 [1955]: 203; Nugent, 2010: 59–63). The movement has been seen 'as a phase in the history of the Protestant conscience, a latter-day Protestant revival' (Hofstadter, 1977 [1955]: 152). At the same time, American sociology emerged from strivings toward Christian social reform (p. 198). Sociologists had personal and ideational connections with the

---

[11] For reasons of brevity, I will use only the concept of Progressivism.

so-called Social Gospel, a Christian movement that addressed the social questions and problems created by the industrial revolution. The Social Gospel was the religious wing of the US progressive movement (Nugent, 2010: 59–62). It is difficult to say whether Social Gospel influenced sociology or the other way round.

Many of the first generation of professional social scientists were former clergy, or sons of clergy (Smith, 1994: 20). The founder of the sociology department at the University of Chicago, Albion W. Small, was the son of a Baptist minister. As a former ministerial student, he saw sociology as Christian endeavour (Salerno, 2007: 30). Another early sociologist, Charles Henderson, was a university chaplain who taught in the spirit of the Social Gospel (Schwartz, 1997: 285–6; Salerno, 2007: 61). As a young man, George Herbert Mead, whose symbolic interactionism would later have a major impact on qualitative sociology, participated in the Social Gospel together with the philosopher John Dewey (Collins, 1998: 682). Many of the early twentieth century criminologists shared this kind of religious heritage. Austin Larimore Porterfield served for years as a minister before becoming professor of sociology at Texas Christian University, and never stopped preaching on Sundays (Cain, 2005). Clifford Shaw started his education to become a priest, but soon became disillusioned and gave up ministry as a calling (Gelsthorpe, 2007: 520; Salerno, 2007: 144). Edwin Sutherland's father was an ordained Baptist minister and both parents have been described as religious fundamentalists (Snodgrass, 1972: 220). No wonder that Sutherland himself acutely observed the salient role of ministry in early American sociology (Sutherland, 1945: 429). Like him, William I. Thomas, Ernest Burgess and Paul Cressey had ministers or preachers as fathers (Salerno, 2007: 34, 57, 122). The links between early sociology and religion were complex: familial, cultural and tactical (see Morgan, 1969; Swatos, 1983; Turner and Turner, 1990: 23, 34–5). The various movements of Christian socialism and sociology even shared a method: the social survey (Bulmer, Bales and Sklar, 1991), more of which will be said later.

One of the recurring themes in Social Gospel and Christian sociology circles was the critique of the 'robber barons' of the capitalist economy. For example, the Social Gospel leader Rauschenbusch emphasized the unrecorded sins of corporations (Rauschenbusch, 1922 [1917]). He wanted to show that crime was not particularly associated with the lowest strata of society. As noted earlier, one of the important bases of the abnormality paradigm was the presumed connection between crime and lowest class membership. If it could be shown that middle and upper classes were also criminal, a crucial element holding the abnormality paradigm intact would collapse. Later, the populist and progressivist attack against robber barons metamorphosed into the analysis of the white-collar offender and his hidden crimes.[12]

Transformation of the Lombrosian criminaloid

As early as in 1901, the sociologist Henderson lectured about the immoral acts of white-collar criminals, noting that 'they were more likely to evade detection' and thus to remain unrecorded, hidden offenders (Gaylord and Galliher, 1988: 18–9). Another early sociologist, Edward Alsworth Ross, published a monograph named *Sin and Society* in 1907, a book that was a classic of the progressive spirit and a precursor of modern white-collar crime studies. Ross emphasized that the modern criminal was not like 'Fagin or Bill Sykes', referring to the stereotypical underclass crime characters of the novelist Charles Dickens. Instead they are

[O]ften 'good men', judged by the old tests, and would have passed for virtuous in the American community of seventy years ago. Among the chiefest sinners are now enrolled men who are pure and kind-hearted, loving in their families, faithful to their friends, and generous to the needy. (Ross, 1973 [1907]: 14.)

Ross wanted to see behind the facades of the middle and upper class person, he could almost 'smell the buzzard under his stolen peacock plumes' (Ross, 1973 [1907]: 38). The 'latter-day sinner' was a fake conformist, and no one could 'outdo him in lip homage

---

[12] Critics have argued that during the nineteenth century, society and culture were permeated by religion to an extent that is difficult to appreciate today. The early American sociologists 'were protestant Christians because most American intellectuals of the late nineteenth century were (at least nominally) Protestant Christians' (Swatos, 1983: 34). Religious movements were also independently adopting sociological tones and their leaders called themselves 'sociologists', blurring the distinction between the two (Swatos, 1983: 44). The case remains unsolved. It would be of some interest to examine empirically whether the first generation sociologists, whether in America or elsewhere, were more likely to be sons of clergy than scholars entering other fields such as medicine, law, psychology or engineering.

to the law and the prophets' (Ross, 1973 [1907]: 87). In his autobiography published three decades later, Ross wrote that in *Sin and Society*, he had simply 'modernized the message of Old-Testament prophets'. On the other hand, he claimed that the book was 'straight sociology', not ethics (Ross 1977 [1936]: 107–10). This was not a contradiction. The analysis was sociological, while religious rhetoric was used for purposes of impact and popularization. He was looking for concepts and metaphors to describe a new area of inquiry. Apart from the religious concept of 'latter-day sinner', he used the twin concepts of overt offender and *covert offender* to describe what today would probably be called the recorded 'conventional' offender and the unrecorded white-collar offender. Covert offenders were *partial villains* who lacked the social stigmata of traditional criminals. Some pages later Ross moved to the dichotomy of plain criminal and *quasi-criminal* before finally deciding on the concept of the *criminaloid* (Ross, 1973 [1907]: 26–8, 46).

That concept was borrowed from none other than Cesare Lombroso. Lombroso had described the criminaloid as someone who was not a born criminal, but very susceptible to environmental criminogenic influences. Ross took the concept but changed its meaning.[13] For him, the criminaloid was the white-collar offender whose crimes had not yet 'come under the effective ban of public opinion', so that the offender enjoyed immunity (pp. 47–8) under the 'protective mimicry' (p. 59) of seemingly law-abiding behaviour. '[The criminaloid] counterfeits the good citizen. He takes care to meet all conventional tests—flag worship, old-soldier sentiment, observance of all the national holidays, perfervid patriotism, party regularity and support' (pp. 61–2). Ross also underscored that white-collar criminaloids were not pathological or degenerates. 'In their crania Lombroso would miss the marks of atavism' (pp. 28, 55). Indeed, Ross may have been the first author using, in a criminological context, the metaphor that would later be central in the moral interpretation of hidden crimes studies: *shades of grey*. 'In a word, the big and formidable sinners are *gray of soul, not black*' (p. 26, emphasis added). Ross critiqued the moralistic pretensions of the middle and upper classes and ridiculed

---

[13] Arguably Ross selected the wrong Lombrosian concept. What he meant was Lombroso's latent criminal, but adopted the term criminaloid because it sounded more striking.

punitive moral entrepreneurs who attacked easily visible vices such as prostitution, gambling, drinking but left the real criminals untouched (pp. 88–9). He labelled people committing vices as non-conformists instead of sinners or criminals, and saw shades of grey where others had seen black and white.[14]

Sutherland and white-collar crime

Edwin Sutherland's groundbreaking analyses of white-collar crime mark the point where earlier popular and religious polemical traditions were transformed into a scholarly study of 'crimes committed by persons of respectability and high social status in the course of their occupation' (Sutherland, 1983 [1949]: 7).[15] Like Ross, Sutherland was born in the midwest and his intellectual outlook was shaped by the social transformations of rural America (Shover and Cullen, 2008: 168–9). In addition, the *data* he used were made available historically by the progressive movement in US politics. As noted above, Thorsten Sellin was moved to distrust official crime statistics because of the legislative activism brought about by the progressive era in US politics. The same legislative activism largely constituted the empirical sources on which Sutherland drew in his analyses of white-collar crime.[16] Moreover, he used investigative journalism, which is often associated with the progressive era. Thus, from the point of view of crime measurement, the progressive climate of opinion had at least three important influences on criminology. First, it supported a moral climate that inspired scholars to expose hidden delinquents. Second, it expanded criminalizations and thereby revealed the artificiality of deviance. Third, it created agencies that investigated probable offences and thus produced alternative sources of crime statistics.

---

[14] While Ross took steps towards conceptual normalization of criminality, he did not advocate lenient punishments. Referring to the white-collar offender, he wrote about the 'sacred duty, not lazily to condone, but vigorously to pursue and castigate the sinner' (Ross, 1973 [1907]: 77).

[15] To a degree, the Sutherlandian research tradition remains 'populist' and morally guided to this day (Shover and Cullen, 2008).

[16] For example, the creation of the Federal Trade Commission in 1915 as an extension of the earlier Bureau of Corporations (1903), and cases based on the Sherman (1890) and Clayton (1914) antitrust acts; on their links to Progressive political movement, see Nugent 2010, 37, 59, 78, 103. Sutherland's sources, see Sutherland 1983 [1949], Part II.

Developed by sociologists, the new scientific approach to white-collar crime was a means of redescribing crime as normal. The expansion of criminology's empirical basis from official crime statistics can be seen in this context. Sutherland's classic monograph on white-collar crime begins with a critique of official statistics on recorded crime. Sutherland exposes the official statistics as a 'biased sample of all criminal acts' (Sutherland, 1983 [1949]: 5). He furthermore observes that the abnormality paradigm of crime rests on the observation that crime is concentrated in the lowest social strata:

> The assumption in these theories is that criminal behaviour can be explained only by pathological factors, either social or personal. The social pathologies which have been emphasized are poverty, and related to it, poor housing, lack of organized recreations, lack of education, and disruptions of family life. The personal pathologies which have been suggested as explanations of criminal behaviour were, at first, biological abnormalities; when research studies threw doubt on the validity of these biological explanations, the next explanation was intellectual inferiority, and more recently emotional instability. [. . .] The thesis of this book is that these social and personal pathologies are not an adequate explanation of criminal behaviour. (Sutherland, 1983 [1949]: 5.)

Others who followed Sutherland also made the point that white-collar crime refuted the link between pathology and crime causation. Vilhelm Aubert, the Norwegian criminologist who would influence the Nordic hidden crime survey tradition (Chapter 5), started as a white-collar crime researcher, and used white-collar crime to argue for the normality of crime (Aubert, 1952: 265-6). In 1952, Aubert may have become the last author to use the concept of 'criminaloid' to describe white-collar offenders, but he wrapped the concept in inverted commas (Aubert, 1952: 269). The criminal was now revealed to be 'a normally organized person social-psychologically' (Hartung, 1953: 32). The mid-twentieth century works by Sutherland (1949), Aubert (1952) and Hartung (1953) testify to how the progressive expansion of the crime concept, initially influenced by populist and religious traditions, had become a research programme in normal science.

In the first decades after the invention of the self-report delinquency survey, at least till the 1950s, the self-report crime survey was perceived as part of the study of white-collar crime. The white-collar criminal was, in a sense, the prototype of the hidden criminal whose immoral exploits were not to be found in the criminal justice statistics. One of the building blocks of any deviance normalization is that the behaviour in question is not seen as particularly associated with the lowest strata in society, or with biological abnormality. This is why concepts like white-collar crime and corporate crime paved the way to redescription of crime as prevalent and normal. This is so even though the early researchers of white-collar crime strongly condemned the behaviour of the 'robber barons'.

The immediate foreground

Above, I have described cultural currents and moral conflicts that directed scholarly attention when they were seeking to solve a problem posed by their science: how to break the official control barrier of crime measurement. Next, I will resume the internal narrative to describe the situation at the immediate threshold of Porterfield's breakthrough in 1940. This narrative also includes near misses and dead ends, even people who got the 'right solution' but were answering the 'wrong question'.

Social survey

The concepts we use to describe methods of social inquiry change historically. The concept of 'survey' is a good example. Today, that word typically refers to asking people to respond to a questionnaire (in whatever form ranging from self-administered paper questionnaires and telephone interviewing to web surveys). Often such surveys are based on random samples representing the target population. In earlier days, the concept 'survey' did not refer to a mode of data collection. 'Surveys' were fact-finding missions that collected information about a limited geographical area by any means available; the word also implied that the ultimate purpose of the fact-finding was social reform. Often the early surveys utilized a structured thematic list (a schedule) of facts to be collected, but it was normally completed by a data collector. There were no standardized questions to be answered by 'respondents' in the modern sense (Platt, 1998: 44–5).

In the US, social surveys in the old meaning of the word go far back in time, at least to the 1865 Doolittle survey of the native American tribes (Chaput, 1972). The committee in charge of that survey sent questionnaires to proxy reporters like 'Indian agents' and army officers. The questions dealt with the social conditions of the tribes. However, the actual social survey tradition is often traced back to the work of Charles Booth who surveyed the social conditions of metropolitan London during the 1880s and 1890s. His work was followed by an avalanche of local surveys from the 1890s to 1920s (Bulmer, Bales and Sklar, 1991: 29). The most famous exemplars were the *Hull House Maps and Papers* of 1895 in Chicago and Seebohm Rowntree's survey of York in 1899 (Converse, 2009: 16–7, 22).

The social surveys typically relied on various types of 'enumerators' and 'visitors', such as school board visitors, who would report on the living conditions of the poor, not unlike the 'Indian agents' of the Doolittle survey. The informants used by the social surveyors were in many cases sent by the expanding state that spread horizontally to new territories (the US expansion to the West) and vertically to new social strata (the British school legislation sending the school visitors to the slums). The social surveys from Booth to early 1930s thus relied on what could be described as proxy reporting method as opposed to asking people directly about their lives.[17] Here it can be seen how the survey tradition depended on the development of the state that created the conditions of empirical data collection by external conquest or internal auditing of the lowest classes. The rise of compulsory education is pertinent in this respect. It created the school classes where youths could be studied, sent the school board visitors on their observation trips, and increased literacy, a crucial condition for the later development of the self-administered delinquency survey.

The Du Bois survey in Atlanta

Aiming at social reform, the social survey movement was particularly interested in measuring the extent of poverty. It was closely related to philanthropic and ameliorative goals, and its ultimate aim was 'changing the community consciousness' (Converse,

---

[17] Some early social surveyors noticed that they could rely on direct questioning of people. In 1901, Seebohm Rowntree, who surveyed York, made the pragmatic discovery that answers to direct questions were reliable when checked against other sources of data, like neighbours and employers (Bulmer, Bales and Sklar, 1991: 22). The era of social surveys closed in the 1930s as they were replaced by directly asked questions and surveys based on random samples instead of total coverage of a limited area.

2009: 25). Some early social surveys were specifically targeted at crime. In this respect, the surveys of W. E. B. Du Bois (1868–1963) in Atlanta are noteworthy. These surveys largely utilized official prison and crime statistics, but Du Bois additionally used the proxy reporting method where chosen informants reported about the criminal behaviour (or 'morals') of people in a given area. Because Du Bois sought to disprove exaggerated claims about the criminality of African Americans, he was able to see that statistics of recorded crimes were constructed by the criminal justice system, and could therefore reflect biases and/or changes in how social control was targeted. For example, he noted that increase in the number of recorded crimes by African Americans could reflect the increasing 'efficacy of the judicial system in ferreting out and punishing crime' (Du Bois, 1904: 10). He wrote that crime statistics are 'too general and too much mingled with extra-moral causes and motives to be trustworthy' (Du Bois and Dill, 1914: 11), thus presaging the critique of official statistics by criminologists like Sellin and Verkko.

Did Du Bois have an intuition as to how to transgress the official control barrier in the study of crime-related phenomena? In 1904, he conducted student surveys among African American youths in Atlanta public schools (Du Bois, 1904: 54–5). He received 1,500 responses from school children and 584 responses from 13–21-year-old students. Apparently Du Bois did not ask the respondents to report their own delinquent behaviour, but he did ask about contacts with the courts and the police. Twenty three per cent of his respondents had seen courts in session (in what role, was not specified). Four per cent said that they had been 'wronged by policemen', while 70 per cent observed that they had 'never been helped or protected' by the police (Du Bois, 1904: 54). While there was no explicit or stated aim of measuring the extent of unrecorded crime, the Du Bois survey represents an early attempt to by-pass the criminal justice system in gathering criminological data.

'No-one knows, for no data are available'

Towards the end of the social survey era,[18] a line of local crime surveys branched from the main tradition. Among the better known

---

[18] Here, the social survey era refers to the local fact-finding mission type of survey that preceded the modern survey that is based on standardized directly asked questions and random sampling of populations.

examples are the Cleveland, Missouri and Illinois crime surveys. The local crime surveys of the 1920s and 1930s sprang from initiatives by civic and professional organizations such as bar associations, and sometimes they were triggered by individual incidents of crime. The crime surveys were called surveys, but the concept of survey was used in the sense of the social survey movement, meaning a multifaceted fact-finding mission by a group of researchers and practitioners. The most typical methods were the use of official statistics on reported crimes, and proxy surveys among criminal justice professionals.

The most thorough surveys, like the Illinois crime survey, conducted extensive questionnaire-based researches among criminal justice professions and jurors. The Illinois survey conducted a large-scale survey of various professions with more than 10,000 questionnaires sent out. Citizens who had served as jurors in 1927 were targeted as well. The survey of jurors was anonymous. While the respondents were not asked about their own criminal victimization, intimidation or offending, they did report other people's dishonest behaviour (Fischer, 1929: 236–42). The local crime surveys did not include what we would today call anonymous self-report or victimization studies.

Dominated by lawyers, the recommendations of the local US crime commissions were more likely to be punitive than normalizing or humanizing. According to Edwin Sutherland, the crime commission surveys of the 1920s shared a common theory of crime causation. This was the 'loophole theory' according to which crime exists because so many offenders escape conviction due to the inefficiency of the criminal justice system (Sutherland, 1927: 481). The policy recommendations, many of which were implemented, followed from this. Today, criminologists would probably describe many of the recommendations as punitive. Several states amended or enacted habitual criminal legislation, often following the 'four strikes and you're out' principle. In some cases, minimum sentences were specified, measures taken to speed up the trial process, and criminal cases were given priority over civil cases. New crime definitions such as 'automobile banditry', or unauthorized possession of an armoured vehicle, were introduced. Funds were channelled to the production and use of official crime statistics. The role of alienists (psychiatrists) was strengthened in the criminal justice system (Pfiffner, 1929; Sutherland and Gehlke, 1933: 1158–9).

In his review of the Missouri crime survey, Edwin Sutherland observed that the surveys were dominated by lawyers and other local elites. In a sarcastic tone, he described the social forces behind the surveys as follows: 'chambers of commerce, traffic clubs, bankers' associations, Rotary clubs, Kiwanis clubs, women's clubs, councils of social agencies, and many other groups' (Sutherland, 1927: 480). He was ridiculing such local elites. Chambers of commerce and country clubs were the kind of social coteries that were attacked by the future founders of the hidden crime research tradition, like Sutherland and Porterfield, whose intellectual horizons were influenced by the anti-establishment, populist and progressive traditions of the American midwest. The crime surveys of the 1920s represented everything that Sutherland was to attack in the next decade, the 1930s: focus on conventional crime, lack of interest in the crimes of the powerful, emphasis on official statistics, lack of causal rigour, and the professional hegemony of law and psychiatry. The critique of lawyers (punitivity) and psychiatrists (treatment ideology) was important for the sociology's takeover of criminology.

The researchers of local crime surveys were aware of the problem of hidden crime. In 1933, when Sutherland himself contributed to a kind of nation-level crime survey, he bluntly wrote that 'crime cannot be measured directly' (Sutherland and Gehlke, 1933: 1123). In the Illinois Crime Survey, W. C. Jamison acknowledged that

> before an adequate plan for the control of crime is possible, something must be learned of the actual amount of crime. How many crimes are committed each year and of what nature? Where are they most numerous? No one knows with certainty, for no data are available. (Jamison, 1929: 579.)

Authors of the chapter on juvenile delinquency, Clifford Shaw and Earl Myers, noted that official statistics are 'necessarily incomplete' because they contained only apprehended offenders:

> It is well known that there are offenders, even some who persistently engage in delinquent practices, who are never known to the police or the Juvenile Court authorities. Furthermore, in some communities certain types of offences are so prevalent that there is very little intervention on the part of the police. This is especially true in certain districts contiguous to railroad yards where stealing from freight cars is more or less accepted by the community and the police. It is obvious that in such districts the number of cases brought to court or handled by the police is only a small proportion of the total number of children actually engaged in delinquency. (Shaw and Myers, 1929: 645, see also p. 670.)

The 'lying to win approval' scale

During the 1920s, when the local crime surveyors were using official statistics, a group of researchers was pondering how children's norm-breaking behaviour could be studied directly. The Institute of Social and Religious Research (ISRR), financed by John D. Rockefeller, has been described as the most sophisticated sociological research institute of the early part of the interwar period (Turner and Turner, 1990: 41). The Institute was formed as a unit that utilized the data collected by the Interchurch World Movement, which had attempted the most ambitious version of the Booth-style social survey: the survey of every evangelical church in America. The ISRR transformed the early Booth-style social survey into modern empirical research. In the context of its Character Education Inquiry (CEI), the ISRR researchers developed what is today known as the social desirability scale. It measures the extent to which survey respondents want to give 'socially desired' answers as a 'front' that hides his or her true behaviour or attitudes. If someone responds 'true' to social desirability items such as 'I have never in my life jaywalked' or 'I have never had negative feelings towards other people', he/she scores high on social desirability. Scoring high on social desirability suggests that the person's other answers to the survey are invalid. Today, the social desirability scale is often used as an in-built validity threat detector in surveys.

During the late 1920s, the Character Education Inquiry project developed the 'lying to win approval' (LWA) scale, which is very much like a modern self-report delinquency scale, with the notable difference that its function was not to measure delinquency. The LWA scale included items such as these: 'Have you ever disobeyed any law of your country or rule of your school?', 'Do you stick with your gang when they go wrong?', 'Did you ever take anything (even a pin or button) that belonged to someone else?', 'Did you ever hurt or cause pain to a dog, cat, or other animal?' and 'Did you ever break, destroy, or lose anything belonging to someone else?' (Hartshorne and May, 1930: 98–100). The stealing and property destruction items of the LWA scale were very similar to later self-report delinquency scale items.

In the LWA scale, respondents answering that they had never stolen anything scored a 'lie point'. Respondents claiming that they had never destroyed other people's property also scored a 'lie point'. The general propensity of lying to win approval was the sum of such norm-abiding answers. How does this relate to self-report delinquency scales later developed by criminologists? Did the developers of the LWA scale *know* that petty theft and property destruction was universal or very prevalent among school-aged children? They had in fact asked a sample of psychology students to answer the questions truthfully. What they found was that a very small proportion of students claimed 'a perfect childhood' (Hartshorne and May, 1930: 102). Since these results were apparently not published item-wise, we have no data about responses to crime-related items. We can only deduce that since the CEI researchers kept the crime-related variables in the LWA scale, they had found high prevalence of self-reported adolescent theft and property destruction in a student sample.[19] Apparently, the CEI team did not present item-specific simple prevalence figures because they conceptualized their instrument as measuring the propensity to lie instead of measuring real behaviour.

There was a strong presence of psychology in the ISRR research projects, with scholars like Edward Lee Thorndike influencing the programme. Psychology was not as morally driven as sociology. During the first part of the twentieth century, psychologists were intensively engaged in developing various kinds of *personality measurement* scales, some of which overlapped with the measurement of behaviour. When delinquency was addressed, it was often by conducting tests in populations of known delinquents as opposed to controls; the prevalence of delinquency was not, as such, the primary question. Methodological work on self-reported behaviour was carried out by psychologists and social psychologists as well; it was, for instance, observed that students would answer more truthfully to self-report questions on cheating if anonymous conditions were guaranteed (Spencer, 1938).

However, the living tradition of criminological self-report research did not grow from psychological work, even though in the 1950s the scale-development approach was amalgamated to the criminological self-report research (see section 'The Americanization of the hidden crime survey in the 1950s' below). The crucial difference was that the psychological tradition was not born out of

---

[19] Technically, it is not necessary that activities described in a social desirability scale have 100 per cent real prevalence, because respondents who have a tendency to lie are revealed by the complete scale, not by individual items. However, the scale developer must choose behaviours that he/she knows or believes to be very prevalent but condemned by norms.

mistrust of official statistics. The psychologists were out to measure dimensions of personality instead of prevalence of crime. Their approach was not policy oriented to the degree that criminology was. For example, the ISRR researchers studied cheating because they wanted to reduce cheating, not in order to show that norms about cheating were too harsh or outdated. They feared that their morally neutral approach would be mistaken as endorsement: 'In asking constantly how much or how often, we are not in the least belittling the spiritual significance of any kind of behavior [...] we are merely drawing attention to its prevalence' (Hartshorne and May, 1930: 13). The ISRR researchers were not innovating ideologists and public sociologists with a mission to redescribe previously condemned behaviours as 'normal'.

The Michael-Adler Report

In 1931, the US Bureau of Social Hygiene commissioned Jerome Michael and Mortimer Adler, a lawyer and a philosopher, to evaluate the status of American criminology. The resulting report is today known as the Michael-Adler report, a devastating criticism of criminology's 'pretensions to call itself a science' (Goff and Geis, 2008: 351).

On reading the Michael-Adler Report, one is struck by the fact that its authors have relatively little to say about the measurement of crime. To begin with, they defined criminals by reference to successful prosecution of suspects. 'The most certain way. . . to distinguish criminals from non-criminals is in terms of those who have been convicted of crime and those who have not' (Michael and Adler, 1933: 3). One reason was that in the absence of conviction, criminality 'must nearly always remain in doubt'. In their view, criminals and delinquents could not be studied before they have come into official custody (p. 5). They thus represented the institutionalist, or law-based, as opposed to the realist, or behaviour-based, approach to the problem of crime measurement (Biderman and Reis, 1967). On the other hand, Michael and Adler knew that a 'comparatively small proportion of the persons who commit crimes are convicted', and even suggested that this was a socially functional situation (Michael and Adler, 1933: 36). Because of this, they felt some uneasiness about their pragmatic institutional definition of the offender as a person who is apprehended, prosecuted, and successfully convicted. This problem re-emerged when they discussed the problem of differentiating criminals and non-criminals:

> The major problem can be stated in the question: can criminals be differentiated from non-criminals? . . . What factor or factors differentiate criminals from non-criminals? This latter phrasing of the question must not be permitted to obscure the fact that at present we do not know whether criminals can be differentiated from non-criminals in any way whatsoever except by reference to the criminal law. . . Some basis for sharply differentiating criminal behaviour from non-criminal behaviour and criminals from non-criminals is *sine qua non* of the development of the science of criminology. (Michael and Adler, 1933: 92; the citation combines regular text and footnote text.)

The question, can criminals be differentiated from non-criminals, was a focal concern for the scholars who would, in the next 20 to 30 years, contribute to the rise of the self-report delinquency survey.

According to Goff and Geis (2008), the Michael-Adler Report influenced the development of criminology in two respects during the 1930s. First, the report is known to have inspired Edwin Sutherland to develop his theory of differential association. Apparently, the report also inspired Sutherland to reflect on the role of theory in criminology. Thus, in defending criminology against the report (Sutherland, 1973 [1933]: 238), he referred to Goring's refutation of the Lombrosian abnormality paradigm as an example of theoretical progress.[20] Second, the report inspired Thorsten Sellin to reject institutional (or law-based) definitions of crime as basis of behavioural research (Goff and Geiss, 2008: 351). However, Sellin had been 'moving towards the crime', and away from the use of official statistics, before the Michael-Adler Report was published (see section 'The view from within: Moral statistics and the official control barrier' above). Sellin was influenced by his empirical observations that official control was socially biased against African Americans, and by the work of Nordic and other European moral statisticians on the constant ratio doctrine. However, the Michael-Adler Report may have further pushed Sellin to toughen his anti-legalistic position on the question of crime measurement. Whether the report also

---

[20] See, however, Beirne 1988 on Goring's adherence to the abnormality paradigm.

influenced Sutherland's pioneering experiments with student self-reports cannot be ascertained.

From Berlin to Chicago

If a scholar wants to study delinquent behaviour directly, by-passing data sources produced by the social control of such behaviour (criminal justice and clinical data), a natural solution is to observe forms of deviant life worlds without intermediaries. One could, for example, let the delinquents speak for themselves. The rise of qualitative methods in sociological criminology was thus partially motivated by the same concerns as the discovery of the self-report survey: the need to break the official control barrier. Both qualitative study and the quantitative self-report survey would ultimately rely on self-reports.

At the beginning of the twentieth century, the idea of qualitative description of deviant life worlds arose both in Berlin and Chicago. In Berlin, the writer Hans Ostwald initiated an ethnographic project, the *Gross-Stadt-Dokumente*, that charted the murky underworlds of *fin-de-siècle* Berlin and Vienna. Written by several journalists and scholars, the *Gross-Stadt-Dokumente* were published between 1904 and 1908 in Berlin. Many of them were underworld ethnographies or life stories of criminals (Fritzsche, 1994: 393). It is hardly a coincidence that this groundbreaking German project was launched at the same time as Magnus Hirschfeld conducted his pioneering self-report crime surveys (see section '*Per scientiam ad justitiam*' above). Ostwald was a member of Hirschfeld's liberal pressure group, the Scientific Humanitarian Committee. The purpose of both Hirschfeld's survey and Ostwald's qualitative approach was to humanize and to normalize forms of life labelled as deviant and criminal by mainstream society.

In 1914, the library of the University of Chicago purchased all 51 issues of Ostwald's *Gross-Stadt-Dokumente* (Jazbinsek, Joerges and Thies, 2001: 6). It is today known that these influenced the rise of the Chicago School of Sociology which emphasized qualitative methods such as ethnography, participant observation, interviews, and autobiography. In a fascinating archival study of library lending cards, Jazbinsek, Joerges and Thies (2001: 8) observed that scholars such as Ernest W. Burgess, William I. Thomas, Walter C. Reckless and Louis Wirth were reading Ostwald's documents. Of course, apart from direct influences, the social context of the

Berlin humanitarian-scientific circle and the Chicago School of Sociology directed their attention to specific topics and methods. The pluralistic efflorescence of the modern metropolis did not fit the rigid expectations of the abnormality paradigm. It must have seemed to acute observers that the various 'deviant' life forms of the great city were somehow called forth by the environment itself. There were simply so many lifestyles in evidence that they could no longer be described as abnormal.

In criminology, Clifford Shaw and Henry McKay applied the Chicago qualitative perspective to the sphere of delinquency. They pioneered the 'boy's own story' method of criminological research. Works such as *The Jack-Roller* (1930) and *Brothers in Crime* (1938), representing the life history method, are classics of criminology. Their creation was based on the ability of researchers to build trustful relationships with delinquents. According to McKay, Shaw was 'at his very best when interviewing juvenile delinquents from whom he got "the whole story" very quickly and without any duress' (McKay as cited in Snodgrass, 1972: 140). Clearly, Shaw was collecting self-reports about delinquency, and harnessing confession to the purposes of criminology. What separates him from the hidden crime survey was that he did not aim at quantitative measurement of crime in a given population. However, he showed that truthful self-reports were possible. When Austin Porterfield in 1943 published the findings from the first criminological self-report survey, he argued for their validity by citing the 'boy's own story' type of research by Shaw and McKay (Porterfield, 1943). Shaw himself would later inspire new developments in the quantitative self-report tradition (see section 'Sutherland experiments in the 1930s' below).

The works of the Berlin and Chicago schools showed that the confessional method worked, and that criminal behaviour was normal in a given cultural and economic environment. They offered an alternative to psychologically oriented abnormality paradigm: the 'normal criminal' (Snodgrass, 1972: 180–1, 184; Shaw et al, 1938: 351). Deviance was humanized and even celebrated (Snodgrass, 1972: 153; Salerno, 2007: 25, 171) as in the Romantic tradition. The idea of the normal criminal was a rhetorical redescription by innovating ideologists. However, the normality of the normal criminal did not at this stage refer to the number of crimes he (or people typically) committed. The statistical normal-because-prevalent rhetoric would be deployed by the quantitative wing of the normalization movement.

Sophia Moses Robison

The history of the discovery of the hidden crime survey is dominated by men, largely because academic careers were difficult or impossible for women in the early and mid-twentieth century. There is, however, one female scholar whose work influenced the discovery of the offender-based hidden crime survey: Sophia Moses Robison.

Can delinquency be measured?

In 1936, Sophia Moses Robison published a book called *Can Delinquency Be Measured*, which is a landmark study in crime measurement. In a way, it can be seen as a kind of 'missing link' between the old social survey tradition and later hidden crime surveys. Her book was a 'New York juvenile crime survey' in the old sense of the social survey as a fact-finding mission with ameliorative and sometimes religious purposes. Indeed, Robison's work was inspired by her involvement with settlement house work (Saul, 1981: 69), a movement that was closely linked with the Booth-style local social survey tradition. Like many of the early pioneers of the hidden crime studies, Robison combined humanism with rigour in science. Her outlook on life was philanthropic, moral and humanistic (Saul, 1981: 70–2), yet she was impressed by the kind of positivism promulgated by the Michael-Adler Report (Robison, 1936: 5, 10).

In *Can Delinquency Be Measured*, Robison posed the problem of delinquency measurement in a manner that called for a shift away from official statistics. She wanted to know the real relationship between apprehended and non-apprehended delinquency (p. 18). In so doing she challenged the classical constant ratio doctrine of criminal statistics. Her thesis and major result was that the likelihood of a delinquent to be officially recorded as delinquent was a variable:

Neighborhoods have varying population with regard to race, nationality, and associated customs, which affect the amount of delinquency officially registered, although the behavior of the children may remain the same. These differences in the amount of delinquency officially registered will reflect chiefly the different customs regarding children and resources for their care but not necessarily the differences in the proportions of children who perform the wide variety of acts which, under some circumstances, call public attention to their need of care as delinquents. (Robison, 1936: 4, see also pp. 33–6.)

Robison's method was to compare cases taken to court with a fuller sample that included all (or most) institutions which took care of delinquent youths in New York, including various unofficial facilities and charities. She was able to show that delinquents brought to court were in many respects a biased sample of all delinquents with some institutional contact. For example, females, younger age groups, and children from white Protestant families were underrepresented in the officially recorded delinquent population when compared with the full institutional population (pp. 57–60). African American youths were overrepresented in the court population (pp. 77, 195–6). Cases dealt with by the criminal justice system and the unofficial agencies were not different in terms of severity (pp. 205–6). Instead, social factors influenced '*the labeling of behaviour as delinquent or non-delinquent*' (Robison, 1936: 36, emphasis added; see also Sellin, 1928). These included group mores towards children or sub-groups of children, the availability of unofficial agencies in different parts of the city, and the differential propensity of families to seek outside help (Robison, 1936: 206). Robison observed that changes in the intensity of police control affected the likelihood of offences becoming known to the police, referring in particular to a 1930 'zero-tolerance'[21] campaign by the Coney Island police (p. 123). Opportunity structure, such as the presence of railroad yards in the neighbourhood, influenced people's reporting propensity as well (pp. 120–1).

Robison additionally observed that the official registration of a child's delinquency is affected by family income because wealthy families are able to deal with children's delinquency by private means (pp. 28–9). She therefore concluded that crime is not concentrated in the lowest social strata, a line of argument shared by many hidden crime research pioneers such as Hirschfeld, Sutherland and others. However, Robison did not use the normal-because-prevalent argument. In this respect, her work did not partake in the moral spirit of early hidden crime research. Her work was rather a 'demolition work', a criticism of official statistics that paved the way for alternative paradigms in delinquency measurement. She concluded that 'the court figures cannot be used to represent any definite fraction of the total problem', thus refuting the classical constant ratio doctrine of early moral statisticians and

---

[21] This more recent concept was not used by Robison.

criminologists (p. 206). Statistics based on the operation of the criminal justice system were unreliable as sources of quantitative crime data.

Reception of Robison's work

Robison's biographer, Shura Saul, wrote that 'the power of her dissertation was smashing, stunning, and it was so accepted by her colleagues' (Saul, 1981: 72). This statement needs some qualification. Reviews published in the most influential scientific journals were appreciative but critical.

The critics did not see Robison's study as calling for, let alone presaging, methodological innovations. Instead, they claimed that Robison was expressing views already known by everyone. Among her many critics was Samuel Stouffer, an important intellectual mandarin of quantitative sociology in mid-century America. In his lengthy review of Robison's book, published in the *American Journal of Sociology*, Stouffer claimed that 'in attacking the reliability of delinquency statistics based on court records Mrs. Robison has said little that is not common knowledge', even though she did manage to illuminate the problem in a novel way (Stouffer, 1937: 586). Stouffer went on to say that 'the "total volume" of delinquency cannot be measured, for the obvious reason that no written records can include all cases of youthful infractions of designated regulations' (p. 587). Stouffer additionally argued that 'an index which is useless as an absolute measure may be useful as a relative measure', meaning that official statistics could capture differences between areas even though they were strictly speaking invalid as descriptions of the total volume of delinquency in every area. Stouffer thus defended the constant ratio doctrine to salvage official statistics as a source of delinquency studies.

Sociological critics were motivated because they saw the Robison study as a challenge to Shaw and McKay's delinquency area studies. Stouffer in particular mounted a spirited defence. Otherwise remembered as a bulwark of quantitative sociology, he sharply defended qualitative and ethnographic delinquency research against Robison. The review published in the *American Sociological Review*, written by Ferris F. Laune, was short and hostile. In his view, the book was 'a result of an emotional reaction to the area studies of Shaw and McKay', and he concluded that the study 'does not at any place seriously challenge them' (Laune, 1937).

The psychiatric criminologist William Healy also reviewed Robison's work. Like Stouffer, he emphasized that what Robison said 'was already known to workers in the field, at least to those who had their eyes open' (Healy, 1937: 237). With barely disguised satisfaction, Healy interpreted Robison's work as a debunking of statistical and sociological analyses of crime. 'The sociological statisticians have something to chew over', he concluded. A more positive review was offered by C. E. Gehlke (1937), who reviewed Robison's work for the *Journal of the American Statistical Association*. He observed that Robison was rather successfully empirically attacking the constant ratio doctrine as an increasingly outdated justification for the use of official statistics in delinquency analysis. Gehlke suggested that the doctrine was more valid in temporal comparison than area comparison. He regarded Robison's book as a good piece of critical work. His positive reaction is not perhaps surprising, as Gehlke had been Sutherland's co-author in the *Recent Social Trends* article commissioned by president Hoover's administration (Sutherland and Gehlke, 1933). A review by Wiley Sanders, appearing in *Social Forces*, concluded that 'what proportion of actual delinquent behavior is not recorded by any agency is, of course, impossible to derive... in the strictest scientific sense, of course, delinquency is impossible of measurement' (Sanders, 1937: 577).

There is a paradox in the reviews of Robison's book. The reviewers apparently sensed that something important was being done, but still wanted to convince the readers, and perhaps themselves, that Robison offered nothing new. Were they baffled by the fact that a Jewish woman, aged 48, mother of five, and a social activist (Dinerman, 2009), had produced such an impressive analysis? With the possible exception of Laune's review referring to 'emotional reaction', there appears to be no evidence that Robison's identity influenced the way her work was received.

A road not taken: The concept of Central Register

Robison's main conclusions in *Can Delinquency Be Measured* were largely critical and negative: the criminal justice statistics were shown to be inadequate in crime measurement. However, during subsequent years she developed a positive programme that aimed at laying new foundations for delinquency research. She did not take the path that would lead to the sample survey based self-report delinquency studies. Instead, she pursued a parallel line of inquiry, developing the concept of the *Central Register*.

The idea of the Central Register was to record every detected juvenile offender before he or she was transferred to any kind of agency, be it the juvenile court, mental hygiene clinic or something else (Robison, 1960: 45–56). The concept was first piloted in Washington DC, in 1943–44, involving all public agencies dealing directly with allegedly delinquent children. The criteria of delinquency were relaxed to gain maximal inclusiveness. Any kind of behaviour that 'might be dealt with under the law' was included (Robison, 1960: 47). The Washington pilot again showed that juvenile court statistics were grossly insufficient as a measure of delinquency. Less than half of all known delinquents were known to juvenile court. Similar results later emerged from the New York Central Register experiment of 1950–52. In 1960, Robison optimistically suggested that a full-blown Central Register 'will achieve community-wide knowledge of the incidence of delinquency' by including 'all children at risk in the community who are in conflict with the law' (Robison, 1960: 50). Future Central Registers would achieve unprecedented coverage by penetrating the body social through three points of entry: the police, the school, and the parent-agency link. The last referred to parents contacting unofficial agencies such as private child guidance clinics. She wrote:

A community device like the Central Register will ultimately make it possible to conduct continuous and systematic research into delinquent behavior, based on better knowledge than is now available in the official statistics. With a reservoir such as the Central Register, problems of representative sampling would be at minimum, and manageable research projects could be formulated. (Robison, 1960: 53.)

Robison was out to achieve the same goals as the hidden crime survey researchers: a nearly total exposure of the dark figure of crime, and a flexible resource of research. Indeed, Robison's concept of the Central Register invites comparison with Foucault's concept of Panopticon. Like the Benthamite prison with a central and all-seeing observation post, Robison's Central Register would be a standardized epistemic reflection of a society's institutional archipelago for delinquents. However, the Robisonian Panopticon had an in-built design flaw that made it seriously myopic. The problem was that the Central Register did not include hidden delinquents. Her 'unofficial delinquents' were not true hidden delinquents, because they were processed by other institutions such as social work agencies and church-based organizations. Her critical work (*Can Delinquency Be Measured*) and her positive programme (the concept of Central Register) perfected the kind of hidden crime analysis that used alternative statistical records to supplement criminal justice sources. With hindsight, it can be argued that during the postwar years, this line of inquiry was eclipsed by the rise of the sample survey based self-report delinquency study as a solution to the problem of hidden crime. Why did the alternative statistics approach fail? First, it lacked the kind of flexibility and transferability that is typical of self-report surveys. By definition, Central Registers would remain anchored to the institutional archipelago of a given locality. In contrast, the self-report survey could be used anywhere and fast, at least if schools or similar institutions were available as points of entry. Second, the Central Register did not fully solve the problem of hidden crime; it just pushed back the frontier between recorded and unrecorded cases. Third, the hidden crime survey liberated delinquency measurement from the problematic dependence on legal definitions, which were replaced by an operational definition embedded in the standardized survey instrument. This again increased the transferability and flexibility of the sample survey.

Even though the Central Register concept could not solve the problem of hidden crime, Robison's work contributed to the 'turning point' (Laub, 2004) of criminology, the discovery of the self-report delinquency survey as a means of measuring the extent of hidden crime. Ultimately, her study shows how the methodology of crime measurement was based on historical changes in social and institutional practices. The philanthropic, religious and socially ameliorative movements of the nineteenth century had helped to create the charitable institutions whose records were then used to check the inclusiveness of the criminal justice records. Similarly, the hidden crime survey would lean heavily on the availability of children in the school system.

Sutherland experiments in the 1930s

In her book *Can Delinquency Be Measured*, Robison had reviewed possible alternative sources that could be used to measure the full extent of hidden delinquency. She mentioned the idea of using the offender as a source of data about his or her offending, noting that 'without doubt many children are aware of delinquencies of their own and of their acquaintances which are never adjudicated, either officially or unofficially' (Robison, 1936: 43). However she also assumed that such a source would be impossible to use in as large a community as New York City. In his review of Robison's book, Samuel Stouffer suggested that '[locally] it may be possible to collect a limited amount of new firsthand data based on a much broader definition of delinquency than would be feasible for an entire city' (Stouffer, 1937: 588). Robison also mentioned a scholar who was already conducting experiments with self-reports. In a footnote, she wrote that Professor Edwin H. Sutherland 'has attempted to work out a method of collecting this kind of data' (Robison, 1936: 43). It appears that Sutherland conducted small-scale self-report survey experiments among his students during the 1930s, even though he did not publish his findings.

Experimenting with self-reports

Did Sutherland actually collect self-report delinquency data? Probably he did. It is known that he asked Indiana University faculty members to keep records of thefts by their children (Snodgrass, 1972: 222), a kind of proxy survey method. In his various writings throughout the mid-1930s there are scattered traces of early experiments with self-report hidden delinquency surveys. In a 1936 address to the Milwaukee police, he revealed the findings of what may have been the first ever criminological self-report survey of non-sexual delinquency:

Of a class of forty, ten did not hand in papers, and since I had no signatures, I could not tell whether they were lily whites or had so many and so serious thefts that they refused to tell. Of those who did hand in reports, only one insisted that he could remember no thefts. (Sutherland, 1936, in Snodgrass, 1972: 222.)

Sutherland's pioneering experiments contained most of the typical elements of later self-report studies: targeting a specific population, anonymous responding, life-time recall period, and a confession of crimes based on standardized questions that are the same for all respondents. Apparently he did not report prevalence rates, at least not his address to the Milwaukee police, but the rates can be calculated from his figures. His response rate was

75 per cent. In the responding population (N = 30), the lifetime prevalence of theft was 97 per cent. Based on the number of non-respondents, the true prevalence had to be somewhere between 73 and 98 per cent. Sutherland's conclusion was that the true prevalence was in fact somewhere very close to 100. Speaking in the same year (1936) to the Indiana State Teachers Association, he said:

> It is quite apparent that in the United States today *all young people*, and perhaps old ones as well, are more or less 'delinquent'. In various universities I have asked students to write anonymously the list of thefts committed since early childhood. Practically *all of them* have had thefts to report, just as *all of us* would have. (Sutherland, 1973 [1936]: 143, emphases added.)[22]

The following year, in his classic study *The Professional Thief*, he wrote that 'everyone has an inclination to steal and expresses this inclination with more or less frequency' (Sutherland, 1972 [1937]: 213). In writing this, he probably had his own self-report experiments in mind. If so, he transferred findings from the classroom to a context in which he discussed serious professional theft. Be that as it may, petty and occasional delinquency was extremely prevalent beyond reasonable doubt. This fact was inconsistent with the notion that offenders were a radically distinct group from the non-offenders. Of special interest is that Sutherland's Indiana address contained the *moral reading* that would later attract many scholars to self-report studies: crime is so prevalent as to be normal. For example, when Nordic self-report delinquency research began in 1959, small samples of university students were used, and the project was morally embedded in the quest to rhetorically redescribe delinquency as normal (see Chapter 5).

Context of Sutherland's experiments

Sutherland's development of hidden crime indicators took place in a distinct historical context of disciplinary turf warfare. The emphasis on the high prevalence of middle and upper class delinquency was an attack against the abnormality paradigm of crime, which was associated with psychology and psychiatry. The attack against

---

[22] Sutherland went on to emphasize the petty nature of this delinquency, and he also recognized the obvious differences in incidence.

pathological explanations was part of 'sociology's coup of criminology' (Laub and Sampson, 1991: 1421).

The notions of hidden crime and selective detection were weapons in this onslaught. As early as in 1931, Sutherland had critiqued studies claiming to observe a link between low intelligence and crime. Witness how he argued his case:

> A second reason for discounting the early conclusion regarding the importance of feeblemindedness as a cause of delinquency is that the delinquents who have been tested are always a *selected portion of the entire delinquent population* and are probably selected partly because of their feeblemindedness. Delinquents who are smarter than policemen are less likely to be caught than those who are less intelligent. Mental tests of police in Los Angeles, Palo Alto, Detroit, and Cleveland indicate that, if this proposition is correct, *a very large portion of the general population could commit delinquencies and not be caught.* (Sutherland, 1931: 364, emphases added.)

Note how Sutherland uses the concept of hidden crime to attack the abnormality paradigm and its individual-level explanation of crime. He uses witty social satire to press his point, describing the police as so unintelligent that most delinquents must remain undetected and unrecorded. Later, he used the notion of ubiquitous crime in his critique of the Gluecks whose multi-factor theory was psychologically oriented. He stated that 'an individual can never be proved to be a non-delinquent' (Snodgrass, 1972: 247). If you look hard enough, everyone is a hidden delinquent. In his white-collar crime studies, he mainly used official records but additionally referred to non-governmental sources. For instance, lie-detector tests made in Chicago banks had revealed that 20 per cent of the employees had stolen bank property. Similar tests in a chain store had shown that 75 per cent of the employees had stolen money or merchandise from the store (Sutherland, 1983 [1949]: 7–8). During the 1930s, Sutherland may even have asked people point blank about crimes in their profession. In 1940 he wrote that 'white collar criminality is found in every occupation, and can be discovered readily in a casual conversation with a representative of an occupation by asking him, "What crooked practices are found in your occupation?"' (Sutherland, 1940: 2).

Sutherland was an eager critic of psychological and psychiatric explanations of crime (Galliher and Tyree, 1985; Laub and Sampson, 1991). Showing that many white-collar people were criminal and showing that almost all of his students had stolen at some time in their lives were means of critiquing the individual-level explanations of the psy-sciences. If we ask the Skinnerian question, what was Sutherland doing when he discovered white-collar crime and the hidden crime survey, a good answer can be found in the early pages of his classic monograph *White Collar Crime*. He critiqued the conception that crime was caused by pathological factors, be they social or individual (Sutherland, 1949: 5). White-collar crime showed that a 'person of the upper socioeconomic class engage in much criminal behaviour' (p. 7). The twin strategy of white-collar crime studies and hidden crime survey experiments thus served the purpose of cutting the link between crime and poverty (Snodgrass, 1972: 229).[23] As observed above, it is important for the cultural normalization of a behaviour type that it is no longer seen as typical or exclusively lowest class behaviour. During the first decades of self-report delinquency surveys, the method was often seen as linked to the study of white-collar crime. These two traditions, which today are almost completely separate, shared a context of discovery in the disciplinary schism between sociology and the psy-sciences.

Sutherland did not publish his self-report survey experiments, even though he referred to them in his lectures and books. The first systematic self-report studies were conducted by another American scholar whose social background was quite similar to Sutherland's: Austin Larimore Porterfield.

Harnessing confession: Austin Larimore Porterfield

In 1940–41, the Texan sociologist Austin L. Porterfield conducted a small-scale survey that was to become a classic in criminology. Porterfield asked college students to report anonymously about their delinquent behaviour. His work differs from Sutherland's prior studies in important respects. First, he went public with the findings. Second, his samples, albeit small by modern standards, were probably slightly bigger than those used by Sutherland. Third, he contrasted the 'full' view of crime, revealed by survey, with a biased and selective sample or recorded offences. And perhaps most

---

[23] Recall that Robison also attacked the link between crime and poverty by indicating that wealthy families are able to divert their delinquent offspring from the attentions of the criminal justice system (see above). Sutherland was one of the scholars who helped Robison in her PhD thesis.

importantly, he built the moral frame that would inspire the first generation of criminological self-report delinquency researchers: the idea that because delinquency was very prevalent, it was normal.

Facts in frame

Porterfield's groundbreaking survey was initially reported in his article 'Delinquency and Its Outcome in Court and College', published in 1943 (Porterfield, 1943). However, his scholarly vision is best exemplified by his monograph *Youth in Trouble* (1946). The moral frame of Porterfield's self-report survey, as presented in the second chapter of his book, cannot be fully grasped without describing the first chapter, entitled 'Delinquents and complainants in court and community'. It is about the people who report children to the police and the juvenile courts. This is the first paragraph in full:

A real factor in the conflict of children with a community is the community itself, and particularly that section of community's population which is most likely to complain. This hypothesis is supported by a study of 1,500 cases of children whose accusers in a juvenile court could be identified—a study which proceeded on the assumption that [. . .] we may judge by the nature of the complaints something of the nature of the person who complains. And we may conclude, from our data, that *no small part of the conflict with youth grows out of the peevishness, impatience, irresponsibility, and, in many cases, the criminalistic attitudes of the complainant.* (Porterfield, 1946: 15, emphasis added.)

In the following pages, Porterfield marshals evidence on how adults have unjustly reported juveniles to authorities. The offences are often petty and sometimes irritating, but the whole point is the irresponsibility of parents and others who relegate children to courts and jails. In technical terms, Porterfield shows in great detail how social control creates the population of recorded offenders. Crime statistics are therefore also social constructs.

In the next chapter Porterfield reports the findings of his self-report survey of college students. The questionnaire followed logically from the topic of the previous chapter. Porterfield analysed what kind of offences were committed by recorded delinquents and included those offences to his questionnaire to be used in a community sample. In 1940–41, he asked about the pre-college delinquent behaviour of 100 men and 137 women. In 1941–42, he asked about both pre-college and college delinquent behaviour of 100 men. Based on anonymous responding, the surveys were conducted in three schools in northern Texas. Strikingly, the results indicated a *'universal prevalence of past delinquency among college men and women'* (Porterfield, 1946: 38). To give just a few examples from the more serious offences among the pre-college men, 22 per cent had driven when drunk, 13 per cent had set fires in buildings, 62 per cent had participated in ordinary fighting, 8 per cent had committed burglary, 10 per cent had shoplifted, and 6 per cent had attempted to rape (Porterfield, 1946: 40–1). One pre-college male respondent even reported having committed a murder, a finding that Porterfield did not discuss.

The prevalence of delinquency was rather similar among college students and recorded offenders. Porterfield interpreted this finding as follows:

Delinquents are not a sub-species of *Homo Sapiens*; neither are the 'best' citizens. The antisocial behavior of both students and court children suggest the same fundamental wishes: new experience, adventure, stimulation, challenge, recognition, personal response—in short, the whole range of the human emotions. (Porterfield, 1946: 45.)

Porterfield also noted that official delinquents have probably committed a greater average number of offences (Porterfield, 1946: 42), so that they really differ in this respect. However, in his view, the notion of delinquents as fundamentally 'other' was destroyed by the self-report survey method. The abnormality of the delinquent group was socially constructed by peevish and hypocritical local elites.

Reception by contemporaries

On reading reviews of Porterfield's book, it is apparent that none of the people who reviewed it immediately after its publication sensed that 'a turning point' in criminology (Laub, 2004) was in the making. In *American Sociological Review*, Lowell S. Selling (1947) noted laconically the 'interesting' use of 'a control group' in Porterfield's research. He wrote that the book is useful for a layman but 'the serious sociologist must continue to gain his most useful data from standard texts'. L. Guy Brown's (1947) review in the *American Journal of Sociology* was similarly short.

F. C. Sumner, Professor of psychology at Howard University, reviewed Porterfield's book for the *Journal of Abnormal and*

Social Psychology. He was among the few who perceived the wider moral lessons of the book. He clearly understood the connection between Porterfield's hidden crime survey and the concept of 'white-collar crime', and concluded his review as follows:

> The book as a whole merits inclusion among significant recent studies of juvenile delinquency. Its bias to the sociogenesis of all criminal behavior will serve as a much needed antidote to the tendency of psychiatrists to diagnose overfrequently the inmates of training schools for juvenile offenders as constitutional psychopathic inferiors. (Sumner, 1947: 377.)

As a psychologist Sumner could appreciate the anti-psychiatric implications of hidden crime surveys showing high prevalence of offending in all social strata.

Mabel A. Elliott, a sociologist from the University of Kansas, is an interesting reviewer of Porterfield's work. Her initial review was negative. She began by stating that 'this little book leaves much to be desired so far as scientific analysis is concerned' and noted that Porterfield 'condemns both private and public institutions' (Elliott, 1947: 171). She described the core results of Porterfield's self-report survey but was not particularly impressed. Two years later, Elliott (1949) returned to the topic, but now her tone had changed. She now regarded Porterfield's findings as *'the most startling'* facts about delinquency. She recapitulated that Porterfield's hidden delinquents were 'class officers, honor students, ministerial students, athletes and musicians', and their offences ranged from 'truancy to serious sex offences, shoplifting and murder'. Furthermore, there was 'no close relationship between income and delinquency'. The major conclusion was that *'respectable people are relatively lawless'* and that *'criminal procedure is shot through with hypocrisy'* (Elliott, 1949: 249–51, emphasis added).

What had happened between Elliott's first and second review? It appears that in her first review, she did not yet use or possess the *moral frame* of early hidden crime surveys, which stressed the criminality of hypocritical middle and upper class people. Apparently, she adopted the moral frame some time between 1947 and 1949. This may have something to do with her increasingly critical view of the American criminal justice system (McGonical and Galliher, 2009: 62–5). In this anti-punitive context she realized the policy use of the hidden crime survey and became a disseminator of the normal-because-prevalent argument. Possibly her change of mood was facilitated by Wallerstein and Wyle's article 'Our Law-Abiding

Law-Breakers' (see section 'The law-abiding law-breaker' below), which had appeared between Elliott's first and second review. In 1952, Elliott incorporated a chapter on hidden crime surveys in her criminology textbook *Crime in Modern Society*, including a discussion of the Wallerstein and Wyle study. The book also included a section titled 'The Average Person is a Lawbreaker'. There Elliott listed various types of crimes committed by otherwise respectable people, some of which were satirical offender types such as treasurers of church organizations, city managers and college students (Elliott, 1952: 79–80). As an early interpreter of the moral message of the hidden crime survey, Mabel Elliott thus shares many of the typical features of the tradition.

Porterfield as social satirist

According to Porterfield, the reason why some children appeared in court and others in college was the unjust targeting of social control based on the social position of the child and his family. This constellation was highly germane to satirical treatment. The delinquent could be defined as a young person 'who is not old enough to run for legislature, but who has offended some part of a rather peevish and irresponsible community, and been charged with the necessity for being responsible and other than peevish himself' (Porterfield, 1946: 46). Porterfield had many concrete examples:

The Ku Klux Klan, never noted for a child-centered program, used to complain because boys [. . .] were suspected of breaking into the Klan Hall. (Porterfield, 1946: 22.)

[The recorded delinquents] are of less social importance than the clerks and managers of five-and-ten-cent stores who turn them in for petty shoplifting. (Porterfield, 1946: 46.)

While the parents of the [recorded delinquent] may be asking the court to send him to the training school, the parents of the [unrecorded delinquent] are planning to send the lucky boy to college. (Porterfield, 1946: 48.)

[The unrecorded delinquent] too, has taken excursions into the underworld and has seen the chief of police drunk at the 399 Club, but he also moves in highly respected circles in the community. (Porterfield, 1946: 49.)

The Klan, the petty store managers, the parents who ask their children to be jailed, and the drunken police chief—*they were all hypocrites*. Clearly, Porterfield was a satirist par example, a social critic in the prophetic and Biblical tradition, exposing the hypocrisy of the 'righteous people'.[24] Porterfield's biographer, Leonard Cain, cites a story by a former student, that Porterfield sent students to write down the licence plates of local cars frequenting a particular local motel. One wonders what to make of this, but it is possible that Porterfield was experimenting with yet another method of hidden crime research: direct observation of illicit activity like extramarital affairs, use of prostitutes, etc. He was out to expose the local elites as hypocrites, and clandestine motel visits would be a good means of discrediting such elites. If true, such activity resembles the muckraking type of exposure journalism which was widely prevalent during the populist and progressive eras in the US.

If we ask the question, what was Porterfield *doing* with the self-report method, the answer must be: he was out to destroy the idea that the typical offender was mentally abnormal. There was no essential difference between the offender and the law-abiding citizen, who was likely to be an undetected offender. Later, during the 1950s, Porterfield wrote about the 'we-they' fallacy, meaning the (erroneous) belief that offenders were essentially abnormal and different from the rest of us. In this context, he noted that the 'we-they' fallacy had proved to be surprisingly resistant in the face of evidence that all social classes committed crimes (Porterfield, 1957: 46).

Social Gospel and midwestern populism

Porterfield, a Professor of Texas Christian University, was influenced by religious traditions. Before his scientific career, he worked for two decades as a pastor, and throughout his career he continued to serve at weekends as a guest preacher (Cain, 2005: xx). According to Cain (2005), he was influenced by the Social Gospel movement that supported the alliance of Christianity and sociology. Especially Walter Rauschenbusch,[25] with his *Theology for the Social Gospel* (1922 [1917]), inspired Porterfield. This book underscored the communal, regular and normal nature of sin. Rauschenbusch

---

[24] Later he would similarly expose the widespread racism in judicial decisions made by local popular elites (Porterfield and Gibbs, 1953).

[25] It tells something about the role of Rauschenbusch that presidents Theodore Roosevelt and Woodrow Wilson consulted him on their social programs (White and Hopkins, 1976: 179).

condemned the hypocritical condemnation of ordinary sinners, because we were all sinners and because 'the sin of all is in each of us' (Rauschenbusch, 1922 [1917]: 91). This religious theme would reverberate in the hidden crime tradition. Interestingly, Rauschenbusch also devoted a whole chapter to 'super-personal forces of evil', or what we would now call *corporate and state crime*. In so doing he raised the question of undetected and unrecorded white-collar crime. This was highly consistent with the spirit of the Social Gospel, social religion in the age of populism and progressivism. As has been described above, the Social Gospel movement was one of the first social movements ever to make extensive use of what was then called the 'social survey'. Social Gospel and settlement house activists gathered information about the moral situation of neighbourhoods, for instance by counting saloons and jail populations (White and Hopkins, 1976: 135–9). Social Gospel can be seen as the religious segment of the American populist–progressive movement (Nugent, 2010: 59–62).

Porterfield's thinking belongs to the American populist tradition. In the 1930s, he was inspired by Charles A. Ellwood and Howard Jensen, whose populism and belief in using sociology to change society reinforced his own predispositions and commitments (Michel and Cain, 1980). Porterfield felt that objectivity required freedom from the 'corruption of vested interests' and that sociology could serve to counteract special interests (Porterfield, 1941: 38, 262). In this he resembled C. Wright Mills who also fought various elites and 'the interests' (Coser, 1971: 278–80). However, Porterfield was not a populist in the sense of demanding harsh punishments for offenders. His work exposed such demands as hypocritical.

What is needed is not to treat the more fortunate [unrecorded] offenders as badly as the less fortunate [recorded offenders] in order to be fair, but to treat the less fortunate with the same consideration that we give to the more fortunate offenders. (Porterfield, 1946: 105.)

In this and many other passages Porterfield sees *luck* as the factor that separates unrecorded and recorded offenders. This was to be repeated many times at least in the Nordic self-report movement of the 1960s (Chapter 5). But Porterfield also formulated another argument which later became important. In judging how severely we should punish recorded offenders, we should keep in mind the great majority who have offended but remained unrecorded.

While direct contacts between Porterfield and Sutherland appear to have been nearly nonexistent,[26] they share a lot in terms of social background. Sutherland's father was a preacher and he himself, as a young man, began his training in religious subjects. This background may partially explain the emotional tone in which Sutherland dissected the offences of white-collar criminals (Geis and Coff, 1983: xv, xx). Second, his early and significant tutors represented the tradition of Christian sociology. When Sutherland first coined the term white-collar criminal, he used the version 'white collar criminaloid' (Geis and Goff, 1983: xvii). The concept 'criminaloid' was adapted from the book *Sin and Society*, by Edward Ross (1973 [1907]). Both Ross and Henderson influenced Sutherland in his youth (Gaylord and Galliher, 1988: 18, 32). As a consequence of this dual impact, Sutherland's work on white-collar crime was '*reminiscent of the preaching of outraged biblical prophets*' (Geis and Goff, 1983: xviii, emphasis added). Because of the general progressive, populist and religious context, Sutherland was certainly not alone in using the prophetic style. Thus, the sociologist Charles Ellwood wrote in 'prophetic mode', while the intellectual style of C. Wright Mills—another populist with midwestern roots—was characterized by 'overtones of hellfire and damnation' (Tilman, 1984: 195; Turner, 2007: 116). Continuing the old progressive-religious tradition of jeremiads against the upper strata of society, Porterfield, Sutherland and Mills may have been the last of this breed before the positivist-empiricist 'Americanization' of social sciences during the 1950s.

Earlier, in fin-de-siècle Berlin, Magnus Hirschfeld had used the self-report deviance survey to expose the facades of middle and upper class propriety. Sutherland and Porterfield were out to achieve the same goal, and invented the same tool without knowledge of German and Dutch precedents. Of course, the background of these American sociologists differed from Hirschfeld. Attacking the hypocrisy of white-collar people was consistent with the tradition of American populism. As described by Snodgrass,

---

[26] The last footnote of Porterfield's classic article is a curious and rather long commentary of Sutherland's theory where the author acknowledges 'thorough agreement with Edwin H. Sutherland's theory of "White Collar Criminality"' (Porterfield, 1943: 208). It is hard to know what to make of it, but it seems almost like a response to a reviewer comment.

Sutherland's agrarian roots, midwestern origin, provincial affiliations, urban resentments and Baptist upbringing made him resemble an 'old-time populist' (Snodgrass, 1972: 229). Shaw, McKay, Sutherland and Porterfield were all raised and located in the central midwest. The emerging sociological criminology came from the rural midwest to challenge the psychological multi-factor tradition of the eastern seaboard (Snodgrass, 1972: 10). Both Porterfield and Sutherland were scholars with rural-populist origins, both were sons of preachers, and both were influenced by the progressive and sociologically oriented religious thought that condemned the hypocrisy of the putatively law-abiding middle and upper classes. Both Sutherland and Porterfield showed that crime is prevalent in all social strata, yet the middle and upper classes all too often managed to avoid detection and prosecution.

The populist or progressive tradition may be a sufficient cultural context to motivate the exposure of hidden delinquents, but it can hardly be seen as a necessary condition. As an empirical finding, the high prevalence of crime is like an invitation to the critique of hypocrites. For example, Tom Harrison, who wrote the introduction to the delinquency report of the UK Mass Observation unit, observed the high prevalence of offending and commented that 'any person who can thereafter feel wholly self-righteous is, in a way, more to be pitied than praised', thus connecting with the critique of hypocrites that recurs in the early hidden crime research (Willcock, 1949: 12). Similarly, the British sociologist John Barron Mays wrote in 1963 that 'illegal conduct permeates the whole of our society' and warned that excessive moralizing reflects 'the *hoary sin of phariseeism* so severely castigated in the New Testament' (Mays, 1963: 39; emphasis added). While these British writers certainly were not 'midwestern populists', they too drew inspiration from religious cultural lexicons.

Boasian relativity

The influence of midwestern populism and Social Gospel traditions are the strongest ingredients in Porterfield's approach to crime. However, there was another intellectual current that was part of the context in which he discovered the self-report survey. During the 1920s, American sociology had cut its earlier ties to biology by strongly underscoring the concept of culture as an analytic concept and object of study (Camic, 2007: 230; Degler, 1991). This turn of events was linked to the work of Franz Boas, an anthropologist, and his pupils such as Ruth Benedict and Margaret Mead. As observed above, the vehement attack of C. Wright Mills (1943) and Edwin Sutherland (1945) against the 'social pathologists' was related to the Boasian notion of cultural relativity. The social pathologist was someone who did not understand that different groups had different values and norms, and the mainstream society was in this respect on a par with all others, including criminal groups. This opened the prospect that in some cases, a conflict between 'criminals' and the law might be solved by changing the law.

In his criminological work, Porterfield did not *explicitly* connect with Boasian relativity. At the time when he was conducting the first self-report delinquency survey, he commented positively on the Boas-influenced 'culture and personality' school (Porterfield, 1941: 229–40). He liked the idea that people's behaviour was caused by cultural learning, even if our culture might define such learned behaviour as abnormal. On the other hand, a nonconformist could change culture. Porterfield suggested that 'we may extend the definition of normality to include not only the conformist but also the creative personality' (Porterfield, 1941: 230–49). By creative personality he meant the nonconformist. The appreciation of the nonconformist was important in Durkheim's effort to redescribe crime as normal; that Porterfield mentioned Jesus of Nazareth as an example is akin to Durkheim giving Socrates as the role model of nonconformism.

The law-abiding law-breaker

In 1951, the American writer James S. Wallerstein published a novel called *The Demon's Mirror* (Wallerstein, 1951). The novel defies genre labels, but today it would probably be described as a mixture of fantasy and science fiction. It is about an ancient magic mirror whose possession gives the power to fulfil dreams, but the main action takes place in contemporary times. This setting allowed Wallerstein to incorporate satirical elements into the storyline. One of the characters in the novel is a professor who preaches Social Darwinist doctrines about the survival of the fittest, but is himself a very sickly person. Another is a corrupt superintendent of a school for delinquent boys, a kind of law-abiding law-breaker (Wallerstein, 1951: 160, 144).

Who was Wallerstein? The dust-jacket of the *Demon's Mirror* introduces him as 'a biological chemist, an inventor with many patents to his credit and author of numerous scientific articles'. He had also 'directed the Randen Foundation crime survey, widely publicized in the Reader's Digest and other journals'.[27]

The Randen Foundation crime survey

The Randen Foundation crime survey was the first-ever general hidden crime survey targeted at an adult population. The polymath Wallerstein thus occupies a central place in the history of the hidden crime survey. The core findings of the Randen foundation survey were published in 1947 by Wallerstein and Clement J. Wyle in an article titled 'Our Law-abiding Law-breakers' (Wallerstein and Wyle, 1953 [1947a]). The oxymoronic title is a good example of the satirical style of the first generation self-report researchers. Wallerstein and Wyle's article continues to be cited by criminologists as the first survey-based study to have measured the hidden crime of adults.

In the Randen Foundation crime survey, Wallerstein and Wyle circulated questionnaires listing 49 types of behaviour that were offences under the penal law of the state of New York. While they did not explain how the sample was formed, they guaranteed that the questionnaires were distributed in a manner that sought to ensure a balanced racial, religious and professional representation (p. 419). Altogether, 1,698 individuals submitted replies. Because the size of the targeted sample was not reported, the response rate is unknown.

The lifetime prevalence rates of various crimes were revealed to be high. For example, 49 per cent of males reported assault, 17 per cent burglary, 13 per cent grand larceny, and 11 per cent robbery. These are high figures in a study based on a community sample of adults. Wallerstein and Wyle noted that the high assault figure may reflect 'the inclusion of such episodes as fist fights and violent shoving in the subway' (p. 421). The study showed that 'the number of acts legally constituting crimes are far in excess of those officially reported', and that crime was prevalent 'among respectable people' (pp. 423–4). In describing the crimes of respectable people, the

---

[27] In my copy of the *Demon's Mirror*, there is a card attached stating 'compliments of the Randen Foundation'.

authors were able to partake in the satirical tradition of early hidden crime surveys. Revelling in the newly found criminality of the middle classes, they wrote:

> Businessmen and lawyers were highest in perjury, falsification, fraud and tax evasion; teachers and social workers in malicious mischief; writers and artists in indecency, criminal libel and gambling; military and government employees in simple larceny, burglary and robbery; students in auto misdemeanors. (Wallerstein and Wyle, 1953 [1947a]: 421.)

The authors interpreted their findings as reflecting the random operation of social control and the criminal justice system. 'The solid truth remains that there is a large chance element in our administration of justice and it's the unlucky ones who are caught' (p. 423). Many citizens committing offences evaded detection 'from sheer accident' (p. 424).[28] Possibly the most important policy implication was advanced in the final paragraph of the article. The authors wrote that, from the angle of criminological self-report research, 'the punitive attitude of society toward the convicted offender becomes not only *hypocritical* but pointless' (p. 424, emphasis added). This argument would reverberate in the later reception of self-report studies among criminologists, especially in the initial phase of Nordic research. It was wrong to punish detected offenders harshly when so many unrecorded offenders went scot-free. It was assumed that there were no qualitative or quantitative differences between the recorded and unrecorded offenders.

When the Wallerstein and Wyle article was reprinted in a criminology reader by Vedder et al in 1953, it was placed in the category 'white-collar crime' instead of, for example, crime statistics or measurement of crime. This reflects the ambivalent status of the hidden crime survey within criminology during its early days. The sub-demarcations of the criminological discipline were fluid, if judged by an anachronistic contemporary standard. The hidden crime survey was often seen as a sub-field of white-collar crime studies, and vice versa: white-collar crime studies were seen and received in the framework of hidden crime studies (see, for example, Elliott, 1952).

---

[28] They did not ask the respondents about getting caught and were thus unable to study empirically the association between offence frequency and registration likelihood.

Three strikes against the abnormality paradigm

'Our Law-abiding Law-breakers' was part of a set of three articles published by the same authors in 1947, all attacking punitive attitudes and the abnormality paradigm of crime.

In the article on 'Biological Inferiority as a Cause for Delinquency' Wallerstein and Wyle (1947b) critiqued the studies and theories of E. A. Hooton, who was a biologically oriented criminologist. Hooton was a typical representative of the abnormality paradigm: he regarded delinquency as a manifestation of constitutional biological deviation. Wallerstein and Wyle argued that the conclusions of Hooton could not be drawn from his own data and results. Their article was a 'demolition job' in a coordinated attack against the abnormality paradigm in criminology. Later, Wallerstein would incorporate elements of this article into his novel *The Demon's Mirror*. Hooton may have inspired the funny character of 'an eminent anthropologist' who, himself a sickly man, preached that 'criminal tendencies were [. . .] hereditarily transmitted by persons of inferior intellect and debased morality' (Wallerstein, 1951: 161). The anthropologist failed to live as he preached: 'Cloistered in the comfort of academic security, he glorified hardship as the driving force of evolution, but became exceedingly annoyed when the hot water was turned off in his bathroom' (Wallerstein, 1951: 137). Since the pioneers of the hidden crime survey were convinced that we are all sinners,[29] this kind of hypocritical morality irritated them. They wanted to expose the facades of the conservative punitivists and the biologically oriented psychiatrists. Wallerstein additionally ridiculed intelligence tests in his novel: the delinquent Tom was tested twice, and found to be both a 'moron' and a 'genius' (p. 171).

The third article of the salvo, entitled 'Roots of Delinquency', was authored by Wallerstein alone. The article on biological inferiority had critiqued abnormality explanations of crime. Here, he presented a positive programme, an alternative explanation of delinquency: Freudian psychoanalysis.[30] Crime represented

---

[29] Wallerstein has one of his characters say, 'we are all sinners' (Wallerstein 1951: 161).

[30] One wonders whether Wyle, a sociologist, disagreed with Wallerstein's Freudianism and is therefore not a co-author in this article. Perhaps they could agree on doing a hidden crime survey, and attacking the abnormality paradigm of crime, but not on promoting Freud as alternative.

'symbolic gratification of a forbidden sexual act blocked by the inhibitions of conscience'. The delinquent was 'deliberately provoking punishment' (p. 405). Crime represented 'the eruption of the psychic tension along the line of least resistance provided by conscience' (Wallerstein, 1947: 404–6). Wallerstein summed up his programme as follows:

> The picture of society divided into a criminally minded underworld and law-abiding good citizens is, of course, a wholly false one. The 'good citizen' differs from the offender only in the intensity of his psychic tension and the extent and direction of his resistance—thus perhaps only in the frequency with which his psychic tension breaks through the bonds of the collective conscience. In a survey of Texas divinity students, Pottersfield [sic] found that nearly all of them had at some time in their youth committed an act for which some other youngster had been committed to reformatory. A similar study on the extent of adult crime was carried out by the Randen Foundation in New York State [...]. It was found that 99 per cent had committed some act punishable by six months or more imprisonment [...]. In the light of these findings, theories of crime and delinquency as a rare and unusual manifestation are hardly tenable. (Wallerstein, 1947: 407.)

The early hidden crime survey was an instrument of attack against the previously dominant abnormality paradigm, and a means of promoting sociological explanations of crime. The invention of the hidden crime survey was thus embedded in two closely related contexts of discovery: the moral critique of punitive over-regulation and the disciplinary battle of sociology to achieve hegemony over criminology. How does Wallerstein's advocacy of Freudian theories fit this picture? It appears to be in some contrast with the general anti-psychological and anti-psychiatric attitude shared by many hidden crime researchers. In the next two sections I will tackle this anomaly from two points of view. First, I will briefly examine how Freudians accommodated themselves to new findings showing the generality of deviance. Second, I describe how Merton used Wallerstein and Wyle's research as a means of warding off disciplinary embraces by Freudians.

The role of Freudian cultural impact

The discovery phase of the hidden crime survey (1930–60, see Figure 4.1 below, p.121) coincided with the heyday of Freudian cultural impact in the US. The emerging finding of self-report delinquency surveys, that there was a huge multitude of undetected offenders, actually refuted a core Freudian theory of crime, namely the idea that criminals were motivated by their wish to be punished. The hidden crime survey showed rather that many offenders were happy *not* to be detected and punished (see, for example, Aubert, 1972 [1954]: 117).

However, the Freudians were able to interpret the new findings as supportive evidence for their framework. Describing psychiatry's views on crime, Manfred Guttmacher claimed that the survey-based high prevalence findings had been 'largely anticipated by psychiatrists' (Guttmacher, 1958: 633). By psychiatrists he meant Freudian psychoanalysts:

[P]sychoanalytic studies of normal individuals have revealed a quantum of aggression and hostility in everyone. Indeed, most persons have sadistic fantasies and murderous dreams. The fascination that newspaper accounts of crime, crime novels, and crime dramas have, for vast numbers of people, is surely dependent, in large measure, upon the *ubiquity of antisocial impulses*. (Guttmacher, 1958: 633, emphasis added.)

Guttmacher wrote about Freud as 'the master' and described Freud's crime theory according to which some offenders committed crimes because they wanted to be punished (Guttmacher, 1958: 634, 639). It sounds credible that the Freudian 'climate of opinion' during the 1950s made the reception and dissemination of the normality paradigm easier. Freudian psycho-culture encouraged people to think that everyone was potentially slightly deviant. Such a context supported innovating ideologists who wanted to redescribe certain types of criminal behaviour as normal. Still, the riddle remains: why Freudianism could be combined with normalization (Wallerstein, 1947; Guttmacher, 1958) while most of the early self-report researchers rejected explanations operating at the level of individual pathology? This dilemma is solved by two contextual specifications.

First, psychiatry was not monolithic. During the 1950s, there were at least two psychiatric paradigms: the so-called first biological psychiatry, and the Freudian psychodynamic psychiatry. *The* psychiatry which was attacked by scholars like Sutherland was the 'first biological psychiatry', with its 'sexual psychopath laws' and huge lunatic asylums. The abnormality paradigm of crime was associated with that tradition. Freudianism was, in many respects, a countermovement to the first biological psychiatry, even though it managed skilfully its relations to the medical model of mainstream psychiatry. In other words, the ire of the sociologists largely bypassed Freudianism, at least in the 1950s.[31]

Second, the Freudian adaptation of crime survey findings may simply reflect the extreme flexibility with which that movement canvassed 'supporting evidence' and aligned with the prevailing *zeitgeist*. Thus, in the 1960s, the famous psychoanalyst Carl Menninger would start from the normal-because-prevalent argument in his attack against hypocritical punitivism, *The Crime of Punishment* (Menninger, 2007 [1966]: xxix, 5). Indeed, Menninger was a latecomer to this platform: he was preceded more than two decades by the first generation of hidden crime survey researchers.

During the 1950s, sociologists were as critical as ever of encroachments from psychology, but Freudian thought was for many the least unacceptable kind of psychology. The basic idea was that psychology is bad for sociology, but, if you must have some, take Freudianism (see Mills, 1958 for a fairly typical discussion; cf Steinmetz, 2007: 338). Freudians of course were not passive in their relation towards social scientists. They were interested in co-opting sociologists to a common cause of accepting Freudian theories. One of the occasions in which Freudians invited sociologists to 'peace talks' is of particular interest here because Robert Merton, acting as sociology's ambassador, used self-report delinquency findings to forestall excessive cooperation between psychiatry and sociology. This incident, described below, additionally shows that crime survey findings were perceived as strategically important by hardcore sociology theorists.

Merton, the 'Little Paper' and sociology

In May 1955, the Children's Bureau of the US Department of Health, Education, and Welfare organized a conference 'on the relevance and interrelations of certain concepts from sociology and psychiatry for delinquency'. The psychoanalyst Erik Erikson and the sociologist Robert Merton emerged as leading exponents of their respective disciplines. Erikson first explained his views on

---

[31] In the 1960s, the radicalization of sociology changed this. In the Nordic area, the hidden crime survey movement was hostile to Freudianism as well, probably because *any* kind of psychiatry could be used to support indeterminate sentencing and the 'treatment ideology'. See Guttmacher 1958, 648, for a Freudian argument in favour of indeterminate sentencing.

delinquency, using psychoanalytic vocabulary. He saw delinquency as a subconscious reaction to psychic problems, a kind of a behavioural language that could be interpreted by a psychoanalyst. 'To be delinquent [...] sometimes seems preferable to the anxiety which is set free by a more objective appraisal of one's contradictory identity fragments' (Erikson, in Witmer and Kotinsky, 1956: 12). Erikson supported the Freudian theory of criminal motivation according to which criminals commit crimes because they want to be detected and punished and cited newspaper clippings about delinquents who had 'wanted to be caught' (pp. 13, 49).

In turn, Merton began in a slightly irritated tone, saying that 'it might be useful to polarize the discussion at the outset and then see what happens' (Merton, in Witmer and Kotinsky, 1956: 24). He then proceeded to several critiques of psychological explanations of delinquency (pp. 25–9). First, he noted that psychologists' conception of social environment was naïve, in that they equated social environment with the immediate surroundings of the child (like 'broken home', 'slum area'), and neglected the role of the social structure. He suggested that the social environment should be subjected to equally detailed analysis as the inner psychic reality of the individual. Second, he noted that researchers should be more analytic in terms of the dependent variable, because 'delinquency' was 'a designating tag or label' hiding substantial variation. Belief in a single explanation of delinquency was like the belief of early medical scientists that there must be a single cause of all kinds of diseases. Instead, researchers should seek explanations of various types of delinquency. Third, Merton referred to his own anomie theory of delinquency. Delinquency results because cultural expectations are out of joint with structural possibilities to fulfil those expectations. This theory was a critique of the abnormality paradigm because it showed that delinquency is a socially induced deviation from social norms.

Having presented these general critiques of the abnormality paradigm, Merton offered an additional argument: the high prevalence of offending. He critiqued the statistics on recorded offences as a data source of delinquency research. Such sources were 'social bookkeeping data'. He said:

From the sociological standpoint, 'juvenile delinquency' and what it encompasses is a form of deviant behavior for which the epidemiological data, as it were, may not be at hand. You may have to go out and collect your own appropriately organized data rather than take those which are ready-made by governmental and other agencies. (p. 31.)

As an example of the kind of data collection he had in mind, he referred to 'the little paper entitled "Our Law-abiding Law-breakers" published some 8 or 10 years ago by James S. Wallerstein and Clement J. Wyle' (p. 31). He additionally acknowledged Porterfield's prior studies. The relevant lesson of these studies was summarized as follows:

> The same action may be defined as a technically allowable departure from overly exacting rules or as an expression of a deviant social type that is tagged as delinquent or criminal. All this indicates that if these deviant acts do in fact turn up in strata of society where those who perform them are unlikely to be tagged as juvenile delinquents or as criminals, then the forces making for deviant behaviour are by no means confined to those strata where these acts are likely to become part of the public record. We lose sight of this as long as we confine our inquiries to officially available statistics on officially defined delicts of one sort or another. (Merton, in Witmer and Kotinsky, 1956: 32.)

Not surprisingly, Merton's initial comments were subjected to a barrage of questions from the seminar participants. Peter Neubauer wanted to know how normal and abnormal behaviour could be defined. Merton offered a functionalist demarcation criterion: 'The sociologist regards those behaviors as normal that do not make for certain kinds of instability in the social system, in precisely the same way as the psychologist regards those as normal' (Neubauer, in Witmer and Kotinsky, 1956: 34). By implication, undetected mass delinquency could be sociologically normal if it did not cause instability in the social system.

Bernard Lander followed up with an observation that was pertinent from the point of view of hidden crime studies. He noted that Porterfield and others had shown the high *prevalence* of occasional offending. But in his view, the crucial question was the *incidence* and *versatility*[32] of offending. Nearly all people commit occasional offences, but few are repeatedly or habitually criminal:

> This difference would be very significant in distinguishing between the kind of individuals whom we define as delinquents or criminals and whose behaviour we want to study etiologically and those individuals

---

[32] *Incidence* here refers to the number of offences committed by a person, while *versatility* refers to the number of different offence types committed by a person.

who have committed felonies but still could not be called delinquent or criminal. (Lander, in Witmer and Kotinsky, 1956: 35.)

Lander's question raised the spectre of the frequent offender that would trouble the Nordic hidden crime pioneers during the 1960s. Merton said that all life types were social but did not respond to the quantitative challenge of Lander's question. It appears that the sociological normality rhetoric used the empirical findings of hidden crime surveys selectively. The *empirical* high prevalence finding was used because it fitted the Durkheim-Merton normality paradigm. When confronted by the challenging empirical reality of frequent offenders, Merton retreated to a non-empirical line of defence where the object of sociology was *defined* as social.

On reading the conference proceedings, one gets the impression that Merton was engaging in a subtle stalling operation against psychiatry and the interdisciplinary goals of the conference organizers. He accepted the (mainly Freudian) psychological or clinical approaches as sources of hypotheses. For instance, he suggested that individual personality types may be selectively preferred or rejected by pre-existing social formations (Merton, in Witmer and Kotinsky, 1956: 66). This idea seems quite modern, even 'anticipatory' of recent research on social selection processes. But towards the end of the conference, Merton increasingly cautioned against too intensive integration of psychological and sociological perspectives. 'The tactic that could be most helpful, it seems to me, would be for us to join together and fuse our respective sensitivities from time to time but, in the main, to continue to develop the conceptions most pertinent to each field' (p. 79). 'Premature commitments' to disciplinary integration should be avoided (p. 92). Sociologists and clinicians were two 'ways of life' and 'guilds' (p. 79). He assured that he was not breaking down bridges between the psychological and the sociological, but suggested that bridge-building might have to wait for a time when both shores would have firmer bases (p. 79).[33]

---

[33] Especially the psychological shore has undergone drastic change from the mid-1950s when the Erikson-Merton conference was held. The Freudian theory and conceptual vocabulary has largely been abandoned in favour of more descriptive clinical concepts. This development resulted from the rise of the so-called second biological psychiatry, and from empirical and historical critiques of Freudianism. With hindsight, Merton's refusal to accept 'premature commitments' appears to have been a wise decision. On the other hand, this meant that the integration of the psychological and social perspectives was later largely realized

In the later editions of his classic 1938 article 'Social Structure and Anomie', Merton cited Wallerstein and Wyle's work approvingly, quoting their conclusion that 'unlawful behaviour, *far from being an abnormal* social or psychological manifestation, is in truth a very common phenomenon' (Merton, 1968: 198, emphasis added). The early hidden crime surveys were strategic resources for the sociological conception of delinquency.

Cambridge-Somerville Youth Study

The Cambridge-Somerville Youth Study (CSYS) was one of the important criminological projects of the twentieth century. It was an early example of experimental criminology (Cabot, 1940; Powers, 1949), but it was also among the first studies that by-passed criminal justice statistics in the measurement of crime. The research was related to a 'program of character-building and delinquency prevention' directed toward underprivileged boys who lived 'amidst the congestion and squalor of the high delinquency areas' (Murphy, Shirley and Witmer, 1946: 686). In the project, case workers interacted closely with the boys and were able to collect information about their delinquent behaviour. In spite of this unique data, the early articles based on the CSYS are somewhat unsatisfactory concerning how the data on undetected offences was actually collected. In the study by Murphy and colleagues, the number of undetected offences was calculated from the case histories written by social workers involved in the project. Thus, there is some doubt whether the CSYS can be seen as a standardized self-report survey. Be that as it may, it appears that much of the information about the undetected crimes came from the boys. The researchers write that the case workers were able to secure the boys' confidences, and the problem of crime exaggeration by the boys is also discussed (Murphy, Shirley and Witmer, 1946: 686–7; see also Cabot, 1940 and Powers, 1949). The project was a practical attempt to reduce delinquency. The pioneering assessment of the extent of hidden delinquency study was an offshoot of this primary interest.

In 1946, the project researchers published results on the prevalence of unrecorded crime in a group of 114 boys. Of the 4,400 minor offences committed by these boys, 1.5 per cent led to official action and less than 1 per cent resulted in court complaint. Of the

without sociologists: by behavioural scientists, public health researchers and criminologists studying the interaction of individual traits and social influence.

616 serious offences, 11 per cent resulted in court complaint. These figures testified to a staggering amount of unrecorded crimes among the boys. The researchers did not report the prevalence levels of specific offences. In discussing the findings, Dr Helen Witmer underscored the implications for describing crime trends:

> So frequent are the misdeeds of youth that even a moderate increase in the amount of attention paid to it by law enforcement authorities could create the semblance of a 'delinquency wave' without there being the slightest change in adolescent behavior. (Witmer's discussion comment in Murphy, Shirley and Witmer, 1946: 696.)

The CSYS indicated that official and unofficial delinquents were similar in many respects. Their average intelligence was similar. There were also 'cultural' and 'neurotic' offenders in both groups. The former were boys who committed delinquencies because they followed the 'prevailing juvenile patterns of their communities'. The latter were driven to crime because of serious personal and social adjustment problems (Murphy, Shirley and Witmer, 1946: 690, 698). When compared with Porterfield and Wallerstein studies, the intellectual style of the CSYS was less morally loaded. In the CSYS, the normality interpretation was more like an etiological argument, not an argument from high prevalence. As explained by the project director Edwin Powers in 1949:

> The medical analogy that a delinquent boy is a 'sick' boy leads one further astray. The evidence seems to show that delinquent behavior, as a rule, is more likely to be related to normal, impulsive response to a particular culture [...] rather than to any serious emotional conflict or abnormality. (Powers, 1949: 82.)

While the existence of socially driven healthy offenders supported the conception of normal delinquency, another finding appeared to contradict it. The CSYS researchers observed that delinquents who ended up in court were, on average, more delinquent than unrecorded offenders in the sample (Murphy, Shirley and Witmer, 1946: 686). Austin Porterfield was among the first to recognize the importance of this finding. As a guest editor of the *Journal of Criminal Law, Criminology and Police Science*, he commented positively on the Cambridge-Somerville Youth Study (Porterfield, 1947: 425–6). He admitted that the CSYS included a crucial variable that was omitted from his own prior studies:

> One item which [the CSYS] includes and which is not included in my own is the *frequency* with which a given individual commits one or more of fifty

acts [...] the transgressions of the official offenders were more frequent and more serious that those of the unofficial group. (Emphasis in original.)

The mean number of offences committed by official delinquents was 2.6 times higher than the corresponding figure for the non-court offenders. The observation that a minority of frequent offenders committed most offences was thus made early in the hidden crime survey tradition. However, the high prevalence of (petty or occasional) offending was the core which fascinated many scholars. Interpretive uses are constrained but not determined by empirical findings.

Normalization of sex: The Kinsey Report

In 1946, Austin Porterfield and Ellison Salley published an interesting article in the *American Journal of Sociology*. They had conducted an anonymous survey of divinity students and revealed that the prevalence of pre-marital sex was surprisingly high. The design of this study, as well as its rhetorical strategy, was a replica of Porterfield's earlier study of self-reported crime. The authors argued that if the conservative divinity students were so liberal in their behaviour, the overall population had to be even more so. They concluded that the conservative and punitive norms regulating sexual behaviour were outdated when judged against the backdrop of people's empirical behaviour. It was 'becoming increasingly difficult to define sex delinquency in any special sense, and perhaps meaningless to do so' (Porterfield and Salley, 1946: 209). Old norms condemning pre-marital sex were outdated. Porterfield was using the same strategy Hirschfeld used four decades earlier: in order to show the futility of a repressive norm, show that the condemned activity is prevalent and therefore normal.

But the breakthrough of sex normalization was not to be linked with Porterfield's name. The landmark was Kinsey's study of human sexuality, first published in 1948 as the monumental *Sexual Behavior in the Human Male* (Kinsey, Pomeroy and Martin, 1948). The book was groundbreaking both substantially and methodologically. With the unprecedented goal of representative sampling, it was based on anonymous self-report interviews of 5,300 white males largely recruited from the north-eastern part of the US (p. 6). Starting from July 1938, the first interviews came from college students, a typical sample feature of academic self-report experiments, but later the sample included every segment of the population (p. 11). The interviews were conducted by members of the research team. The most important principle of Kinsey's team was not to have any preconceptions of what was normal or abnormal, prevalent or rare:

> No preconception of what is rare or what is common, what is moral or socially significant, or what is normal and what is abnormal has entered the choice of histories or into the selection of the items recorded on them. [...] Nothing has done more to block free investigation of sexual behavior than the almost universal acceptance, even among scientists, of certain aspects of that behavior as normal, and of other aspects of that behavior as abnormal. (Kinsey, Pomeroy and Martin, 1948: 7.)

Kinsey's sampling method was not based on random sampling of individuals; instead, it was more like a non-random cluster sample of various groups. By interviewing groups and people who volunteered to participate and who were willing to talk about sex, he quite probably oversampled people who were more sexually active than average persons (Michael et al, 1994: 21,173–4). While this is interesting as such, the relevant question from the point of view of the present study is: what was Kinsey doing with his figures? What was the moral framework in which he presented, and was read to present, the facts of sex?

Object of Kinsey's attack

To understand the context of Kinsey's discovery, and what he was doing by his research, we need to recapture how intensely sex was controlled in the early part of the nineteenth century. Kinsey wrote:

> English-American legal codes restrict the sexual activity of the unmarried male by characterising all pre-marital, extra-marital, and post-marital intercourse as rape, statutory rape, fornication, adultery, prostitution, association with a prostitute, delinquency, a contribution to delinquency, assault and battery, or public indecency—all of which are offenses with penalties attached. However it is labelled, all intercourse outside marriage is illicit and subject to penalty by statute law in most of the states of the Union, or by the precedent of the common law [...]. In addition to their restrictions of an heterosexual intercourse, statute law and common law penalize all homosexual activity, and all sexual contacts with animals; and they specifically limit the techniques of marital intercourse. Mouth-genital and anal contacts are punishable as crimes whether they occur in heterosexual or homosexual relationships and whether in or outside marriage. Such manual manipulation as occurs in the petting which is common in the younger generation has been interpreted in some courts

as an impairment of the morals of a minor, or even assault and battery. [...] There have been occasional court decisions which have attempted to limit the individual's right to solitary masturbation; and the statuses of at least one state rule that the encouragement to self masturbation is an offence punishable as sodomy. (Kinsey, Pomeroy and Martin, 1948: 263–4.)

Whether or not this captures correctly the law during the 1940s, this is what Kinsey's team was attacking. The repressive regulatory framework was ideologically buttressed by conservative religious thought and the abnormality paradigm of deviant behaviour. The connection between excessive regulation of sex and the abnormality paradigm was general, but perhaps most evident in the case of masturbation. Kinsey spared no ammunition in making his case:

Throughout history, both the Jewish and Christian churches have condemned masturbation as either immoral or unnatural. [...] Every conceivable ill from pimples to insanity, including stooped shoulders, loss of weight, fatigue, insomnia, general weakness, neurasthenia, loss of manly vigor, weak eyes, digestive upsets, stomach ulcers, impotence, feeblemindedness, genital cancer, and the rest, was ascribed to masturbation. Feebleminded and insane individuals were held as horrid examples of the result of masturbation. [...] Patients in [mental] institutions were observed to engage in frequent masturbation, and this seemed sufficient proof that the insanity was a product of the sexual behavior. Since the lives of university scholars were not so easily observed, it was not so generally known that masturbation occurred quite as frequently among them. (Kinsey, Pomeroy and Martin, 1948: 513.)

Reference to the professorial penchant for masturbation exemplifies the satirical stylistic elements in Kinsey's work, not unlike Hirschfeld's and Porterfield's. Deviance is most effectively normalized if it can be uncoupled from its association with lowest class behaviour. Exposing middle and upper class people as hidden deviants was intended to normalize behaviours previously defined as delinquent. Cultures bent on defining activities as abnormal are also prone to call forth 'facade normality', that is, hidden deviants pretending to be normal (Link, 1997: 78). This is why the quest to normalize crime was often linked to satire.

Tolerance and understanding

Kinsey and his team's findings showed that just about all kinds of sexual behaviours were much more prevalent than hitherto believed.

The kinds of sex that were forbidden by social mores and local laws were also prevalent. The conclusion was clear: *'no segment of society accepts the whole of the legal code, as its behaviour and expressed attitudes demonstrate'* (Kinsey, Pomeroy and Martin, 1948: 265, emphasis added). Moreover, it was revealed that lower classes were more liberal in their attitudes, and sexually more active, than the upper classes. This resulted in a culture conflict when upper class people judged their inferiors on the basis of their own class-bound mores.

Kinsey ridiculed the upper class judges who believed that the police were apprehending, and bringing to court, all of those who are involved in the infraction of the sex laws. Such a judge was ignorant of the massive prevalence of hidden sex delinquency. The aim of detecting and processing all sex delinquents was a futile dream because of the massive normality and high prevalence of such delinquencies:

It will be recalled that 85 per cent of the total male population has pre-marital intercourse, 59 per cent has some experience in mouth-genital contacts, nearly 70 per cent has relations with prostitutes, something between 30 and 45 per cent has extra-marital intercourse, 37 per cent has some homosexual experience, 17 per cent of the farm boys have animal intercourse. All of these, and still other types of sexual behavior, are illicit activities, each performance of which is punishable as a crime under the law. (Kinsey, Pomeroy and Martin, 1948: 392, 663.)

Kinsey explicitly stated that behaviours such as homosexuality and animal sexual contact were part of the normal continuum of human sexual behaviour (p. 677).

In his book *The Origins of Scientific Sociology*, published in 1963, the British sociologist John Madge reviewed a series of important studies reflecting what he saw as the scientific breakthrough of sociology. In his view, this breakthrough had taken place in the post-war years, with Kinsey's study as one of the key turning points. A crucial indicator of pure science was distance from moralistic goals. Madge repeatedly underscored the purely scientific spirit of Kinsey's project: Kinsey 'set himself the task of what seemed to be the fairly definite and simple task of accumulating an objectively determined body of facts about sex which would strictly avoid social and moral interpretations of the facts' (Madge, 1963: 334). An important 'un-moralizing' resource that Kinsey brought to the discussion of sex was the purely statistical interpretation of normalcy. Kinsey declared that 'the difference between normal and abnormal behavior is merely a matter of statistics' (p. 338). As a taxonomist with background in insect research, Kinsey defined normality in terms of frequency of occurrence. But the adoption of the statistical norm did 'not confuse them [the Kinsey research team] into attaching an ethical value to their concept of normality'. They thus eschewed 'the moral judgment with remarkable thoroughness' (p. 358). Yet Madge acknowledged the emancipating impact of Kinsey's statistical conception of normality, revealing how the statistical conception of normality combines descriptive and prescriptive meanings. The un-moralizing nature of Kinsey's analysis meant that various manifestations of sex could not be condemned religiously or moralistically. The report therefore had a 'tremendous impact':

> Here, in a report of scientific integrity, avoiding euphemisms or moralization, was the evidence that sexuality takes many forms and that many practices formerly whispered were regularly indulged in by *apparently good citizens*. The permissive connotations of the presentation were not lost on the millions who read the reports or the condensed versions carried in the popular press. [...] The reports have played an important part in the reduction of sexual anxiety and the dissemination of tolerance and understanding. (Madge, 1963: 375–8, emphasis added.)

These effects were the kinds of results the first hidden crime survey researchers wanted to produce. They wanted to reveal the real behaviour of the 'apparently good citizens', to reduce punitivity, and to support tolerance and understanding. There is no logical reason why Kinsey's style of argumentation could not be applied to any (prevalent) type of behaviour proscribed by society. Arguably, Kinsey's strategy of rhetorical redescription had already been applied by criminologists like Porterfield, Sutherland, Wallerstein and Wyle. The resemblance with Porterfield's argumentation is especially striking. Like Kinsey, he critiqued local upper classes for their hypocritical penchant to repressive measures against lower class people. Both used the weapon of satirical style as a means of rhetorically redescribing previously condemned activities as normal. Witness the above cited joke about masturbating professors lecturing about the dangers of masturbation. The upper class or city-bred judge is also a rather comical figure in the Kinsey Report, always demanding harsh punishments for offences that are prevalent and normal (Kinsey, Pomeroy and Martin, 1948: 677). Indeed, there are plentiful references to clerical and religious people in the Kinsey team's 800-page book *Sexual Behavior in the Human Male*;

recall how Porterfield and Salley (1946) had sought similar satirical impact by exposing the premarital sex of divinity students. The satirical exposure of hypocrisy has always been closely linked to rhetorical redescription of behavioural forms.

In some respects, the hidden crime survey researchers had anticipated Kinsey's work. But at the same time, the post-Kinsey development of the self-report delinquency survey during the 1950s was influenced by the Kinsey report. At least Clifford Shaw is known to have suggested, some time in the early 1950s, that criminology needed a 'Kinsey Report of its own', which would reveal the high prevalence of hidden crime among the general population. While the Kinsey Report should not be equated with the primary discovery of the self-report delinquency survey, it appears to have been important for the second generation of hidden crime survey researchers such as Short and Nye (Meier, 1988: 242–3; Short and Hughes, 2007: 627). Apparently, Sophia Moses Robison was engaged, in the early 1960s, in 'Kinsey-type' research in hidden delinquency as well (Sellin and Wolfgang, 1964: 41). In the 1960s, the Nordic hidden crime survey researchers related their own work to Kinsey's, at least when pondering the cultural impact of what they were doing (Christie, 1967: 71). Thus, while Kinsey was not the first self-report delinquency survey researcher, his cultural impact was so extensive that, after him, criminologists often related their work to what Kinsey had done.

The Americanization of the hidden crime survey in the 1950s

Austin L. Porterfield's 1941 book *Creative Factors in Scientific Research* was a pamphlet against scholars like William F. Ogburn and Charles Lundberg, who were prominent advocates of positivism during the 1920s and 1930s. The book started with a quotation from the 1929 presidential address for the American Sociological Association, where Ogburn had predicted and hoped that in the future era of scientific sociology, the role of 'intellectuality' would decrease while a positivist 'disciplining of thought' would gain ground. While praising Ogburn's speech for bringing the 'struggle between the factions' of US sociology into the open (Porterfield, 1941: 3–4), Porterfield himself represented the anti-positivist faction. His own creative discovery, the self-report delinquency survey, emerged for him in this tension field: it combined a quantitative tool (survey) with a critical-populist aim of changing the way people think about crime. However, this fragile combination was not to last; there was no room for a 'third way' between morally committed research and positivism. During the 1950s, the juggernaut of positivism would grind the morals out of the tool.

As described by Haney (2009), the American social sciences were 'Americanized' after the Second World War. European-style grand theorizing was rejected and replaced by quantitative and empirical research. Theories became, or were expected to generate, hypotheses that could be tested empirically. Older philanthropic, progressive, moralistic, populist and Social Gospel traditions were largely abandoned. With leaders such as Talcott Parsons, Robert Merton and Paul Lazarsfeld, sociology started to imitate the strikingly successful natural sciences. The study of 'big issues' was replaced by clearly delimited topics. The methodology of measurement and operationalization of theoretical concepts was emphasized. Sociology was meant to be incremental, advancing knowledge by gradually accumulating a multitude of small-scale studies. Additionally, the Americanization of social sciences meant that sociologists were supposed to withdraw from public debates and moral issues (Haney, 2009: 200–7). Sociologists started to talk to each other on technical matters instead of addressing the larger public or community. They started to avoid moral messages and rejected 'moralistic humanism'. It was increasingly believed that society no longer needed the 'passion of the moralist' (Haney, 2009; also Camic, 2007; Steinmetz, 2007).

The Americanization of social sciences has been linked to the US war experience: during the war effort, big research projects, such as the Manhattan project, had shown the great military and strategic significance of science. The methods of quantitative survey were also brought to the battlefield. In 1945, the *United States Strategic Bombing Survey* (1947) (USSBS) conducted a large-scale survey in the occupied areas of Germany, probing the morale and behaviours of Germans during the bombings. Some of the behaviours, such as listening to Allied radio broadcasting, had been illegal at the time of their commission, making the questions in a sense self-report delinquency items.[34] The USSBS used interview questions strictly

---

[34] Needless to say, acts defined as illegal by the Nazi regime, such as listening to Allied radio broadcasting or sabotage of war industries, are not morally condemnable; this point is about asking people to confess deeds that were technically illegal at the time.

as tools, to measure the association between the intensity of bombing and the morale and behaviours of enemy civilian populations. In principle, this showed that the delinquency survey could be used as a value-neutral tool. The point here is not to argue that the USSBS was somehow directly involved in the development of the modern self-report delinquency survey. Rather, it reveals some of the social and economic factors behind the Americanization of social sciences. During the post-war years, the scientific development of the hidden crime survey was similarly detached from general moral and policy concerns. It was uncoupled from any explicit moral or political agenda. The moral fervour that inspired the early 'heroic' hidden crime researchers, from Hirschfeld and Sutherland to Wallerstein and Wyle, came to an end during the 1950s. The style of reporting lost nearly all traces of social satire. The method additionally became an object of study as its methodological qualities were researched. I will describe this turn to scale development and psychometrics by focussing on the work of James Short and Ivan Nye on one hand and Harrison Gough on the other.

The Short-Nye papers

During the 1950s, more scholars were engaging in the development of the criminological self-report delinquency survey, but two names stand out: James F. Short and F. Ivan Nye. Short was influenced by Clifford Shaw's above cited view that criminology needed a Kinsey Report of its own (Meier, 1988: 242–3). With this inspiration, Short began a more systematic work on self-report delinquency scales in 1953. During the period 1954–58, he and Nye published a series of papers and articles based on what they called 'reported behaviour'. From the point of view of the present research, which focuses on the moral and policy frames of data interpretation, and the historical context of discovery, the studies of Nye and Short are a turning point. On reading the Short and Nye papers, one is struck by the nearly complete absence of the moral frame which animated the 'heroic' phase of earliest self-report research. The idea that the criminal justice system suffers from biases is still there, but Short and Nye do not press this point like the first generation of hidden crime surveyors.

Short and Nye updated and upgraded the self-report delinquency research to a new level in several respects. First, they initiated what today would be called scale development, that is methodological work to construct optimal means of measuring behaviour by survey questions. Second, they moved from description to explanation, using the method to study the causes and correlates of delinquency. Third, they started using normal everyday language in phrasing their delinquency items, thus freeing the method from correspondence with the legal categories of the criminal law. This was a means of making the measurement more accurate and realistic.

Scale development

Short and Nye made the self-report delinquency survey a scientifically and psychometrically 'respectable' enterprise. They applied recent developments of scale construction, especially the so-called Guttman scale, to crime measurement. The logic of the Guttman scale required them to treat delinquent behaviour as a continuum starting from relatively non-serious offences. Thus, innovations in the methodology of scale development helped Nye and Short to break away from the 'simple dichotomy of delinquents and non-delinquents' (Aebi, 2009: 27). This was consistent with the moral and anti-psychiatric spirit of early self-report survey research, even though Short and Nye refrained from drawing explicitly moral lessons they way earlier researchers had done (and the way Nordic scholars would again do in the 1960s).

Short and Nye additionally differed from previous researchers in that they explored the reliability and validity of the self-report method. They introduced reliability checks to questionnaires. First, they used what today would be called the social desirability variables: 'behaviour items considered by the general public to be undesirable but considered by the writers to be universal' (Nye and Short, 1957: 327; Short and Nye, 1957–58: 211–12). In other words, if a respondent claimed never to have defied parental authority and never to have jaywalked, the response could be classified as unreliable (see also section 'The immediate foreground' above). Second, they disqualified probable exaggerators, respondents who claimed to have committed every kind of delinquency with maximum frequency. Third, respondents with a clearly inconsistent response style were excluded. Fourth, respondents who obviously had serious problems with reading were excluded. With the partial exception of social desirability scales, all these methods have subsequently been incorporated as features to self-report surveys.

The Short and Nye studies verified many of the findings made earlier by the first generation of self-report crime survey experimenters. Based on non-institutionalized and non-clinical samples, they concluded that 'delinquents are fairly evenly distributed among socioeconomic levels' (Nye, 1956b: 169). The method 'eliminates socio-economic biases related to differential punishment procedures by police and the courts' (Nye and Short, 1957: 331). They recognized that the biases introduced by the selective criminal justice process were not necessarily based on 'evil' motives such as prejudice, hypocrisy or discrimination (Short and Nye, 1957–58: 210). Furthermore, their equal social distribution result came with some reservations. Short and Nye delimited the scope of the self-report survey to exclude the most serious types of crime. They stated that the equally criminal nature of social groups did not exclude the possibility of qualitative differences (Nye and Short, 1957: 331; Short and Nye, 1957–58: 209). The latter point was an important caveat, a crack that would limit the rhetorical space available for crime normalization movement.[35] The possibility that *serious crime* could be differentially committed by various social strata would later contribute to a renewed interest in official statistics.

The disappearance of the strong normality rhetoric was thus largely an intra-scientific process as US researchers became increasingly aware of the limits of the self-report method. This was associated with stylistic changes. During the 1950s, the 'cutting edge' of self-report delinquency research largely abandoned satirical prose, moral fervour, and policy engagement as stylistic conventions. The feasibility of crime survey had become a methodological question of reliability and validity. Doing hidden crime surveys was no longer seen as public criminology, a means of shaping public consciousness.

Causal analysis

The early pioneers of the hidden crime survey had been largely content to describe the prevalence of various offences in their research populations. Short and Nye's approach led them in new directions. When measured with scales, delinquency became a continuous variable that could co-vary with other phenomena. Some

---

[35] The Cambridge-Somerville Youth Study group had made similar observations in their 1946 publication (see above and Porterfield, 1947).

of the covariates could be causal factors of criminal behaviour. When the analysis of such causal factors was freed from the selective filter of the criminal justice system, one could examine the pure causation of delinquent behaviour. As described by Nye in 1957:

> A distinction should be made between delinquent behaviour and delinquents. Delinquent behavior is violation of important rules of laws. A delinquent is a child so designated by legal process. [...] Interest here is not in what action the authorities take, but in the factors which prevent or permit delinquent behavior. (Nye, 1956b: 162–3.)

Apart from by-passing the official control filter of crime data, the survey gave researchers the crucial option of incorporating questions about potential predictors and correlates of delinquency into the self-report questionnaires (Krohn et al, 2010). This may sound self-evident from today's perspective, but it was new in the 1950s.

Some of the specific hypotheses examined by the Short and Nye team are strikingly modern. For example, Edwin Pfuhl explored whether media exposure was associated with delinquent behaviour, with a special emphasis on interaction with delinquent friendships (Pfuhl, 1956). A similar contemporary feel is evident in Nye's 1956 paper 'The Rejected Parent and Delinquency', which explored the notion that delinquent children tend to reject their parents, net of parental proneness to reject the children (Nye, 1956a). Here, children are not seen merely as recipients of parental influences. Instead, they have their own personalities that guide their reactions to significant others, and that evoke reactions in other people such as parents, teachers and employers. Thus, family dysfunction can be a consequence, as well as a cause, of delinquent behaviour (Beaver and Wright, 2007). Research in how people self-select themselves to various environments, and influence their environments, has increased during the recent decades.[36]

Harrison Gough and the delinquency continuum

The main conclusion of the Short and Nye studies was that the self-report delinquency survey was scientifically sound and practically feasible. 'It is our conclusion that major categories of deviant

---

[36] On reading empirical sociological research conducted in the 1950s, one sometimes gets the feeling that the social turbulences of the 1960s interrupted promising lines of inquiry that were resumed a couple of decades later, sometimes by other disciplines than sociology or criminology.

behaviour can be studied in a general population provided proper attention is given to public relations and provided the anonymity of the individual is protected' (Short and Nye, 1957–58: 212). At the same time, other scholars were doing similar work. The psychologist Harrison Gough developed and tested the personality measurement instrument known as the California Personality Inventory (CPI) at the University of California, Berkeley.

The CPI included a subscale named the 'socialization scale', which was intended to tap the dimension of normative behaviour. It appears that Gough used the concept of delinquency to refer both to external breaches of norms and to a personality predisposition to do so. The latent variable causing the covariation of the socialization scale item responses was a predispositional personality factor that *explained* crime and delinquency. The scale was thus not explicitly developed to measure delinquent behaviour. However, many of the socialization scale items were about the criminal and norm-breaking behaviour of the respondent. There were questions about giving teachers a lot of trouble, being in trouble with the law, being sent to the principal in school, being in trouble because of sexual behaviour, excessive use of alcohol, truancy and stealing (Gough and Peterson, 1952: 209).

Three aspects of Gough's work are of interest with respect to the present study. First, Gough produced his theory of delinquency on the basis of George Herbert Mead's social interactionism. Like Sutherland, he saw delinquency as socially produced and learned in the process of upbringing (Gough, 1948). He was offering a sociological theory of antisocial behaviour as opposed to psychological or psychiatric theories referring to individual abnormality. Second, like other early self-report researchers, he rejected the idea that people could be sharply and neatly categorized as delinquents and non-delinquents. 'An adequate theory of delinquency cannot be an "either-or" theory, postulating a simple dichotomy between "delinquent" and "nondelinquent" personalities. The psychological conceptualization of delinquency must recognize gradations and degrees of variation' (Gough, 1954: 381). Gough thus offered a conceptual tool, *the continuum*, to replace what he saw as misplaced dichotomies of the abnormality paradigm. He saw the continuum idea as a sociological conception (Gough, 1960: 23). As a data interpretation frame, the continuum was more subtle than the normality interpretation, because it did not downplay or deny individual and group-level variation in delinquent behaviour.

The idea of the crime continuum as such was not new,[37] but Gough had something none of the earlier criminologists had: empirical measurements in multiple community samples.

Third, Gough validated his scale by comparing results in groups that 'sociologically' differed from one another in terms of rule-breaking. He reasoned that gradations of delinquent propensity would correspond to 'realities of the sociocultural environment'. A scale measuring people's delinquent propensity should position individuals along the continuum 'in general accordance with the verdict which the sociocultural environment has handed down concerning them' (Gough, 1954: 381; Gough, 1960: 23). Here, Gough departed from the mainstream of sociological hidden crime surveys. After all, those surveys were at least partially designed or prepared to show that the external labelling of individuals did *not* correspond with their true delinquency. In contrast to this view, Gough believed that convicts were really more criminal than non-convicts, and therefore his scale should reveal a consistent result. He also hypothesized that upper class people were less criminal than people on the lower rungs of social stratification.

The development of the CPI and its socialization scale offered an opportunity to test these hypotheses. The instrument was tested in multiple sub-studies targeting different levels of the hypothetical delinquency continuum. The tested groups included, for instance, the following: early onset detected delinquents, inmates of various prisons, late onset detected delinquents, teacher-nominated probable future delinquents, high school students with disciplinary problems, unwed mothers, psychology graduate students, machine operators, high school students, semiskilled workers, prison guards, electricians, civil service supervisors, college students, business executives, wholesale salesmen, banking executives, teacher-nominated probable future non-delinquents, and nominated high school 'best citizens' (Gough, 1960; Reckless, Dinitz and Murray, 1957a; Reckless, Dinitz and Murray, 1957b). It is a fitting testimony to the

---

[37] See the above discussion of the abnormality paradigm and its internal development towards increasing subtlety, a development seen in both German and British criminology (Galassi, 2004: 177–8; Garland, 1985: 184). Aebi (2009) has additionally stressed that technical developments in scale development, such as the Guttman scale, supported the idea of continuum as opposed to dichotomical concepts.

Americanization and empiricism of the second generation self-report researchers that groups such as these no longer inspired satirical comments. Very likely, the first generation scholars would have liked to expose nominated high school best citizens, bankers and wholesale salesmen as hidden delinquents. Now, the thrust of the analysis was quite different. The groups listed above were observed on the delinquency continuum in that order. In other words, officially detected offenders scored lowest on the socialization scale while nominated high school best citizens scored highest on socialization (and inversely, lowest on delinquency).

Thus, with respect to Gough's hypotheses, the results were affirmative. When measured with the socialization scale, the tested groups ranked very consistently along the delinquency continuum. The correspondence between the test ranking and the sociological hierarchy was, in Gough's estimation, remarkable (Gough, 1960: 25–6). Criminologists like Reckless and Dinitz also used the CPI delinquency subscale, and their findings further corroborated that the 'labelled' social gradient in offending was consistent with the real delinquency of social groups. Reckless and Dinitz compared the delinquency scores of delinquent and non-delinquent boys in a high delinquency area, and observed that non-delinquent boys in such areas scored lower CPI delinquency scores than officially tagged delinquents. This suggested that the personality of these boys functioned as a protective factor against delinquency, suppressing the adverse influences of social environment (Reckless, Dinitz and Murray, 1957a; Reckless, Dinitz and Murray, 1957b). The same study additionally suggested that non-delinquents had higher IQ and other ability scores than delinquents (Dinitz, Kay and Reckless, 1957), suggesting that both non-cognitive (personality) and cognitive individual-level features could function as protective factors against delinquency in environments that offered delinquent opportunities. The finding was based on data uncontaminated by the official control filter. In the Reckless and Dinitz studies, the non-delinquent group was nominated by teachers, whose perceptions were thus independently verified by self-reports based on the socialization scale. Teacher perceptions of delinquency appeared to be accurate, not prejudiced or stereotyped.

The validation studies of the California Psychological Inventory bypassed the criminal justice system as a source of individual-level data. Gough and others approached the various groups directly. The skewed social gradient in crime revealed by official statistics reflected an underlying reality in the self-reported criminal propensity of various social groups. This was at odds with the moral spirit of the early hidden crime survey research that underscored the normal-because-prevalent argument. It seems that there were at least two empirical extensions of the hidden crime survey which tended to produce anomalous findings for the normality frame. *First*, asking respondents to report the number of times they had committed offences tended to reveal the existence of the frequent offender as distinct from 'ordinary' people. This was shown as early as in the Cambridge-Somerville Youth Study (Murphy, Shirley and Witmer, 1946) and duly acknowledged by Porterfield (1947). *Second*, extending the hidden crime survey to groups of people who were previously known to be delinquent tended to corroborate differentials that were not based on biased control. Especially when 'problem groups' were *compared* with various types of 'normal' controls, as in the CSYS and CPI test studies, the social gradient reappeared as something real and stubborn. Empirical research thus yielded findings that were at odds with the normality notion of delinquency. During the next decade, the Nordic self-report delinquency researchers would confront similar tensions between findings and moral frameworks. The Nordic experience is described in detail in the next chapter. They initiated self-report research inspired by the normality framework and struggled to accommodate findings with it. But before describing the Nordic sequel to an American discovery, I will first summarize the canonical tradition created by that discovery, and briefly discuss some post-1960 developments.

Canonization and predecessor selection

In the formation of an intellectual tradition or school of thought, the process of predecessor selection is central (Camic, 1992). This is performed by scholars citing prior research, and by outsiders who construct traditions by seeing separate works as similar in content or purpose. While this process is always to some degree a selective construction, it is also constrained by the factual content of existing research. For instance, in the case of the hidden crime survey, there is no doubt that it was invented by a small group of US criminologists. Their similarity was constructed initially by two factors. First, they were trying to solve a particular intellectual problem: how to transgress the official control barrier of crime measurement. Second, their work was embedded in a shared policy goal of redescribing crime as normal. In the second phase, external commentators stepped in to canonize the tradition.

By the 1950s, the classical canon of the hidden crime discovery had been formed. Its hardest core coalesced around Porterfield's studies and the Wallerstein and Wyle article on 'Law-abiding Law-Breakers'. The discovery of hidden crime as a measurable entity was commonly attributed to these studies. Often, the article on hidden delinquency by Murphy, Shirley and Witmer (1946) was additionally cited. This set of three articles became the official ancestral line of the criminological hidden crime survey research tradition. One of the earliest codifications of the canon was Mabel A. Elliott's textbook *Crime in Modern Society*, published in 1952.[38] Like all traditions, the list of hidden crime survey classics was partially a social construction that omitted forgotten predecessors, 'near misses' and alternative paths of inquiry. The forgotten forerunners included people like Du Bois in the US, von Römer in the Netherlands and Hirschfeld in Germany. Sutherland was largely erased from the strict 'lineage' of the hidden crime survey canon because he did not publish his student experiments in the 1930s. The prize had been his for the taking. Perhaps he had prevaricated, or saw the analysis of corporate crime as more important.

There is a 'dark side' of predecessor selection: the exclusion of some work from the tradition (Camic, 1992: 424). The canon of criminological self-report tradition largely omitted work that was conducted within psychological and psychiatric traditions. For example, the 'psychiatric interviews' conducted by the Gluecks are largely absent from the canon and citation patterns of the early criminological self-report tradition even though their interviews included a Kinsey-style self-report element (Glueck and Glueck, 1968 [1950]: 60–4). Several factors contributed to this. First, the organizing concept of the psychological tradition was the individual and his personality, not crime. Second, the early psychological self-report questionnaire studies were not developed as means to transgress the official statistics barrier in crime measurement; in contrast, the criminological self-report survey was an answer to the internal crisis of the moral statistics tradition. Third, there was a

---

[38] For other early citation patterns referring to these three studies, plus often some additional studies, see Sutherland and Cressey 1955, 39–40; Perlman 1959, 6–7; Sellin and Wolfgang 1964, 40–1; West 1970 [1967], 40–1. During the 1960s the first Nordic studies are frequently cited as well.

strong moral and policy component in the creation of the criminological self-report delinquency survey. Fourth, the criminological tradition developed as anti-psychology and anti-psychiatry (see also Galliher and Tyree, 1985; Laub and Sampson, 1991). It was invented and used as an antidote to the abnormality paradigm of crime.[39]

The results and interpretations of the first self-report delinquency surveys were received by contemporary audiences in the context of other findings. The idea that norm-breaking behaviour is very prevalent was supported in the late 1940s by the white-collar crime concept and the Kinsey sex studies. Both indicated massive prevalence of deviant behaviour among social groups previously thought norm-abiding. The connection between hidden crime surveys, white-collar crime studies and Kinsey studies was made by contemporary commentators. For instance, Elliott's textbook placed all these in the context of hidden crime studies (Elliott, 1952: 33–42, 61). Similarly, the psychiatrist Manfred Guttmacher linked Kinsey's researches with Sutherland's white-collar studies and Wallerstein and Wyle's survey findings. These showed the 'prevalence of deviant and legally-prohibited behavior in all groups of the population' (Guttmacher, 1958: 633). The same connection was made by people who had contributed to the invention of the self-report delinquency survey (Sutherland and Cressey, 1955: 40; Robison, 1960: 11).

The discovery of the hidden crime as a measurable entity resulted in the turning point of criminology: the era of the self-report delinquency survey (Laub, 2004). This methodological innovation solved a riddle that had haunted moral statisticians for a century: how to measure crime quantitatively as it exists beyond the official control barrier. During the century that followed the 'avalanche of published numbers' in the 1820s, most moral statisticians had kept on repeating that unrecorded crime was beyond their reach. Others tried various solutions, resorting to using the police as informants, engaging in direct observation (as in the UK Mass Observation: see Willcock 1949), or making local reporting propensity studies. Some, like Sophia Moses Robison, remained within the

---

[39] Another case of creative exclusion of predecessors is the curious deletion of references to the *Gross-Stadt-Dokumente* by some Chicago sociologists, a fact partially explained by their desire to appear more 'scientific' than their Berlin forerunners (Jazbinsek, 2001: 14–15).

control-based data domain, but sought to make it better by including all kinds of control agencies. Yet others came up with the 'right' solution, but were answering the 'wrong' question (the lying to win approval scale and the lineage of social desirability measures).

The lineage of quantitative, offender-based self-report survey is ideal-typically and schematically shown in Figure 4.1. The figure highlights the breakthrough phase, which lasted roughly from 1930 to 1960. It focuses on the immediate lineage while excluding some important aspects of the context of discovery, such as the disciplinary warfare between sociology and the psy-sciences. Moreover, the schematic figure brackets an important precondition of the discovery: the availability of the standardized survey as a technique that could be expanded to new topics (Converse, 2009).

The history of the discovery of hidden crime as an entity that could be measured independently of criminal justice and clinical data sources was, to a significant degree, an internal process where the discipline of criminology solved a problem it posed to itself. I would even go so far as to say that this methodological innovation marks the moment when 'moral statistics' was definitely transformed into criminology.

Paradoxically, this internal transformation was aided by an external context of disciplinary warfare and moral politics. The discovery that the sample survey could be the solution took place in a morally loaded context. Most of the first generation crime survey researchers wanted to produce findings that would embarrass their adversaries: the punitivists and the psycho-scientists. There were three tools that they used in this attack. First, the *normality argument* stipulated that because crime was very prevalent among 'respectable' people, recorded offenders were not abnormal. Second, according to the *random control argument*, the targeting of crime control was not guided by the criminality of its objects. Control was thus random with respect to criminal involvement, if not in other respects. Third, the *hypocrisy argument* suggested that punitive attitudes towards recorded offenders were hypocritical because we, the condemners, are likely to have committed the same crimes but escaped detection because of biased control or luck. These interpretations were consistent with the moral content of Durkheimian-Mertonian sociology paradigm, which redefined deviance as normal. The hidden crime survey was used by sociology in its effort to take the 'ownership' of crime from psychology and

The Americanization of the hidden crime survey in the 1950s   121

```
┌─────────────────┐  ┌─────────────────┐  ┌─────────────────────┐
│ Circle of the   │  │ The internal    │  │ Progressive and     │
│ Scientific      │  │ crisis of moral │  │ Social Gospel       │
│ Humanitarian    │  │ statistics:     │  │ traditions of moral │
│ Committee,      │  │ how to break    │  │ and public          │
│ Berlin 1897-    │  │ the official    │  │ sociology:          │
│ Hirschfeld,     │  │ control barrier │  │ sensitization chain │
│ von Römer,      │  │ in crime        │  │ from 'robber barons'│
│ Gross-Stadt-    │  │ measurement,    │  │ and 'criminaloids'  │
│ Dokumente       │  │ c. 1830–1940    │  │ to 'covert          │
│                 │  │                 │  │ delinquents' and    │
│                 │  │                 │  │ 'hidden delinquents'│
│                 │  │                 │  │ exposing the        │
│                 │  │                 │  │ hypocrisy of        │
│                 │  │                 │  │ punitivists         │
└─────────────────┘  └─────────────────┘  └─────────────────────┘
```

1930 — Chicago school of sociology, 1915- Shaw, McKay — Sellin — Sutherland

1940 — Robison — Porterfield

1950 — Wallerstein and Wyle — Short and Nye, Gough, Reckless and Dinitz, and others — Aubert

1960 — Circle of the *Nordic Draftee Research Programme*, 1959- (Andenaes, Christie, Sveri, Anttila, Greve and others; first cross-national comparative self-report design)

Proliferation and expansion of self-report delinquency research in an 'Americanized', positivist form; normality frame abandoned as its validity is limited by research

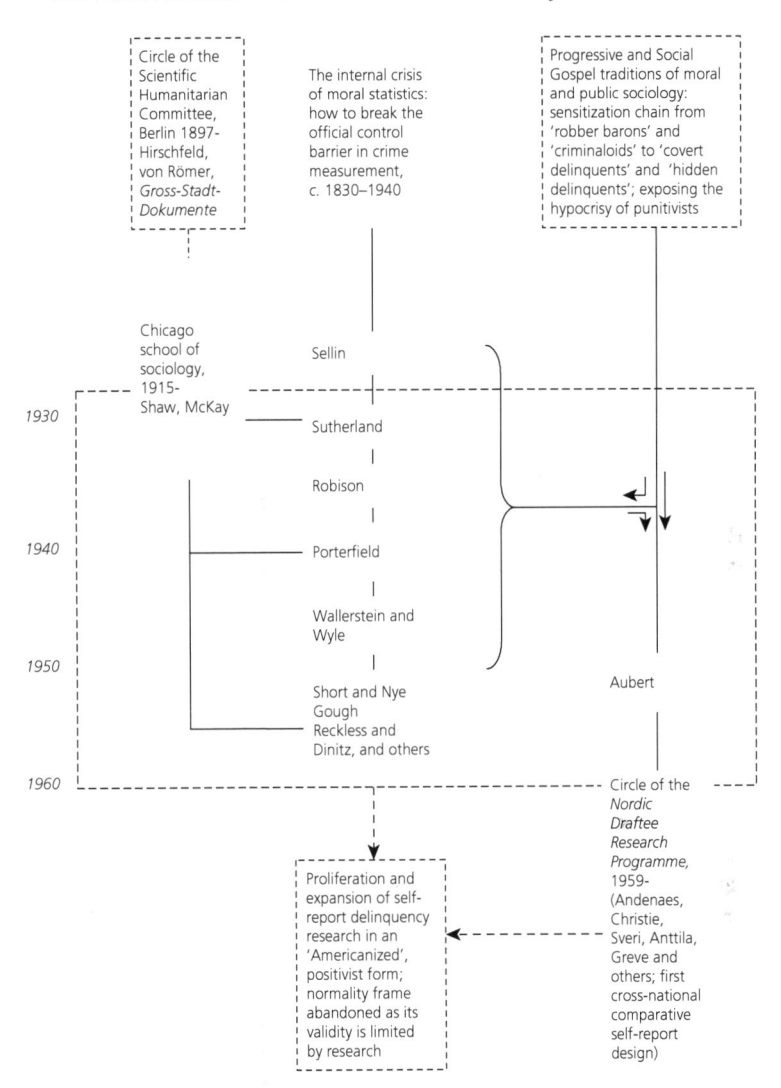

Figure 4.1 Breaking the official control barrier of crime measurement: the discovery of hidden crime as an object of standardized, survey-based quantitative measurement, USA, 1930–1960. A schematic representation. The box indicates the breakthrough phase of discovery, with the normality frame as an important context and aid of methodological discovery.

psychiatry (see also Laub and Sampson, 1991). This is how the hidden crime survey was used by its discoverers. The survey was a weapon in a war waged simultaneously on two fronts or levels: against punitivity, and against the abnormality paradigm. Both of these intellectual attacks had professional dimensions. Sociologists were attacking lawyers (punitivity) and psy-sciences (abnormality paradigm).

Central developments after 1960

What happened to the self-report delinquency survey tradition after 1960 in the US, or globally, when the heroic and moral discovery phase (1930–60) was over? This lies outside the purview of the present study. The Americanization of the social sciences ended the 'heroic', morally and politically oriented phase of the offender survey. However, there is a need to make some observations about the post-1960 developments because they are of intrinsic interest and because they form a contrast to the Nordic entry to the field, which is described in detail in the next chapter. The major trends after 1960 can be concisely summarized as follows: *expansion* in the quantity of research, *proliferation* to new areas and countries, drive towards nationally *representative* samples, focus on *causal* research and theory testing, increasing *value-neutrality*, *methodological* work and the specification of the *scope conditions* of the method. As these developments unfolded, the offender survey became a neutral method in the toolkit of criminology. Moral rhetoric, satirical attacks against the middle classes, and disciplinary conflict were left behind. Conceivably, during the 1960s some of these activities were taken over by the qualitatively and theoretically oriented labelling theory and anti-psychiatry.

After the discovery of the hidden crime survey, criminologists were free to test any theories whose explanatory concepts could be measured in surveys. This led to an explosion of theoretical developments. This is not the place to examine these in detail, but two related research frontiers need to be mentioned. *First*, one of the important post-1960 US developments took place within the debate on the social basis of delinquency. In the 1950s, it was often argued that all social strata were equally delinquent, and this notion was buttressed by the rise of labelling theory in the 1960s. Later on, evidence gradually indicated that social differences existed in the domain of delinquency as well (Braithwaite, 1981). Especially frequent delinquency was more prevalent among the lower social strata (Elliott and Ageton, 1980). Similarly, variables tapping serious social exclusion yielded higher class-delinquency correlations than stratification measures. *Second*, since the hidden crime survey was born out of distrust of official statistics, it was natural to use the method in the study of labelling processes. After 1960 a steady sequence of studies explored this. Typically these studies came up with the finding that becoming officially tagged as delinquent was primarily caused by the seriousness and repetitiveness of delinquent behaviour (Hindelang, Hirschi and Weis, 1979: 1009–10; Elliott and Ageton, 1980: 107; Krohn et al, 2010).

Both of these developments—the re-emergence of the class-delinquency link and the stubborn link between offending and labelling—supported the comeback of register-based studies of recorded offenders. A landmark study in this respect was the *Delinquency in a Birth Cohort* by Wolfgang, Figlio and Sellin (1972). From the point of view of the self-report delinquency survey, the re-emerging prestige of register-based studies was linked to increasing awareness of the scope conditions of the survey. In particular, the limits of conducting self-report research in mainstream institutions such as schools were increasingly acknowledged. After all, the most active offenders tend to be absent from such institutions (Cernkovich, Giordiano and Pugh, 1985; Hagan and McCarthy, 1999: 5–8; Kivivuori and Salmi, 2009). As the self-report delinquency survey became one of the standard tools of criminology, its scope conditions were increasingly specified.

Another consequence of the self-report survey was that social structural explanations of delinquency were supplemented by social psychological variables. Individual-level factors became thus more prominent in the explanation of delinquency. The development of social control theory, general strain theory, labelling theory, and rational choice (deterrence) theory were all supported by the availability of the self-report delinquency survey (Krohn et al, 2010). In each case, progress was made because the theoretical concepts could be flexibly measured and tested in the survey. The individualization of delinquency explanation is an ironic development from the point of view of the first generation of hidden crime surveyors who drew inspiration from the normality framework. At the most simplistic level, the normality framework argued that since we are all delinquents to an equal degree, crime could not be explained by individual differences. The drift towards variation-detection and the incorporation of individual-level predictors therefore seriously destabilized the normality framework.

Probably the most ironic part of the new individualization involved the question of cognitive capacities (intelligence). Earlier, the intelligence-delinquency link, as detected in recorded offenders, could be discounted because offenders with low cognitive capacity were more likely to be apprehended, while clever perpetrators avoided detection. Now, as self-report studies by-passed the official control barrier, the link between delinquent propensity and low cognitive capacity became more robust (West and Farrington, 1973: 193–4; Hirschi and Hindelang, 2002 [1977]: 136). Buttressing the re-emergence of psychological deviation, the survey thus helped to undo the normality frame that inspired its birth. It could do this because of the extreme flexibility of the survey method in testing various hypotheses. There appears to be no limits to such applications. Recently, the self-report survey has been combined with biological markers to examine the role of genes in delinquency causation (Guo, Roettger and Cai, 2008).

In Europe, the Nordics were the first to adapt the American discovery of the hidden crime survey. Why this was the case is the topic of the next chapter. The British entered the self-report delinquency survey scene slightly later than the Nordics, in the mid-1960s. Funded by the Home Office, the *Cambridge Study in Delinquent Development* was launched in 1961 under the leadership of Donald J. West. Originally, that study was not primarily inspired by the hidden crime survey tradition. Its inspiration was causal analysis based on prospective longitudinal research design, and its paradigmatic exemplars were prior US studies by the Gluecks, the McCords and Lee Robins (West, 1982: 3). In the first CSDD monograph, which described the first measurement of the 411 London boys included in the study (West, 1969), the concept of self-reported delinquency was not listed in the index, and the book did not take issue with the themes and topics of the classical hidden crime survey domain, nor its Americanized 1950s version; overall, the book appeared to link with the 'psychiatric caseworker' tradition instead of standardized measurement. In contrast, the second monograph, co-authored by West and David Farrington (1973), linked with the self-report delinquency tradition, referring explicitly to the Short and Nye papers and to Finnish and Norwegian predecessors. West and Farrington also raised the question of the class-delinquency link and the question of whether official control was random or biased. What they found was that delinquency was associated with low parental income, large family size, parental criminality and behaviour, and low non-verbal IQ. Furthermore, they found that being labelled as delinquent reflected delinquent behaviour (West and Farrington, 1973: 157–62).

With respect to collecting nationally representative samples of youth, British researchers may have been the first. In 1963, H. D. Willcock from the UK Social Survey conducted a self-report delinquency survey with aims of national coverage (Willcock, 1974).[40] Willcock is an interesting figure because he was involved with the UK Mass Observation of delinquency in the late 1940s, then interpreting the high prevalence findings with the classic notions of 'normality of crime' and 'hypocrisy of the middle classes' (Willcock, 1949). In the 1960s, he re-emerges as the person who conducted Britain's first nationally representative standardized self-report delinquency survey. This time, there appears to be no trace of any aim to redescribe crime as normal.[41] Furthermore, his 1963 research influenced the questionnaire used in the *Cambridge Study in Delinquent Development* (West and Farrington, 1973: 153).

One of the crucial strengths of the self-report delinquency survey is that it facilitates international analyses of crime. Such analyses are notoriously difficult if official statistics are used because national differences in penal laws and law enforcement practices introduce multiple pitfalls for comparative analysis. When researchers can define their concepts independently from the official control barrier, comparisons become easier. Against this backdrop, international applications of the self-report method were relatively slow to emerge. The *International Self-Report Delinquency Study* was launched in the early 1990s at the initiative of Josine Junger-Tas.[42] However, much earlier the Nordics had been quick to realize that the new method freed them to compare nations in an unprecedented way. The next chapter is about the Nordic Draftee Research project, the world's first internationally comparative self-report delinquency survey. The Nordics entered the scene of self-report delinquency surveys heavily inspired by the normality framework, and were soon entangled with anomalous findings.

---

[40] The first nationally representative US study was conducted in 1967 (Williams and Gold, 1972).

[41] The same applies to Belson's study of theft among London boys, the data collection of which took place in 1967–68 (Belson, 1975).

[42] A NATO Advanced Research Workshop organized by Malcolm W. Klein in 1988 inspired this development. Klein's (1989) report does not elaborate on the role of NATO apart from its funding role.

5

He Who is Without Sin Among You Let Him Cast the First Stone: Deployment of Hidden Crime Studies in the Nordic Area

In the US, the moral tradition of the early hidden crime researchers died with the Americanization of the social sciences during the post-war era. Science, methodology, scale development and causal analyses replaced the effort to influence public opinion. The hidden crime survey was no longer used as an instrument of 'public criminology'. But the policy-oriented tradition of research did not completely disappear. The Nordics, when they started the self report research tradition, were inspired by its practical usability in moral and policy debate. This chapter recounts the birth of the Nordic self-report delinquency research tradition. It is a case study of a partially successful rhetorical redescription of crime as prevalent and normal. This redescription was part of a more general effort to make criminal policy more humane during the 1960s.

Garland (1985; 2001) has described the penal context in which the original discovery of hidden crime survey took place: the penal-welfare complex that lasted in the US and the UK from the early twentieth century to the 1980s. This complex had replaced an earlier 'Victorian' complex that was legally oriented and rested on 'just desserts' and harsh punishments. The penal-welfare complex saw crime as a result of individual and social pathology and shifted the attention of the penal complex from the offence to the offender. To combat crime, individually tailored treatment and sanctions were needed in combination with social work and reform. To some extent, this grand narrative applies to Nordic countries as well, even though there were national variations. Especially in Finland, the 'welfare' part of the penal-welfare

*All translations from original non-English sources are by the present author.

equation was underdeveloped. The prison rate was high, property offences harshly sanctioned, and the penal culture was dominated by old school law professors who advocated harsh punishments. This was the setting where the protagonists of the hidden crime survey entered the scene.

Twelve-year hunt for the dark number

In the Nordic area, the Norwegians were the first to initiate self-report delinquency surveys. This was followed by a flurry of activity with national measurements in all Nordic countries save Iceland. During the years 1961–64, the Nordics launched an ambitious comparative self-report research programme based on draftee data. If the extended period of data analysis is included, the first period of Nordic hidden crime surveys lasted until 1974. While the Nordics were following a path opened by US criminologists, they were the first to conduct an internationally comparative hidden crime project. In this section, I recount this ground-breaking effort, described as the '12-year hunt' for the dark figure of crime. In the Nordic experience, the emerging research programme of self-reported delinquency was interpreted from the point of view of criminal policy. The self-report studies became one of the central arguments supporting a less punitive criminal justice system. Thus, 'the 12-year hunt for the dark figure' was not based on scientific curiosity alone. It was initiated because it was seen as politically and morally meaningful. The rise of the hidden delinquency survey is a good example of criminological thought-in-action.

First experiments in Oslo, Uppsala and Gothenburg

The first Nordic self-report delinquency survey was conducted in 1959 when male law students in the University of Oslo, Norway, responded anonymously to questions about their criminality. Initially, the researchers did not intend to publish the results (Andenaes, Sveri and Hauge, 1960). Their study thus came close to suffering the same fate as Sutherland's similar experiments with student surveys in the 1930s. But when the Norwegians saw what they got, they decided to publish. The prevalence of criminality among the law students was high. For instance, 12 per cent had participated in breaking and entering, 30 per cent had shoplifted, and 22 per cent had committed other types of theft.

Towards the end of the same year (1959), Swedish researchers conducted a similar study among law students in the University of Uppsala (Nyquist and Strahl, 1960). A further replication was conducted in Gothenburg where students of medicine responded anonymously to questions about their crimes (Forssman and Gentz, 1962). Using variants of the Norwegian questionnaire, the Swedish studies similarly observed high levels of lifetime participation in mainly property-related offending. An important aspect of these early experiments[1] was that the targeted populations (university students) represented upper and middle classes whose hidden criminality was thus being exposed.

Impressed by their results and the feasibility of the self-report method, the Norwegians suggested that similar studies should be replicated in bigger samples (Andenaes, Sveri and Hauge, 1960: 102). This initiative resulted in the innovative Nordic Draftee Research project.

The Nordic Draftee Research programme

The Nordic Draftee Research programme (NDR, 1961–64) was the first ever international comparative self-report delinquency survey. The site of research was chosen well: young men were researched in the pre-military screening (draft) sessions. This was a good idea because it was legally compulsory for all young men to show up at the drafts session. At the same time, the Scandinavian Research Council for Criminology (SRCC) was being established. Under its auspices, the Norwegian draftee-based model was exported to other Nordic countries. Finland followed the Norwegian example in 1962, while Denmark and Sweden conducted similar surveys two years later in 1964 (Stangeland and Hauge, 1974). Young men attending the pre-military screening sessions in Copenhagen, Helsinki, Oslo and Stockholm responded anonymously to a self-report delinquency survey.[2] The Norwegian questionnaire was used, with some national variations. There was no sampling: all men attending were targeted. Apart from the basic aim of

---

[1] With 125 (Oslo), 98 (Uppsala) and 164 (Gothenburg) respondents, these studies can be seen as small-scale student experiments in the Sutherland-Porterfield tradition.

[2] Some rural municipalities were included as well. Additionally, Norway's 1967 national measurement is here regarded as a continuation of the NDR.

comparing the crime situations of the participating countries, project researchers wanted to assess the validity of recorded crime statistics and to examine patterns of crime (Stangeland & Hauge 1974: 39). In what follows, 'NDR' is used as an abbreviation of Nordic draftee self-report delinquency research programme.

The findings of the NDR measurements corroborated the findings of earlier pilot studies. Lifetime participation in crimes was high in all participating cities. In Copenhagen, 39 per cent of the men attending pre-military screening had shoplifted at least once in their lives. The corresponding figures for Oslo, Helsinki and Stockholm were 45, 40 and 49 per cent (Greve, 1972: 53). As observed by the Finnish report, 'illegal acts are rather common among the youth of the present-day society' (Anttila, 1966: 16). Almost everyone had committed some type of property crime (for contemporary interpretation of findings, see Greve, 1972; Stangeland and Hauge, 1974; for a reinterpretation, see Kivivuori, 2007).

Importantly, the NDR questionnaire did not include any self-report questions about violence. This is an interesting omission, especially as Porterfield, Wallerstein, Wyle, Nye and Short had included violence items to their delinquency scales. Violence items could have shown lower prevalence levels than the various types of petty theft included in the NDR questionnaire. On the other hand, had violence items been included, and had they been included in the sum variables tapping into general delinquency, 'the number of self-admitted law-breakers would perhaps have reached 100%' (Anttila, 1966: 16), the ultimate dream of any scholar wanting to redescribe crime as normal.

Normality of crime as a policy frame

Defining the task at hand

After the Second World War, the social sciences of Nordic countries were, at least comparatively speaking, Americanized. Continental-style, philosophically-oriented and literature-based research was replaced by empirical and quantitative approaches. Intellectually, the overriding problem was how to reconstruct and stabilize democratic social orders in the postwar world (Thue, 2009: 95–6). A new generation of social scientists adopted methods, theories, and concepts from American sociology and social psychology and used them as instruments of social analysis critique (Thue, 2009: 123). The general Americanization of social sciences was an important context for the discovery of the hidden crime survey.

In Norway, new methods were used to shed light on the empirical functioning of the 'law in action'. One of the important scholars in this movement was Vilhelm Aubert, whose doctoral thesis on the social functions of punishment, published in 1954, became a landmark study in the application of empirical approaches to law (Aubert, 1972 [1954]). The book included a chapter on the extent of hidden criminality. Aubert reviewed pre-survey sources such as statistical comparisons and reporting propensity studies, but additionally mentioned the Wallerstein and Wyle study (pp. 75–85). He also drew on his own prior studies on white-collar violations of price control and labour regulations; in the study on labour regulation, employers had been asked about breaches of law, an inquiry revealing 'close to 100 per cent "criminality" in the probability sample' (Aubert, 1952: 269).[3] For Aubert, the high prevalence finding was meaningful when contrasted with commonly held beliefs about crime. In making this contrast, he formulated the policy platform of the later Nordic hidden crime survey tradition quite clearly, many years before the first NDR pilot studies.

Thus, Aubert first observed the widespread belief that criminal offenders are qualitatively and essentially different from law-abiding people. He regarded this as an erroneous and ideological conception in the face of new evidence from hidden crime studies (Aubert, 1972 [1954]: 209–10). In his view, the sharp dichotomy of law-abiding people and criminal offenders was sustained because the criminal justice system selected a minority of offenders as objects of official control. Indeed, one of the functions of the criminal justice system was to create a small minority of scapegoats from the vast multitude of unrecorded offenders. The selective and ideological functions of the justice system constructed a *'black and white'* view of society (p. 209), as if society really was divided into a law-abiding majority and law-breaking minority.[4] Aubert concluded that more research is needed to explore the prevalence of

---

[3] This study based on 'fairly intricate interviews' may actually be the first Nordic self-report crime survey, preceding the NDR by a decade.

[4] Influenced by sociological functionalism, it is possible that Aubert adopted this critique from Merton who saw the concept of latent function as an antidote to the 'black and white' ideology (see the discussion of Merton's normality conceptions in Chapter 3 above).

deviance (p. 85), a suggestion fulfilled some years later by the NDR project. The NDR project would develop the 'shades of grey' metaphor as an antidote to the 'black and white' ideology diagnosed by Aubert.

In Aubert's view, the black and white notion of society was partly created by criminology, especially by scholars such as Lombroso and Hooton. While suggesting that psychological and psychiatric theories dominated criminology, Aubert (pp. 210–11) observed that 'newer criminological research' was challenging the abnormality paradigm. An example was the emerging field of white-collar crime studies, showing extensive but hidden criminality in a population that was not commonly regarded as pathological. Thus, the Nordics appear to have understood that the question of hidden crime was meaningful also from the point of view of drawing and defending disciplinary boundaries. And this was so many years before they actually deployed the self-report delinquency survey (in 1959).

During the Nordic Draftee Research programme the policy issues came to the fore and occupied a central place in the reception and dissemination of self-report research. The classic criminal policy message of the NDR project is expressed in the titles of the two books reporting the project findings. In 1972, Vagn Greve published Danish findings in the book named *Kriminalitet som normalitet* (*Criminality as Normality*). In 1974, Stangeland and Hauge published Norwegian and combined Nordic findings in the book *Nyanser i grått* (*Shades of Grey*). The core message of self-report studies was that the criminals were not so different from law-abiding people. Instead, nearly everyone was a criminal to some extent, but the criminal justice system targeted social groups differentially.

Policy context and goals: interview with a Finnish pioneer

The primary researcher of the Finnish NDR project was Risto Jaakkola. The NDR was his first research commission. It made his reputation as a cutting-edge sociologist and a central policymaker in the criminal justice sphere. In February 2010, I interviewed him about the history of the Finnish and Nordic self-report delinquency surveys (Jaakkola 2010).

Jaakkola confirmed that the idea for the NDR came from the Norwegian criminologists such as Christie and Andenaes.

He believed that the methodological concept was originally imported from the US. 'They all went there, they had funds for that.' When I asked about the specific methodological inspiration, Jaakkola observed that the point of the project was not primarily 'criminological' in the strict sense. The ultimate inspiration for the NDR was not the methodology of hidden crime measurement. 'It was not the method as such to which these men were drawn. More like it, the method could be used in bigger projects.' By the bigger project he meant the cause of defending the little people of the lowest strata of society who were not fairly treated by the official criminal justice system. In the Finnish case, Jaakkola confirmed similar motives. When I pressed the point of crime measurement and methodology, he countered as follows:

[In self-report delinquency research], the criminological points have become more central quite recently, which was not the case originally. In the Finnish debate [in the late 1950s and early 1960s] the point was about criminal policy. In that context, anything was applied which could destabilize the punitive attitude towards young offenders and towards property crime as opposed to violence.[5] If we had expectations [prior to the NDR measurement], it was more like it that we could get material and arguments that could be used in this criminal policy debate. (Jaakkola, 2010.)

The hidden crime survey was useful because it provided arguments not only against punitivity, but additionally against treatment that was largely perceived as a facade hiding harsh sanctions:

If one thinks about these results of hidden crime research, that everyone commits crimes but only some are caught, and so on. The seriousness of deviance among the youths who were caught was in no proportional relation with the harsh measures [that were then taken]. In the treatment ideology, it was this general vagueness and non-proportionality where the offence and the sanction were not in sync. [...] The youth [treatment] facilities, if you went to see them, were like prisons, they were really harsh. The boys were made to do senseless work, they were made to craft concrete pipes, these young lads. And they were closed behind bars for the nights. These were actually youth prisons, one could see that right away if one visited them. High walls and everything. (Jaakkola, 2010.)

This describes the policy context of the Finnish deployment of the hidden crime survey. In the early 1960s, the Finnish penal

---

[5] The property crime and violent crime contrast refers to the fact that in the 1950s, Finnish penal law defined harsh penalties for property offences especially when contrasted with violent offences.

complex was a mixture of harshness and weak correctionalist and treatment goals. While national differences undoubtedly existed, the overall policy platform was similar in the other Nordic countries as well. For example, the Norwegians interpreted the NDR findings as calling for the decriminalization of petty property crimes (Stangeland and Hauge, 1974: 121). In other words, the Nordic hidden crime research agenda was not primarily or solely motivated by an empiricist wish to describe neutrally the extent of hidden crime. Instead, it was inspired by the need to make the criminal justice response more humane and more proportional to the empirical reality of the crime problem. In what follows, I take a closer look at how the Nordics interpreted the NDR findings.

Crime is normal

The moral frame of the Nordic self-report delinquency research tradition was born at the very inception of the method (if not earlier, as formulated by Aubert). In interpreting the results of the Oslo pilot study on law students, Andenaes and his collaborators defined the core arguments of the interpretive frame of the NDR researchers. First, they noted that people cannot be neatly divided into 'lawbreakers' and 'law-abiding people' because so many have committed unrecorded crimes. They stressed that occasional criminal behaviour during childhood and adolescence was 'a normal phenomenon' that does not indicate a serious threat to a person's development (Andenaes, Sveri and Hauge, 1960: 110). In 1965, Knut Sveri opined that the core finding of the NDR was the 'normality' of crime among young people (Sveri, 1967: 56; see also Bratholm, 1966: 15). In the Finnish NDR report, Inkeri Anttila wrote:

The findings on unrecorded criminality may be surprising and disagreeable to many people because they confuse a stereotyped picture about criminality and criminals: criminals are 'hoodlums' who will sooner or later get caught and will receive the punishment they deserve. It may not be very easy to accept the fact that the line between criminals and the 'rest of us' is not at all clear, and that very few offenders actually receive the punishment prescribed by the law. (Anttila, 1966: 21.)

The Swedish NDR report writer Birgit Werner began her research article by stating that in these days, 'no-one believes in [the division of people into] black and white, instead what we have is some kind of greyish continuum' (Werner, 1971: 106). A year later, the Danish researcher Vagn Greve developed the 'grey continuum' theme by summarizing the core finding of the NDR project as follows:

> The main result of these [NDR] studies of unrecorded crime is that criminality is *normal*, in the sense that (almost) everyone has broken the law. It would therefore be reasonable if we forsake the traditional division of humanity to *white and black, angels and demons, good citizens and criminals. We are all grey.* (Greve, 1972: 151, emphasis added.)

The Norwegian writers Stangeland and Hauge (1974) also noted that the core relevance of self-report studies for criminal policy was that people were not neatly divided into criminals and law-abiding people. Indeed, they continued Greve's metaphor by naming their book *Shades of Grey*. Instead of black and white, there were differential shades of grey. This conception was shared by Nordic self-report researchers doing research in schools. Based on her pioneering self-report studies in Swedish schools, Kerstin Elmhorn (1969: 127) concluded that 'it seems more reasonable than ever, that individual offences and offenders are judged and treated according to the background of what is *normal*, in the sense of average for the age group in question, and not from the point of view of the *empirically false premise that crime should be something abnormal* and uncommon among young people'.

Stangeland and Hauge additionally argued for the normality paradigm by referring to explanation of crime. They observed that few variables covaried in a significant manner with general delinquency. Men were more delinquent than females, young people more delinquent than adults, and city people were more delinquent than rural people (Stangeland and Hauge, 1974: 119), but these facts were not particularly useful for crime prevention. Stangeland and Hauge (1974: 11) regarded it as very unlikely that researchers could explain why someone commits more crimes than others. In their view, 'the better our methods become, the more clear will it be that there are no simple differences between law breakers and law abiders [...]'. Greve similarly argued that since people cannot be sorted as criminals and non-criminals, explanations of crime should be based on situational instead of life history factors (Greve, 1972: 138).

Unfair to punish the few who are detected

One of the core interpretations of the Nordic self-report tradition was that since a large proportion of offenders remain undetected, unrecorded and unpunished, it was unjust to punish the detected minority harshly. This interpretation was already in existence at the earliest stages of self-report data collection.[6] The Norwegian criminologists who piloted the self-report survey at the University of Oslo in 1959 argued along similar lines: it is unfair to punish harshly the students caught at cheating if we know that cheating is very prevalent (Andenaes, Sveri and Hauge, 1960: 105). Stangeland and Hauge argued that the randomness of police detection was a source of unfairness in the criminal justice response to crime (Stangeland and Hauge, 1974: 120). Elmhorn, the Swedish criminologist who conducted self-report research among a school population, noted in her final report that 'the few that for reasons of general prevention are registered with the police [. . .] are hit unproportionally hard' (Elmhorn, 1969: 127). She advocated the abolition of criminal justice control of under-aged persons even at the cost of some increase in property crime.

Knowledge about the true prevalence of offending was also a means of controlling criminal justice related emotions. The Danish NDR researcher Greve wrote that since 'we are *all sinners* [. . .] we can develop a more relaxed attitude towards recorded offenders' (Greve, 1972: 151, emphasis added). The findings of the self-report studies were expected to function as an antidote to moral panics. As expressed by Stangeland and Hauge (1974: 119), '[The results of NDR] should contribute to a *less emotional attitude* towards registered offenders' (emphasis added). Like the liberal British civil servants studied by Loader (2006), the Nordic NDR criminologists worked against populist emotionalism. In so doing, they continued the tradition of scholars like Porterfield who were ready to condemn moral crusaders attacking easy targets.

Crime is not psychologically caused

Early sociologists such as Durkheim, Ross and Sutherland were extremely critical of the psychiatrically and psychologically oriented abnormality paradigm. Sutherland especially was an ardent critic of psychiatric and psychological explanations of crime

---

[6] In his 1954 book on the functions of punishment, Aubert pointed out that only a fraction of all offences became known to authorities, and that people's behaviour was not primarily determined by the certainty of penal deterrence (Aubert, 1972 [1954]: 86–8).

(Galliher and Tyree, 1985). This disciplinary conflict was an important context in which the Nordics rediscovered hidden crime. The questions of disciplinary predominance and criminal justice policy were closely related.

Starting in the 1960s, Nordic criminologists actively criticized the so-called treatment model of criminal justice. The treatment model was based on the causal theory that criminal activity reflected individual psychopathology. In the Nordic area, the hegemonic causal theory was, until the 1960s, that crime is caused by individual pathology or serious disturbance. This conception was supported by studies of institutionalized offenders. In some countries, offenders could be sentenced to indeterminate periods of 'treatment'. This was increasingly seen as an inhumane and ineffective mode of control (Papendorf, 2006). The critique of the treatment ideology gathered momentum towards the late 1960s, propelled and aided by the more general anti-psychiatry movement.

In Sweden, the opposition to psychiatry climaxed in the debates that followed the 1968 'sociopathy report' by a working group planning the future of psychiatric treatment. The 'sociopaths' of this report were defined as people with anti-social tendencies (like substance abusers) that made them a difficult sub-category of patients in the general drive to liberalize and humanize the treatment of people with mental disorders (Ohlsson, 2008: 198–1, 203). The sociopath report provoked an unprecedented wave of criticism. Many journalists and critics claimed that the concept of sociopath was so broad as to include a great many people (Ohlsson, 2008: 205). These critics felt that the idea of sociopathy pathologized behaviour that was normal by the sheer force of high prevalence.

There was a direct argumentation link between self-report delinquency research and the critique of treatment. The self-report studies indicated that we are all criminals, at least to some extent. This was interpreted as a refutation of the idea that crime was caused by individual psychopathology:

Extreme psychiatric theories [. . .] can be disregarded as theories which have value for the understanding of 'criminality'. The self-report delinquency surveys show that most of the crimes are committed by presumably 'normal' people. The fact that a small minority remains which belongs to the hard-core psychiatry does not alter this fact. (Sveri, 1967: 62.)

The results [of the Finnish NDR] present the 'criminal' in a new light. The existence of such a large number of 'unrecorded criminals' refutes among other things the opinion of some psychoanalytically oriented persons that even a minor crime usually indicates a personality defect. (Anttila, 1966: 20.)

Description, explanation and prevention of crime were intimately interrelated in a consistent chain of argumentation. Thus, according to Anttila, if a young person committed an occasional crime, involuntary 'treatment' or harsh punishments were uncalled for. The problem of the Finnish system was that 'many "normal" boys or girls are registered as criminals and imprisoned' (Anttila, 1966: 20). In 1967, Anttila, who was Finland's most important criminal policy maker during the post-war decades, saw treatment as a 'frontline' between conservatives and radicals. Radicals were against treatment, conservatives for it. The radicals were motivated by a sociological conception of society while conservatives adhered to a psychological or even psychoanalytical notion of society and crime (Anttila, 1967: 245). She speculated that advocacy of treatment was based on 'incapacity to accept new research results', by which she may have meant for example the hidden delinquency studies (p. 251). In Norway as well, criminologists criticized the so-called treatment ideology that was based on individual psychopathology theories (Papendorf, 2006).

Nordic forensic psychiatrists were aware that their profession was under attack, and that the self-report delinquency survey was used as an instrument in this purpose. In 1973, they held a kind of crisis meeting on the justification for the forensic psychiatry profession. There they noted the role of the self-report delinquency survey in the destabilization of psychiatry:

Criminological findings that underlined the great extent of hidden criminality, so that crime had to be considered as culturally determined and many offenders as non-abnormal or normal, raised the question of the appropriateness of the psychiatrist as the authority on criminal genesis. (Svendsen, 1977: 162.)

The anti-psychiatric arguments of NDR researchers show how self-report delinquency research became thought-in-action, a means of normalizing 'deviant' behaviour in a manner that simultaneously discouraged both punitive and treatment-oriented responses to crime. Normality rhetoric was a powerful weapon in the hands of the young innovating ideologists because it attacked simultaneously both wings of the punitive-psychiatric complex: we should not punish what is normal and prevalent, or heal people who are not sick.

Random control hypothesis

In a 1958 article Nils Christie wrote about the 'dark figure' question. He defended the need to study recorded crime (as opposed to unrecorded crime) because 'within certain limits we may assume that people who massively break the law have the greatest likelihood of becoming registered offenders'. Interestingly, he also added that many of the unrecorded crimes were very probably committed by offenders who were recorded in the police statistics (Christie, 1958: 136). A couple of years later, the self-report researchers, one of whom was Christie, would approach the problem of control from a different angle. They wrote that it is possible that some offenders were selected to be detected and registered as if in a random process (Andenaes, Sveri and Hauge, 1960: 111). There is no doubt that some of the NDR researchers expected to find random control. There is an interesting mimeographed document based on a speech given by the Swedish NDR researcher Birgit Werner, reflecting on the hopes and expectations of the early Nordic hidden crime survey researchers:

> Before we started to prepare for this [the NDR] we said: What if we should find out that there is no association between criminal involvement and exposure to sanctions! What if this is a purely random process [*ren slump*]! [...] If this would turn out to be the case, *our research would overthrow criminology and criminal policy as we know it today*. It turned out not to be so bad, or so funny. (Werner, 1969: 117–18, emphasis added.)

This reflection discloses what at least some of the NDR researchers were doing in moral terms when they set about to study the hidden criminality of young men. Werner's testimony suggests that she initially hoped to show the randomness, and therefore the unjust nature, of criminal justice sanctions. But, as Werner noted, reality was stubborn in this respect. Several NDR researchers reported findings that people who were officially sanctioned and recorded were significantly more criminally active than other people (see section 'Anomalous findings' below).

Biased control hypothesis

There are two variants of the 'unjust control' hypothesis. According to the random control hypothesis, discussed above, control is targeted randomly and without regard to people's criminality. According to the biased control hypothesis, some social groups are controlled to a degree that cannot be explained by their criminal involvement. In Finland, this latter question occupied a central place in NDR analysis and impact.

The question of biased control was investigated by Risto Jaakkola (1966) who made his reputation as a prominent sociologist and policy advisor by showing that various social strata were equally criminal while the lowly educated were subjected to more intense control. To begin with, he used the Finnish NDR data to examine the social background of criminality. He observed that there was no systematic pattern, and nothing suggested that the lowest classes were more criminal than middle and upper classes. In some crimes types, the upper classes were more criminal than the lowest classes. Most notably, the lifetime prevalence of shoplifting was twice as high (50 per cent) in the upper class than in the lower working class (23 per cent; Jaakkola, 1966: 27). The situation was the same in alcohol and tobacco smuggling. These findings of excessive criminality in the upper class are unique in the annals of self-report delinquency survey research. Jaakkola then proceeded to analyse the possibility of class bias in social control. He first observed that the more offences a person had committed, the more likely he had been in conflict with the law. Becoming a recorded offender was thus not random with respect to versatility[7] of criminal offending. But when the versatility of lifetime offending was held constant, working class males were more likely to have been in conflict with the law (Jaakkola, 1966: 32). Jaakkola concluded that holding crime constant, 'the higher social classes and the better educated run a smaller risk of having to answer for their crimes' (p. 35).

Anomalous findings

The early Nordic self-report researchers had high ethical standards. While moral and policy concerns influenced the questions they posed to reality, and the take-home messages they picked out from the findings, they always reported the full picture of findings. In the course of analysis, some findings emerged that were anomalous from the point of view of the normality paradigm and the policy frame elaborated above.

[7] Versatility of offending here refers to the number of different offence types committed by a person (as opposed to the number of offences).

Different, after all?

The questionnaire used by the NDR researchers was not very good at detecting and analysing differences in the frequency of offending. The standard recall period was lifetime, while response options were as follows: 'many times', 'once or twice', 'never', and 'don't know'. However, this question structure made it possible to give separate prevalence levels for respondents who had committed the offence once or twice, and for those who had committed the offence many times. The typical finding was that frequent offending was clearly less prevalent than rare offending.

Thus, the Finnish NDR report first highlighted the high lifetime prevalence of petty and occasional offending, but proceeded to show how these prevalence levels dropped when only frequent offenders were included. The report noted that 'the findings suggest that although most boys engage in illegal acts, very few do it continuously' (Anttila, 1966: 16–17). The Norwegians observed a similar pattern. For instance, the 1967 lifetime prevalence of shoplifting one or two times was 28 per cent, while the corresponding figure for shoplifting many times was 10 per cent. The same figures for auto theft were 5 and 2 per cent, respectively (Stangeland and Hauge, 1974: 25). The general conclusion was that 'it is statistically normal to commit crime, but in the main the youths commit few crimes, and not so often' (Stangeland and Hauge, 1974: 27).

In analysis, the NDR researchers often used general indices of crime. This is important because summing individual offence items yields measures with higher prevalence levels. The typical solution was to use the so-called variety type of measure tapping into how many different offence types the respondent had committed (Jaakkola, 1966; Greve, 1972: 51). The Norwegian measure of general criminality was more discriminating, a combination of offence seriousness and offending frequency with possible values ranging from 0 to 75 (Stangeland and Hauge, 1974). However, in the actual analysis, a popular solution was to truncate the distribution of continuous indices by using categorical variables. This move involved a significant loss of information especially with respect to frequent offending. Thus, Jaakkola (1966: 32) dichotomized his variety indices, while Stangeland and Hauge (1974) used four or five categories. In some of the analyses, the frequent offenders included anyone who scored at least 13 points on a scale from 0 to 75.

Since the NDR researchers published the full distributions of their sum scales, it is possible to examine them more closely from the point of view of offence accumulation. Thus, Greve's variety based distribution reveals a fairly modest accumulation of offences to a minority of frequent offenders (Greve, 1972: 51). The top quartile of offenders accounted for 37 per cent of all 'versatility scores'. In contrast, the Norwegian index was more sensitive to the frequency of offending (see Stangeland and Hauge, 1974: 28). In their data, the top quartile of offenders scored 59 per cent of all crime severity/frequency scores. Similarly, 10 per cent of the respondents scored 34 per cent of all severity/frequency scores. The NDR data thus showed that a minority of offenders committed a disproportionate share of offences.[8]

Evidence for the existence of a minority of frequent offenders did not trigger criminal policy interpretation in the same manner as the high prevalence finding. While the facts were laid out in a balanced manner, the interpretive frame made some findings more salient than others. Moreover, it seems that the *internal discourse* of criminologists was more critical towards the normality frame than the 'take home messages' of published reports. For example, in a 1965 meeting of Nordic criminologists, Knut Sveri made it clear that the high prevalence finding related to occasional lifetime delinquency, and consistently used inverted commas when writing about the 'normality' of crime (Sveri, 1967). Furthermore, he correctly pointed out that the 'normality' of crime was, to a degree, a methodological artefact (Sveri, 1967). This was so because it was based on variety type sum scales including a large repertory of petty offences. Using such global scales in a manner that truncated variation in the upper end of the distribution guaranteed that high prevalence, and hence 'normality', would emerge. Patrik Törnudd concurred by noting that if each offence type was separately analysed, none of them might be normal (Törnudd, 1967).

Indeed, the NDR involved several design and analysis-related decisions that, with hindsight, appear to have been congenial to the normality frame: first, the targeting of youths; second, the exclusion of violence from the questionnaire; third, use of sum variables to describe high prevalence of general deviance; and not using these sum variables as continuous variables or as variables revealing offence accumulation to a minority of offenders. Thus, there was selective tension between data and how it was interpreted.

---

[8] The Oslo pilot researchers had also observed that offenders with early onset were more likely to have offended recently as well, suggesting individual-level continuity in frequent offending (Andenaes, Sveri and Hauge, 1960: 110).

While the empirical evidence was open to various interpretations, and these were discussed in internal seminars, the core take home message typically omitted specifications of scope conditions. This should be understood in the historical context of what the NDR researchers were doing with their findings. In the 1960s, the normalization frame attacked, and helped to uproot, outdated visions of delinquents as moral degenerates, monsters or sick people. The normality rhetoric served the goal of humanization. Additionally, the normality concept was used to highlight differences between natural and social sciences.[9]

Accuracy of police control?

In Norway, the random control hypothesis was rejected early on in the analysis of the NDR findings. In 1964, Norwegian radio broadcast a lecture by Nils Christie. In that lecture, Christie said that:

> It is *normal* that an average citizen has broken the law. It is silly to ignore this. However, it is equally silly to continue that reasoning into absurdity. Criminality is not the lifestyle of the average citizen. Not all people have committed equally many crimes. Most people have really modest and few sins on their conscience, but a few people go much further. These latter people have a much greater chance of becoming caught for crimes sooner or later. The registered offenders are therefore *not a random sample* of the general population. (Christie, 1966 [1964]: 59, emphasis added.)

Christie went on to say that it is the registered offenders who must be dealt with by society, and therefore deserve special attention.

The next year, 1965, the Norwegians published an article based on the first draftee data from 1961. The authors of that paper examined the likelihood of police contact by the level of criminal involvement. What they found was a strong correlation: the more a young man committed crimes, the more likely he had become an officially recorded offender. Christie, Andenaes and Skirbekk were quite clear about this:

> The official system of control does not select its cases at random. By and large it is the case that the small group of officially registered criminals have also been involved in the largest amount of crime, as reported through the questionnaires. And, even more important, this relationship is kept up

---

[9] Thus, Greve argued that if everyone in a given community had malaria, it still made sense to describe these people as suffering from an abnormal condition; but not so if everyone was criminal (Greve, 1972: 127).

within all educational levels. (Christie, Andenaes and Skirbekk, 1965: 112–13.)

These results had been foreseen by the Norwegian pilot researchers using a sample of Oslo law students. Andenaes, Sveri, and Hauge had observed that becoming a recorded offender was not a completely random process. In their view the risk of being detected 'self-evidently increases as the seriousness, intensity, and duration of criminal activity increases' (Andenaes, Sveri and Hauge, 1960: 112; see also Stangeland and Hauge, 1974: 86–7). The Swedish NDR report writer Birgit Werner reported similar findings based on the Swedish data. The selection of offenders to the criminal justice system was not random: 'Not only how many crimes have been committed, but also the seriousness of the crimes is relevant. Those who commit serious crimes often become objects of criminal justice action more often than those who commit less serious offences' (Werner, 1971: 140). Finns also observed a rather dramatic correlation with versatile criminality and police detection likelihood: four out of five persons in the highest property crime score levels had been in conflict with the law (Jaakkola, 1966: 32). In the early 1970s a popular Finnish criminology textbook even described the link between offending and elevated detection risk as 'natural' (Anttila and Törnudd, 1973: 62).

It thus appears that the *random control* hypothesis was refuted in all national datasets of the NDR. Findings related to the *biased control* hypothesis were not as clear-cut. In Norway and Finland, official control appeared more biased in terms of education/class than in Sweden and Denmark (Stangeland and Hauge, 1974: 89; Greve, 1972: 119). In Denmark, criminal versatility appeared to be associated with low education and low social class, while youths with institutional backgrounds[10] had above-average prevalence of almost all crime types (Greve, 1972: 76, 96–8, 125–6). Findings such as these went against the grain of the biased official control hypothesis. Differential findings in different countries made Stangeland and Hauge (1974: 89) suspect that none of the analyses was robust, even though the finding had been useful in

---

[10] The Danish NDR was particularly strong in that it included the institutional group and contained a variable identifying it. Greve justly considered youths from 'children's homes' etc. as occupying the lowest stratum of society (Greve, 1972: 91; see also Berntsen, 1967, who appears to have worked outside the NDR circle and its interpretive framework).

social criticism. They suggested that middle and upper classes appeared criminal because the lower classes had cognitive difficulties with survey questions. Additionally, there were class differences in what kind of acts were understood as 'crimes' and 'violence', with upper classes tending to include less serious incidents (Stangeland and Hauge, 1974: 89–91).

Continuing appeal of the random control hypothesis

While the empirical NDR findings suggested that official control was relatively successful at targeting the most frequent and persistent offenders, some of the researchers liked to underscore the randomness of control. Thus, Greve observed that 'If we admit that only a small part of criminals are punished, it becomes less crucial to punish those whose offences are registered by a more or less random process' (Greve, 1972: 153–4). The Norwegians as well continued to refer to the random process by which offences become known to the police. We are all equally criminal, but the wheels of fortune have randomly selected some people to become labelled as official delinquents (Stangeland and Hauge, 1974: 119–20). Writing 20 years after the NDR heyday, Anttila recalled that back in the 1960s, officially registered offenders were severely punished while most offenders were unrecorded 'perhaps only because of good luck' (Anttila, 1986: 17).

Thus, there was a tension between the actual empirical findings and the interpretive frame. The tension resulted from how morally salient aspects were chosen from a wider repertory of available findings. Or, it may be that counter-intuitive statements (like the idea that a person's likelihood of becoming a target of police control is unrelated to his/her criminality) are better remembered than opposite claims.[11] It certainly appears that the NDR findings were, at least in Finland, remembered like no other study from the 1960s. Decades later, when the 1960s generation sociologists looked back, they would refer to Jaakkola's landmark study of hidden crime. Risto Alapuro, professor of sociology at the University of Helsinki, recounted how the Finnish NDR study made a lasting impression by taking the side of the oppressed, and by revealing an empirical fact that was against commonly held beliefs (Alapuro,

---

[11] There is some evidence in cognitive psychology that humans tend to remember counter-intuitive statements better than claims that are fully expected (see Johnson, Kelly and Bishop, 2010).

2000: 71–2). Similarly, Antti Eskola, professor of social psychology at the University of Tampere, recalled how he had popularized Jaakkola's results in a *satirical* TV show; it had been fun because it 'irritated the bourgeoisie'. In his view, the findings were plausible precisely because they went against what the bourgeoisie believed was true (Eskola, 2009: 263). For both Alapuro and Eskola, the quality of *exposure* singled out the NDR study as outstandingly important.

The vivid memory of the first Nordic hidden crime survey exemplifies how ideas can symbolize and flag membership in academic horizontal networks, which in turn provide scholars with collective effervescence and affective energy. As observed by the US criminologists Joachim Savelsberg and Sarah Flood, this influx of energy to intellectual work often comes by means of antagonism to other intellectual currents (Savelsberg and Flood, 2010; see also Collins, 1998). Indeed, the NDR was a project structure that created horizontal networks among Nordic criminologists, but its social significance exceeded the small discipline of criminology. The NDR became a kind of a paradigmatic exemplar of how empirically oriented social science could be used in social criticism.

Additional sources of the normality frame

The hidden crime survey was not the only reason why many Nordic criminologists advocated the normality paradigm. In this section, I discuss three additional cultural lexicons that added power to the redescription of crime as normal. First, and more importantly, concepts derived from sociological theory pointed in the same direction as the hidden crime surveys. Second, after the Second World War, psychological theory defined conformity as a social problem. Third, the question of religious influences is discussed. While these factors were probably relevant for the reception of early self-report delinquency research elsewhere as well, the Nordic scene shows their presence clearly.

Sociological theory

In 1969, a Finnish sociologist, Patrik Törnudd, wrote: 'According to a sociological conception with considerable support, all societies need a certain amount of deviant behaviour. Deviance is something *normal in the sense that it is an integral element of society's mode of functioning*' (Törnudd 1996a, [1969]: 19, emphasis added).

In another article published the same year, Törnudd elaborated on his views. He critiqued the inclination of criminologists to explore and locate the causes of crime, which he regarded as futile. Overemphasis on individual-level causation was itself caused by a failure to understand that crime is 'a necessary social phenomenon upheld by vital social forces' (Törnudd, 1996b [1969]: 23). He proceeded to examine what he called the necessity doctrine of crime. This was largely based on Durkheim's arguments on the normalcy of criminal behaviour. First, crime increases general integration. Second, society needs its norms to be reinforced, and crime serves the function of igniting such reinforcement. Third, crime is a source of innovation to society. Each society thus seeks a point of equilibrium between the level of criminality and repressive measures. For example, a society might repress much of its crime, but this would take place at the expense of social integration and innovation (Törnudd, 1996b [1969]: 29). The normalcy and necessity doctrines additionally meant that a society can (or must) choose how many people are punished and from which social groups or strata those people are selected. The intensity and targeting of social control was thus to some extent detached from the behaviour of individual offenders (pp. 35–6).

The sociological normality thinking combined various Durkheimian motifs such as prevalence, innovation and functionality. An important variation of this conceptual family was the idea of *balance*. This idea was exemplified by Durkheim's famous saint example: even a society of saints would define some petty infractions as crimes. Societies should therefore strike a balance between too many and too few criminalizations by adopting a 'consciously balance-oriented ideology' (Anttila, 2001 [1971]: 42–7). Later similar themes were discussed using concepts like self-regulation and homeostasis. These concepts were less provocative than the concepts of normalcy and necessity. The meaning, or at least the policy conclusion, was however roughly the same. An aberrant shift towards increasing control would be cancelled by the automatic or cybernetic functioning of the system that would start to leak deviants from other joints. Thus, excessive punishments would trigger self-regulation mechanisms counteracting punitivity (Anttila, 2001 [1976]: 185).[12]

---

[12] For a similar Durkheimian balance-oriented argumentation in the US, see Moynihan 1993.

Conformity as problem

Fredrik Thue has recently observed that the Second World War was an 'epochal experience that constantly reverberated with the social thought' of the generation that took over the social sciences after the war (Thue, 2009: 123). Consider, for instance, the crimes and atrocities committed by Nazi Germany during the war. Why had so many apparently 'normal' people followed the commands of a criminal regime? It was logical that, after what happened, many psychologists and social psychologists defined conformity as a pathological character trait. Ability to break social norms was redefined as a feature of mature personality, while excessive conformism was an important social problem to be tackled.

The landmark of this cultural turn was *The Authoritarian Personality* by Adorno et al (1982 [1950]). That study set out to describe and analyse the potentially fascistic individual whose personality was authoritarian and rigid. The innovation of this research was to combine Freudian theory with the methods of academic psychology, most notably scale development. At the heart of the study was the famous F-scale (the F comes from Fascism) which measured antidemocratic and fascistic tendencies. The core feature of the authoritarian or potentially fascistic personality was his rigid attachment to normative behaviour. He/she would look down on and punish those who were believed to be violating conventional values, and to condemn such people on moral grounds (pp. 156, 162). The authoritarian personality was bent on finding 'good enemies' against whom he could vent his own hang-ups and aggressions. 'Conventionalism, authoritarian submission, and authoritarian aggression all have to do with the moral aspect of life—with standards of conduct, with the authorities who enforce these standards, with offenders against them who deserve to be punished.' (Adorno et al, 1982 [1950]: 162–3.) Thus, in analysing authoritarianism, Adorno et al were also dissecting the psychological roots of punitivity. In this respect, their study resembles the studies by Sutherland, Porterfield and Kinsey. All these studies were satirical exposures of 'moral' people who saw themselves as moral pillars of society. Sutherland and Porterfield revealed that behind the facades, upper and middle class people were often criminal; Kinsey revealed that they were sexual; and Adorno et al, probing deep behind superficial facades, revealed that they carried seeds of fascism in their personality. Rarely in the history of social sciences has there been such a concentrated cannonade against petty bourgeois and middle class hypocrisy.[13]

Not surprisingly, the Nordics were also influenced by psychological theories of conformity (Thue, 2009: 109–10). In his 1954 book, which defined the agenda of the Nordic hidden crime survey research, Aubert discussed Freudian theories of crime and punishment. He was critical of the Freudian theory of criminal behaviour,[14] but more enthusiastic about Freudian theories of criminal justice reactions. For example, he commented on people's deep psychological needs to identify 'scapegoats' (pp. 45–7, 208–9). Five years later, the first hidden crime report by the Norwegians noted that law-abiding behaviour was statistically abnormal, and indeed possibly 'a symptom of neurotic, repressed or anxiety-ridden character' (Andenaes, Sveri and Hauge, 1960: 110). In 1960, the Finnish criminologist Törnudd discussed the functions of nonconformity on similar lines. He noted that 'nonconformist' had become a word of praise among liberally oriented intellectuals. This was so because experimental studies had shown that conformism was associated with authoritarian character traits. In contrast, a well-adjusted person was more likely to act in a nonconforming manner (Törnudd, 1960: 48).

However, the influence of psychological theories of conformity on Nordic criminology was limited by other, more central policy concerns. Chief among these was the perceived need to combat the abnormality paradigm of crime, and its practical corollary, the treatment ideology of the psy-sciences. This policy need worked against the psychologization of social problems. But the idea that excessive conformity is a problem would reverberate in the hidden crime tradition (see below).

Invoking religious language?

Apart from its links to sociological theory and disciplinary turf warfare, the development of the hidden crime survey is tangentially

---

[13] It should be noted that the hidden crime survey concept, and its critique of petty bourgeois hypocrisy, predated the Second World War (Hirschfeld, Sutherland, Kinsey, Porterfield). Arguably, the war boosted an existing interpretive frame because Nazism and Fascism could as such be seen as revealing the criminal potential of the *Kleinbürgertum*.

[14] Aubert pointed out that the high prevalence of hidden crime contradicted the Freudian theory, which claimed that criminal behaviour is motivated by the offenders' need to get punished (Aubert, 1972 [1954]: 117).

related to religious practices and discourses. Hirschfeld used Catholic confession as one data source among many others to show that crime was more prevalent than previously believed. The earliest formulations in white-collar crime studies were influenced by the late nineteenth century Social Gospel movement whose extended sin conception included the sins of corporations. Many of the early hidden crime survey pioneers engaged in the critique of hypocritical punitivity. In this respect, their position was close to the New Testament teaching against hypocrisy. Probably the most famous example of this is the scene where Jesus confronts Pharisees who are about to stone a woman accused of adultery by saying, 'He who is without sin among you, let him throw the first stone at her' (John 8: 3–7).

The way the Nordic hidden crime survey findings were received and interpreted by scholars and other audiences was influenced by religious language. The most obvious example is the book by three Swedish lawyers originally published in 1971, which was entitled *Den första stenen* (*The first stone*; Elwin, Hecksher and Nelson, 1975).[15] In the section titled 'The myth of the law-abiding citizen', the book explained the findings of the NDR, and used the interpretive frame of the normal-because-prevalent argument. The standard critique of punitivism and treatment was also offered (pp. 219–23). On reading that book, one gets the impression that some of the interpreters of the NDR were drawn to the moral and policy frame of the tradition while lacking the empirical subtlety of the NDR researchers; in the course of time, something analogous perhaps happened to the researchers (see below).

Occasionally, some of the Nordic hidden crime research pioneers used religious vocabulary in popularizing their findings. In the 1972 book *Crime as Normality*, the Danish NDR researcher Vagn Greve wrote that, based on self-report crime studies, we should forsake the traditional division of humanity to 'angels and demons' (Greve, 1972: 151). In 1975, Nils Christie used religious language to interpret the moral significance of hidden delinquency studies: 'we are all *sinners, the whole flock*', he wrote. However, we had at the same time 'continuously struggled to uphold the fiction that [...] it is about the black and the white, and that the black are punished and it is we who punish. An important function of modern criminology has been to support the *ancient wisdom* that it is rather

---

[15] I am grateful to Britta Kyvsgaard for pointing this book out to me.

about shades of grey' (Christie, 1975: 73, emphasis added). Christie thus attacked the hypocrisy of condemnation. When later challenged by an unexpected critic, he confirmed the biblical source of his metaphors (Christie, 1995 [1992]: 366).

While there was a religious residue in the discourse of the hidden crime surveyors, and in the manner their findings were received, this emphatically does not mean that their actual research project was 'religious' instead of scientific. Their context was the culture of the Nordic countries, which are all overwhelmingly Protestant nations with strong traditions of popular religious movements. The popularization and dissemination of findings must take place using the common metaphors and lexicons that are derived from the surrounding culture.

Later developments in hidden crime data interpretation

The phases of Nordic hidden crime research

The Nordic Draftee Research project did not become a survey instrument with repeated sweeps, as originally planned by its creators. In 1967, Norway repeated the sweep with a refined sampling frame. However, the second Norwegian sweep was the last of its kind for a long time to come.[16] Writing in 1975, Patrik Törnudd observed that the enthusiasm for self-report research had 'died away'. According to him, 'criminologists had to admit that occasional dark number studies could only offer a means of checking the validity of crime statistics, but could never replace these statistics' (Törnudd, 1996c [1975]: 42).

During the second phase of Nordic self-report tradition, covering roughly the years from 1970 to 1990, the method was rarely used, at least when compared with the 1960s and the period after 1990. There were multiple reasons for this development (Kivivuori, 2007: 8–9). First, problems in the perfect standardization of questions made comparative work difficult. Second, quantitative analysis was time-consuming and labour-intensive in the pre-computer and early computer era of the 1960s. Third, the popularity of self-report surveys was increasingly challenged by the rising concept of victim surveys. Fourth, qualitative, critical and

[16] In 2006, Finland replicated the original 1962 NDR measurement to study long-term changes in self-repored delinquency (Salmi, 2008).

historical methods were becoming increasingly popular among social researchers. Fifth, towards the end of the 1960s, the *zeitgeist* changed rather drastically. This is the moment Rafter has called the beginning of agonistic modernism when criminology's scientific outlook was fractured by the advent of feminism, radical politics and student revolutions, the revival of Marxism, sexual revolution and drug cultures (Rafter, 2010: 347). Many Nordic social researchers were radicalized at this time. In a curious way, the early entry of Nordics to the self-report delinquency survey tradition carried the seeds of its own destruction. This was so because the Nordics, perhaps uniquely, *combined* the 'Americanized' positivist outlook with the earlier policy-oriented and morally loaded normality frame. In the early 1960s, they were late enough to be Americanized and empiricist, but early enough to adopt the normal-because-prevalent framework. The scientifically external influence of the anti-positivist and left radical turn in the late 1960s resulted in the rejection of quantitative surveys as American and 'positivist' exemplars lost much of their appeal. Simultaneously, the scientifically internal developments contributed to the same end result as it appeared that the normality quest was not corroborated by empirical findings. Thus, the Nordic abandonment of the self-report tradition was doubly over-determined. Here, contrast with the developments in the UK is instructive. Since the early British self-report research was conducted in the causal framework instead of the normality platform, the findings were not as anomalous. Thus, while West and Farrington (1973: 189) noted that their findings were 'undramatic and unfashionable', this did not lead to the same kind of decline of the self-report delinquency tradition as in the Nordic area.

Eventually, the Nordics returned to their past source of fame. Starting from the early 1990s, the self-report delinquency survey re-emerged as a popular method. In the period 1990–2009, the self-report survey was the most frequently used data source in articles on delinquent behaviour published by Nordic scholars in the most important criminology journals (Kivivuori and Bernburg, forthcoming). This recent phase of 'renaissance' lies beyond the scope of the present study.[17] However, some aspects of the recent developments merit attention because they relate to the normality paradigm of early Nordic criminology. In Sweden and Finland,

---

[17] More on specific Nordic self-report studies and indicator systems, see Kivivuori, 2007: 10–11, 102; Andersson, 2009; Kivivuori, 2009.

the method re-emerged without much ado in early 1990s, following Finland's decision to participate in the first sweep of the *International Self-Report Delinquency Study* (ISRD-1). In Norway, the redeployment of self-report delinquency surveys resulted in a relatively acrimonious debate about the normality paradigm. To some extent, Danish criminologists were drawn to this debate as well. These national differences were hardly coincidental as the normality frame that inspired the NDR was most consistently deployed in Norway and Denmark.

Norwegian debate

The idea that crime is normal has a distinct capacity to trigger scientific debates. A hundred years after Durkheim and Tarde clashed over this question (Beirne, 1993: 164–70), Norwegian criminologists engaged in similar internal combat. The difference was that the debate had an empirical focus in the findings of the self-report delinquency surveys, an asset the moral statisticians of the nineteenth century did not have. Yet, as in the classic French duel, moral questions soon emerged.

In 1992, the researcher Willy Pedersen (1995 [1992]) attacked the 'shades of grey' argument, using new self-report data and showing the accumulation of offences to a minority of frequent offenders. Nils Christie (1995 [1992]) emerged as the defender of the early NDR interpretive frames. He started his defence by an historical contextualization. He pointed out that when the self-report method was first used by Norwegian researchers, society and culture were different. People used to think of criminals as an alien group whose individual characteristics were deeply different from law-abiding people (Christie, 1995 [1992]: 365). The first generation self-report researchers therefore highlighted findings showing that the great majority of young males had committed at least some minor offences. 'We were more interested in the grey aspect than the black aspect', Christie pointed out (Christie, 1995 [1992]: 366). He underlined that the similarity or normalcy interpretation was fruitful [*fruktbare*] in the 1960s. Unfortunately he did not elaborate on the criteria of usefulness or fruitfulness. The context suggests that the aim was to contradict the traditional and conservative visions of the surrounding culture. The NDR was a project that would today be described as public criminology, engaging society to change its sensibility towards criminals. As has been observed above, the early self-report researchers certainly did not falsify or fabricate findings; in contrast, they selected the fruitful facts from a larger repertory of findings. What was defined as fruitful was typically based on policy considerations.

The Pedersen-Christie debate corroborates that the 1960s generation saw its role in society largely in moral terms. They had a vision that guided their criminological research; witness, for instance, Jaakkola's remembrance of the policy-oriented nature of the survey. Against this background it is interesting to note that when attacked by Pedersen, the NDR veterans could have resorted to their own empirical findings. After all, they had observed, and quite clearly reported, that the likelihood of police detection depended on offending frequency: in this respect, police control was not random. Additionally, the NDR researchers had internally critiqued the proper scope conditions of the 'normality' interpretation (see above). Thus, the NDR researchers could have replied to Pedersen, look, our research was balanced and we acknowledged the existence of the frequent offender. Instead, they largely preferred moral and historical argumentation. Indeed, they evoked dark visions of moral depravity: Christie referred to the Holocaust, while another criminologist, Høigård, raised the haunting images of castration and lobotomy (Christie, 1995 [1992]: 368; Høigård, 1995 [1993]: 279). The critic Pedersen had not brought these topics up. The memory of the Holocaust and other atrocities were brought up in a debate about the measurement of adolescent delinquency and the interpretation of rather mundane survey results. Reference to Nazi crimes and punitive excesses were echoes from the original context of discovery in which the hidden crime survey was deployed: the aftermath of the Second World War. For this reason, the 'shades of grey' metaphor meant different things to different generations. For some, it was a description with problematic or poor fit to data, while for others it was loaded with moral meaning and deep social significance.

Pedersen countered by suggesting that Christie and Høigård were using some kind of consequentialist or instrumentalist epistemic criteria of validity, selecting research programmes and facts on the basis of their likely policy recommendations (Pedersen, 1995 [1993]). Indeed, Christie's use of the concept 'fruitful' was open to this suspicion, as if he was choosing descriptions of reality on the basis of expected moral effects. There is an element in the sociological attack against the abnormality paradigm that judges potential facts in accordance to how 'dangerous' they might be in terms of political consequences (Hindelang, Hirschi and Weis, 1981: 16; cf Pietikäinen, 2004). In their final contribution to the debate, Høigård and Christie discussed the notion of fruitfulness as a core criterion of scientific research but did not explicate it in greater detail; by implication, they argued that seeing crime as a social construct was more fruitful than multivariate analyses of crime causation (Høigård and Christie, 1995). Their rhetorical strategy was to equate Pedersen's empiricism with the criminology of the 1930s while their brand of social constructionism was currently leading the way.

The normality frame was a symbolic idea around which the first generation of social science based empirical criminology networks coalesced in the Nordic area, providing scholars with the kind of affective and antagonistic energy that builds 'schools' and circles (Collins, 1998; Savelsberg and Flood, 2010). In the passage of time, that idea could appear strange to new cohorts of scholars who did not share the original social and cultural context of the 1960s.

Pathology of conformity re-emerges

When responding to the critic Pedersen, Christie argued for the deep contextuality of criminological research. In the early 1960s, it had been fruitful to underscore the normality of petty and occasional offending, because the general population had then entertained an inflated view of its own moral high ground. The hypocritical righteousness of the supposedly law-abiding people was pulled down by early self-report research. Interestingly, Christie argued that the situation was now, in the 1990s, starting to resemble this earlier constellation. The dichotomy of 'them' and 'us' was again raising its ugly head, and conformism was returning as an accepted code of conduct. He referred to findings from recent Danish self-report delinquency surveys indicating that the percentage of law-abiding adolescents was increasing.

Christie additionally observed that back in the 1960s and 1970s law students had looked like lawyers while social science students looked like ordinary young people; in contrast, in the 1990s, social science students were beginning to look like lawyers (Christie, 1995 [1992]: 367). This historical anecdote has a ring of satire to it. Recall how Porterfield had exposed the criminality of divinity students. Back in 1959, law students had been the first group whose hidden criminality had been exposed by the Nordic criminologists. Now Christie lamented the rise of conformity among contemporary youth with reference to law students. Indeed, the old hypocrites of the country club and law student variety, disclosed by Porterfield and his Nordic followers, were somehow humane in their hidden depravity. Their delinquency had connected them to the ordinary man and to the criminal. In contrast, today's conformist had something alien in him/her because he/she really was a conformist. In other words, the conforming society was back with a vengeance because *its rise was documented by self-report studies* (Kyvsgaard, 1992; Balvig, 2006; Kivivuori, 2007). The new conformity was menacing because it was no longer hypocritical as in the olden days, when the condemners had been exposed as petty offenders. Now the new Philistines really were law-abiding, making their suspected conservatism doubly disconcerting to the 1960s generation.

Christie was not alone in Nordic criminology in constructing the new law-abidingness as a social problem. In Denmark, Flemming Balvig (2006) advanced similar interpretations. He likened today's law-abiding youth to stock market speculators who invest in their own futures and fortunes, while renouncing any compassion towards chronic offenders (p. 63). This simile is not unlike Christie's satirical observations about students looking like lawyers. The moral commentary on the badness of the new conformity continued the moral programme of the early self-report delinquency researchers, the normalcy paradigm. Indeed, these vicissitudes of the normality approach testify to how interpretive frames are highly flexible with respect to evidentiary bases. Delinquency could be shown to be normal because almost everyone was occasionally a petty delinquent. When this was no longer the case, normality was no longer judged on the basis of what delinquent behaviours were prevalent; instead, the interpretive frame defined the conformist as the problem. Whatever the empirical result of self-report delinquency research, the paradigm of the Skinnerian innovating ideologist stood on an unshaken firmament.

Effects of the hidden crime survey

The question of how new ideational materials influence historical developments is notoriously difficult. The briefest way to summarize the overall NDR impact is probably to say that radical recommendations were not fulfilled, while a more diffuse and less radical reframing of the crime problem probably helped to make the criminal justice system less punitive, at least in Finland.

Decriminalization proposals

Concerning the first of the above mentioned potential impact types, it is instructive to look at the Norwegian recommendations. There the NDR criminologists suggested that petty larceny should be decriminalized. Because such crimes were extremely prevalent and therefore normal, the Norwegians suggested that the police should not investigate minor shoplifting, car and bicycle thefts and some types of burglary. They argued that 'urging the victims to deal with the offenders themselves may be just as good a deterrent as the present legalistic procedure' (Stangeland and Hauge, 1974: 156). Rather than referring to any kind of vigilantism, these suggestions presaged mediation and alternative conflict resolution movements.

The Norwegians were not alone in bringing up the subject of decriminalization.[18] As early as in 1965, Karl J. Lång, an influential Finnish policymaker, suggested that the hidden crime surveys opened the road to decriminalization (Lång, 1967). He observed that such initiatives should be age-graded and mentioned drunken driving as a possible crime that could be decriminalized. Needless to say, these initiatives were not fulfilled then or later. However, there appears to be one partial exception. In 1966 Lång argued against defining sexual intercourse between two adolescents as criminal. Referring to the new findings of the Finnish NDR, he described adolescent sex as normal behaviour (Lång, 2004 [1966]: 30–1). Today, consensual sex between adolescents is not defined as a crime in Finnish penal law, if the maturity level of the 'victim' and the 'perpetrator' is similar. The purpose is to depenalize sex in adolescent dating relationships where age difference exists but is small.

Successful reframing of the crime issue

While decriminalization proposals largely failed, the NDR had a diffuse impact on the general social sensibility towards offenders that probably influenced policy developments. At least in Finland,

---

[18] For a Danish (and more circumspect) discussion of decriminalization, see Greve, 1972: 151–3.

the core arguments of the hidden crime research agenda had an impact on the general sensibilities concerning crime, and even effects on criminal policy. The general thrust of these arguments was towards a more humane and less severe sanctioning of crimes. The normal-because-prevalent argument was successfully deployed to attack psychiatric treatment modalities and sanction harshness. When the history of the successful penal moderation in Scandinavia is examined, the use of hidden crime surveys as instruments of 'public criminology' must be acknowledged.

According to Inkeri Anttila, the main architect of what came to be called rational and humane criminal policy, the NDR studies helped to push Finland out of the age of draconian punishments and dubious treatment aims (Anttila, 2001 [1979]: 150). An important Commission appointed by the Ministry of Justice referred to NDR results when arguing against unconditional prison sentences for young people (pp. 151–2). The Finnish hidden crime researchers were politically active and were thus able to influence political processes. A good example is the 1969 criminal policy programme of the Social Democratic Party. In that programme, it was stated that only a fraction of crimes are reported to the police and therefore contribute to the statistics of recorded crimes. The programme then specified:

The Nordic research of hidden criminality shows that crime among youth is not exceptional. Rather, it is statistically something that the majority of youths do. Contrary to what is commonly believed, the criminal offenders are not a group that constitutes a deviant category of people. Instead, the people who are sent to prisons comprise a deviant group. Research has shown that psychological disorders and low social position are more usual phenomena in the prison population when compared with the general population. The people who are targeted as objects of criminal justice sanctions are not selected equally from the population of all offenders. Instead, the economically and individually least advantaged people are overrepresented in this group. (SDP, 1969.)

It was no coincidence that the NDR was mentioned in the programme because the Finnish NDR researchers actually wrote these lines (Jaakkola, 2010). They had access to highest political influence. The findings and interpretations of self-report surveys were put to policy use. The Finnish NDR was one factor pushing the country towards less punitive criminal policy (Anttila, 1986: 17). In interview, the Finnish hidden crime survey pioneer Risto Jaakkola (2010) noted that the NDR was not only about the science of criminology; rather, it was also about changing society. It is clear that to a considerable degree, this goal was achieved. One factor that may have contributed to success is that the Finnish balance-oriented criminal policy doctrine was not so radical as to suggest decriminalization of common crimes. The balance doctrine was genuinely balanced: it was not a total or abolitionist critique of punishment. From its point of view, excessive leniency could be seen as reflecting, or resulting in, social disequilibrium (Anttila, 2001 [1979]: 185). Characteristically, Törnudd wrote that an organized society cannot 'afford to let statutes on the unlawful appropriation of another's goods fall into disuse', and suggested that occasional crackdowns on minor offences should be implemented 'to maximize the deterrent effect' (Törnudd, 1996d [1975]: 72, 76). Thus, the balance doctrine of criminal justice was consistent with temporary 'zero-tolerance' measures in the context of a low general level of penal repression. The point is that the normality frame, derived from sociological theory and supported by aspects of crime survey data, *influenced policies when they were delivered as a package that moderated but did not deny the role of classical deterrence.*

To conclude, the data of the self-report delinquency survey constituted a kind of *gestalt* figure: the raw sensory information emanating from the data remains constant, but different interpretations can be constituted depending on how the perceiver attends to the figure (Heritage, 1989: 39–40). For example, the NDR produced several empirical findings such as (1) the concentration of offences, and especially serious offences, to a minority of offenders and (2) high prevalence of occasional and petty offending. There appear to be at least three types of bifurcation between these two emphases. First, written commentaries were more likely to stress 'normality' than internal discussions and critiques of the criminological community. Second, with the passage of time, the normality frame gained salience as the complexity of original findings faded from memory. Third, it is likely that the societal reception of the crime survey results was selective in the sense that surprising results 'sunk in' better than commonsensical results.

Intellectual products resemble sacred objects because they are meant to reflect truths that transcend individuals, and because their revealers expect them to command respect in others (Savelsberg and Flood, 2010). Moreover, core ideas guiding scientific research provide scholarly networks with collective effervescence and affective energy (Collins, 1998). As such, they fulfil totemic functions for tribes and networks of scholars. As examples of such symbolic and totemic beliefs, Savelsberg and Flood refer to Durkheim's contention that 'crime is normal', Sutherland's principle that all 'criminal behaviour is learned', and Merton's claim that 'crime is a normal adaptation' to culture-economy discrepancy. The historical analysis provided in this chapter, focussing on the horizontal network that coalesced around the first Nordic self-report delinquency study, corroborates Savelsberg's analysis. Thus, the story of the normality frame probably exemplifies a more general pattern in social sciences and humanities: counter-intuitive statements tend to be popular and well remembered. Consider, for example, slogans like 'prisons are schools of crime', 'crime is socially constructed', 'crime does not exist', and the ideas listed by Savelsberg. While all these have a limited sense in which they are true, their practical efficacy as public sociology is based on interpretive thought-in-action where empirical scope conditions are creatively bracketed.[19]

Because of the historical and punitive context of the 1950s and 1960s, the normality frame became an important tool of public criminology. Self-report surveys were used to stress that most of us are sinners, and that the social control of crime was biased, if not random, with respect to crime. At least in Finland, the new empirical criminology successfully challenged the old guard of lawyers and judges whose control opinions were traditional and punitive. New empiricism went hand in hand with a new kind of liberal sensitivity. The future would show that the crime survey could be harnessed to serve different goals, and to swing back the punitive pendulum.

---

[19] Indeed, it is conceivable that certain faddish general currents in social sciences, like radical constructionism and relativism, achieve popularity because they are counter-intuitive and exaggerated. See also Boudon, 1989: 130–3; Boudon, 2003.

6
Concluding Discussion

Explanations in social science can be divided roughly into two types. First, there are explanations that do not refer to conscious motives of the historical actors. Such explanations work 'behind the back' of the people whose behaviour is being explained. Second, there are explanations that refer to people's conscious motives and moral ideas, which drive them to behave the way they behave. The philosopher Charles Taylor has critiqued social sciences for disliking such moral and intentional explanations. In his words, the typical fashion of social science explanation 'has generally shied away from invoking moral ideals and has tended to have recourse to supposedly harder and more down to earth factors in explanation', such as mode production and economic factors (Taylor, 1991: 19–21).

There is no doubt that people like Sutherland, Porterfield, Wallerstein and the Nordic pioneers of hidden crime research were driven by strong moral motives and ideals. Their urge to redescribe (some types of) crime as normal was linked to the goal of humanizing the treatment and sanctioning of offenders and deviants. It would be unfair to say that they were merely defending their own interests against rivalling disciplines such as psychiatry, or that they were vehicles of capillary power penetrating the body social by means of modern survey techniques, nor were they mere carriers of linguistic discourses or memes. They were flesh and blood, men and women who used the available cultural and rhetorical lexicon in historically specific local battles of resignification and politics. The immediate policy struggle combined two fights: one for humane criminal policy (and against excessive punitivity), and another for sociology (against psychology and psychiatry). The general context was even more complex. Shaped by a particular historical constellation of social and ideological forces, the normality interpretation was a 'negotiated accomplishment of distinct social groups operating in bounded situations' (Measham and Shiner, 2009: 507).

Furthermore, the invention of the modern standardized and confession-based crime survey cannot be described as a teleological unfolding of a potentiality that was destined to result in the modern crime survey. There were crossroads where developments could have taken alternative routes. Local reporting propensity studies, direct mass observation, Robison's concept of the Central Register, and perhaps even the 'psychiatric case-worker' type of intensive interviews, were options that did not flourish in the same way as the modern self-report delinquency survey. If there are elements of seeming necessity, these are probably related to the internal logic of empirical investigation. By this I mean that on many occasions, the hypotheses and expectations of the first generation researchers were not corroborated by empirical findings.

Internal logic: The diffusion of the survey method to new topics

The invention of the hidden crime survey cannot be fully reduced to its immediate policy uses, or to its cultural context. The discovery was also an *internal scientific process*. The crime survey was a solution to a problem that had been discussed for decades among moral statisticians. The problem was: since we know that recorded crimes cannot be used as a proxy measure for all crimes, how could we bypass the official control barrier in crime measurement? One of the findings that led moral statisticians to critique official statistics was the observation that official control was biased against the underdogs of society. In this respect, W. E. B. Du Bois and Thorsten Sellin were central figures: Du Bois even went so far as to use the sample survey to study criminal justice related matters. But more typical solutions to the riddle of the official control barrier ranged from police folklore, reporting propensity studies and direct observation to alternative statistics offered by private or quasi-governmental sources. However, the real breakthrough came with the discovery that people were ready to confess their crimes to researchers if asked directly under conditions of anonymity. This breakthrough has been justly described as a turning point in the development of criminology as a science (Laub, 2004). Arguably, this was the moment when moral statistics were replaced by criminology, now at last freed from the limitations of governmental statistics, clinical data and institutional populations.[1]

The hidden crime survey concept was an amalgamation of two traditions: the criminological tradition and the survey tradition. The survey method started as local 'social surveys' with strong moral and sometimes religious goals. The earliest Booth-style surveys were fact-finding missions that incidentally used questionnaires typically filled in by informants. The modern survey was born in the 1930s and was characterized by two features. First, it addressed social actors directly with standardized questionnaires. Second, it was increasingly based on probability sampling instead of full surveys of local units or the 'quota sampling' of market researchers (Converse, 2009). The hidden crime surveys of the 'heroic' discovery phase (roughly between 1930 and 1960, see Figure 4.1, above, p. 121) combined aspects of the nineteenth century social survey and the modern sample survey. They resembled the early social surveys in that they had a strong moral mission, and in that they used local samples. They resembled the modern sample survey in that the respondents were targeted directly. The classic early hidden crime survey was thus a 'hybrid' form, combining elements of the early moralistic surveys and the later more technical and 'Americanized' sample survey.

The survey method was developing fast from the 1920s and important breakthroughs were made during the 1930s. What then happened was a kind of *adaptive radiation* of the method: it was constantly being applied to new life domains. Converse has described the diffusion of survey method as a 'luxuriant field of self-reports' (Converse, 2009: 402). The survey method spread to various disciplines and to various areas of life. Especially sensitive topics offered an enticing frontier for survey researchers. At first, it was believed that asking about income or occupation was a sensitive field, but it gradually became clear that people were rather willing to 'discuss almost anything' (Converse, 2009: 403). The Kinsey sex studies proved this point.

---

[1] Needless to say, criminologists kept on using official statistics in addition to survey resources. The position of official records actually strengthened when it was realized that survey sources and official records tended to tap into different parts of the crime continuum. Furthermore, survey-based research on police detection likelihood supported the validity of official statistics. This was one of the ironic results of self-report delinquency surveys (see section 'The Americanization of the hidden crime survey in the 1950s' above).

Preconditions of survey penetration

From the internal perspective, the self-report crime survey was a means of transgressing the official control barrier in crime measurement. However, the history of how the barrier was broken may exaggerate the 'degrees of freedom' that resulted from that breakthrough. There were certain social preconditions that had to be fulfilled before the crime survey concept could proliferate.

In many respects, the increasing use of survey methodology has followed the advance of state institutions, both horizontally in terms of geography and vertically in terms of how deeply state institutions penetrate the social fabric. In the first stage of survey advance, various proxy reporters were used: 'Indian agents', school board visitors, social workers, and local priests. In the second stage, when people were directly addressed, most of the activity took place in schools and other educational institutions that cannot be regarded as entirely voluntary for the students.

The link between mass confessional survey and the educational institutions is intriguing, because it appears that whenever schools were created, they were soon used as data collection sites by researchers. Furthermore, the rise of the school created further openings for data collection because it increased the literacy of populations. Literate populations were able to respond to self-administered self-report questionnaires in the orchestrated silence of the classroom. Later on, literate citizens were able to respond to mail survey questionnaires carried to their homes by the post office, a communication network created by the state. Hirschfeld's ability to collect mail survey data among Berlin's blue-collar workers in 1903–04 is a case in point, testifying to how mass literacy paved the way for sensitive topics research. Clearly, the story of the hidden crime survey could be told from the point of view of power analysis, as a history of how forms of knowledge rely on specific power practices. As seen from this perspective, the official control barrier will never be fully transgressed because all attempts to do so will ultimately rest on forms of power.[2]

However, the fact that the centralized state has created the structures upon which methods of science rest does not mean

---

[2] Other important preconditions of survey research include research funding and the institutional frameworks of academic disciplines (Savelsberg and Flood, 2004; Savelsberg and Flood, 2010).

that research results are by definition contaminated or socially constructed by power. The history of the self-report delinquency survey reveals a different picture. The discovery of the offender survey was heavily theory-laden in the normality paradigm, and embedded in a specific moral platform. Yet when the pioneers applied their tool, the paradigm started to yield and bend. This was so because the tool was repeatedly brought into contact with external social reality: the thousands of people who responded to the survey. The most important 'stubborn facts' were the existence of the frequent offender, the class-delinquency link, and the finding that becoming known to the police was related to offending (as opposed to socially biased control and labelling mechanisms). Many of the first generation hidden crime surveyors felt disappointment when findings such as these were at odds with the expectations. Yet, as true scientists, *they* yielded and bended to findings. The discovery of hidden crime shows that, also in the field of human and social sciences, findings are more than social constructs: there are external facts that discriminate between theories.

From abnormality to flexible normalization

The discovery of hidden crime took place in a series of local battles in which groups of scholars wanted to reduce repressive social control practices by showing the normalcy of crime. Their cultural sources were multiple, ranging from statistical fatalism and Romanticism to grand sociological theory, but the new innovation was to show empirically the statistical normalcy of petty and occasional crime. Inspired by moral concerns, they engaged in local battles to reduce the punitivity of repressive normative structures.

In so doing, they probably influenced larger societal and cultural trends. The German literary scholar Jürgen Link published in 1994 a study of Western normalization discourses, *Versuch über den Normalismus*. In his view, normative rules and social norms and laws are human universals, but the discourse and practices of 'normality' have been unique features of Western societies since the beginning of the nineteenth century (Link, 1997: 23, 341). Link suggests that there were actually three kinds of normalization strategies that supplemented the previously existing legal-repressive type of governance. He calls these strategies *pre-normalization*, *proto-normalization* and *flexible normalization*.[3] Each was a combination of ideas and social practices.

Pre-normalization, proto-normalization and flexible normalization are overlapping phenomena, but it helps to consider them in their historical order of appearance. Pre-normalization began in the eighteenth century mainly through practices such as military discipline, standardization of weights, astronomical observation, and pedagogical standardization (Link, 1997: 190). According to Link, the first attempts at standardization of industrial products were related to pre-normalization (Link, 1997: 191–2). Proto-normalization refers to a strategy that wanted to define and delimit the area of abnormality in humans by erecting clear, stable criteria and boundaries of normality. In the field of criminology, the abnormality paradigm of nineteenth century psychiatrists corresponds to Link's era of proto-normalization. Like pre-normalization, this strategy aimed at suppressing variation such as physically and/or morally deformed 'monsters', or atavistic throwbacks to the evolutionary past. In contrast, the flexible normalization strategy expands the area of normality by making its criteria historical, social and fluid. While proto-normalization aimed at clear definition and exclusion of abnormality, flexible normalization relies heavily on the empirical behaviour of people as a resource for a new kind of self-regulation:

Proto-normalization defines its norms *ex ante* and is prepared to enforce those norms repressively on individuals, while flexible normalization infers the norms *ex post* from statistical inquiries and leaves people to self-adjust their behaviour based on their knowledge of statistics. (Link, 1997: 92.)

In other words, the twentieth century witnessed a momentous change in how social regulation functions. Previously, people were expected to follow pre-defined rules. Now, in the age of flexible normalization, people are given empirical data on how people normally or typically behave, and they are then given the freedom to adjust their behaviour to thus defined criteria of empirical and statistical normality. The history of the discovery of hidden crime as a measurable entity can be interpreted from this point of view.

---

[3] In my analysis, I have preferred the simpler conceptual framework where normalization is contrasted with the psychiatric and medical abnormality notions (see Chapter 3).

The discoverers of self-report delinquency survey advanced 'flexible normalization' by showing that petty and occasional crime was empirically very prevalent. They attacked rigid *ex ante* normality definitions and sought to replace them with more flexible *ex post* normality constructs. This is not to say that they caused flexible normalization to happen; more likely, they contributed to a macro-cultural process that was unfolding in any case.

Sociological bid for disciplinary hegemony

As a science, sociology was born from a sharp confrontation with the pre-existing sciences of the individual: psychiatry and psychology. As described by Robert Merton, Durkheim, the founding father, had been 'fighting entrenched groups of psychologists and social psychologists who were questioning the intellectual legitimacy of sociology' (Cullen and Messner, 2007: 21). This context of discovery left an enduring legacy for sociology that truly became an embattled science. Sociologists still tend to dismiss attempts to include psychological elements as 'reductionist', thus upholding the constitutive principle of the profession (Scheff, 1995: 161).

The hidden crime survey was born in the context of this battle, where it was then used as weapon. The survey, showing the high prevalence of occasional and petty crime, was used to attack the abnormality paradigm. Edwin Sutherland especially was inspired by a strong anti-psychiatry ideology, becoming the 'warrior' of sociology's coup over criminology (Laub and Sampson, 1991: 1421–2). He studied white-collar crime to show that social and individual pathology did not cause crime. He used the qualitative case study interview to humanize and normalize the life of the professional thief. He experimented with the self-report method to show that almost all of his middle-class students had committed theft at least once in their lives. James Wallerstein similarly saw the hidden crime survey as a weapon in the fight against the abnormality conceptions of the psy-sciences. His tour-de-force, the Randen Foundation Crime Survey, was a piece of action research, designed to cause shock waves. In his novel *The Demon's Mirror* (1951) Wallerstein used satire and fiction to critique non-sociological criminology.

Non-criminological sociologists did not miss the point. They appreciated the help given by the hidden crime surveys. The findings of high crime prevalence were recognized as anomalous for the abnormality paradigm. Of the great mandarins of the American sociological tradition, Robert Merton was perhaps most keenly aware of this. When skirmishing with the psychiatrists, he engaged in evasive action, warning against the 'premature' integration of disciplines. As a trump card, he drew on the hidden crime surveys of Wallerstein and Porterfield, arguing that crime was so prevalent that it could not be psychologically caused. It should be added that the hidden crime survey was invented at an opportune time when Talcott Parsons was making the classics of European sociology available for US sociologists. Durkheim's discussions about the normality of crime may have been easier to accept because the surveys supported the statistical prevalence of occasional and petty crime.

The battle for disciplinary hegemony was explicit in the Nordic case as well. The early Nordic self-report researchers stated that since crime was so prevalent, it could not be individually or pathologically caused. While some of the critique against psychiatry and psychology may have been scientifically problematic if judged on the basis of what is known today (Laub and Sampson, 1991), it is nevertheless important to recognize that anti-psychiatry ideology was a cultural *context of discovery*, which escorted scholars like Sutherland to important true discoveries.

The populist soil

It has been suggested that the self-report delinquency survey tradition was inspired by American Puritan tradition, which motivated attention to minor and petty infractions (McClintock, 1970: 18). This interpretation is a partial truth at best, and possibly erroneous. As has been shown in this study, the sensibility that inspired early hidden crime research was different: it was about revealing the hypocrisy of those who condemned sinners. *Who is to throw the first stone, if hidden crime research indicates that we are all sinners?* Showing the high prevalence of petty offending was meant as a critique of the rules, or the enforcement of rules; it was not about calling for stricter control. The results of the hidden crime surveys, indicating very high prevalence, meant that calls for 'eradication of crime' were unrealistic. Clearly, the Puritan control motivation theory fails to explain the rise of the self-report delinquency research. If one excludes the internal scientific path to discovery and focuses on the cultural context of discovery, we have to look for traditions that were anti-punitive. In any case, the cultural influences were multiple and complex.

168 Concluding Discussion

In this study, I have argued that the early twentieth century populist and progressive movements were an important context of discovery for the hidden crime survey. This was mainly so because those movements introduced a broader definition of crime than the one offered by the abnormality paradigm of crime. Previously, crime had been seen as linked to lowest social strata and/or to psychological abnormality. The critique of robber barons and corrupt politicians sensitized people to see crime among the middle and upper classes. In this framework, crime became biologically and psychologically normal, even though it was still seen as immoral and sinful. Another habit of the progressive heart was to see respectability as a surface hiding ugly truths. They wanted to expose the sordid reality behind 'supercilious' and hypocritical facades (Hofstadter, 1977 [1955]: 199). Their imagination about crime was clearly not bound by the official control barrier, which was seen as reflecting power biases instead of real behavioural differences. The progressive movement was closely associated with the Social Gospel type of religious thought.

However, there are features in the hidden crime survey movement which are difficult to reconcile with the populist–progressive movements from the 1890s to 1920s. Most importantly, the progressive movement had *moralistic and punitive* aspects. For example, the victory of prohibition in the US has been described as the victory of progressivism (Nugent, 2010: 112–13). The movement sought to transform the 'drinker from the victim of evil to a lawbreaker' (Hofstadter, 1977: 291), thus expanding instead of contracting the sphere of crime. The Ku Klux Klan movement has been described as a rural Protestant offshoot of the progressive era, indicating the punitive and moralistic potentials of the Populist movement (Hofstadter, 1977: 291–7). It is quite clear that the anti-punitive and tolerant attitude of the early hidden crime researchers was highly inconsistent with such movements.

The innovation of the hidden crime surveyors was that they transformed the populist suspicion of ubiquitous criminality into an instrument of more humane treatment of offenders. In other words, the spirit of early hidden crime surveys was *populist in cognition* but *anti-populist in moral evaluation*. Like populists, the hidden crime survey pioneers felt that crime was very prevalent in all social circles. But unlike populists, they did not draw the conclusion that a moral crusade against crime was needed or feasible. Instead, they aimed at soothing the heated retributive emotions by arguing that high prevalence of crime constituted normality and normality called for tolerance. Two historical developments, or contexts of discovery, helped to make the change from punitive populism to crime normalization. First, there was the strong Christian component in early American sociology: the religious cultural lexicon had much to offer for social critics who satirized hypocrites. Second, and more importantly, sociology's sustained attack against the psy-sciences and the abnormality paradigm made heavy use of the idea of normality. Helped with these cultural lexicons, the hidden crime survey showed that it was possible to practise populism without punitivism.

Can self-report surveys increase crime?

When the self-report crime survey was being introduced in criminology, there were fears that the findings could lead to a collapse of morality. Thus, Nils Christie pondered in 1965 whether the findings, when publicized, reduced people's respect for the law and increased deviance. As a case in point, he referred to the 'effects of the Kinsey report' (Christie, 1967: 74). Similar fears were expressed in Finland (Anttila, 1966: 19). The logic was that if people are told that so many are breaking the law, the previously law-abiding might start following other people's example.

Is there any reason to believe that this might actually be the case? If researchers announce that crime is very prevalent, will this lead to an increase in crime? The idea seems almost preposterous, especially if aggregate level crime trends would be explained by the cultural impact of a limited number of surveys. It is fairly well established that crime was increasing in Western Europe during the post-war period (Estrada, 1999: 23), but typically crime surveys were launched later, and it is doubtful if extensive segments of populations were aware of such studies. Yet, there are theoretical reasons not to discount the hypothesis completely. At least three research programmes suggest that there can be a causal link between high prevalence announcement and offending behaviour.

(1) *Neutralization theory*. This theory suggests that culturally available techniques to redescribe crime as prevalent and normal can impact the level of crime. As noted above in Chapter 2, neutralization theory sees offenders as 'innovating ideologists' who try to redescribe types of illegal behaviour as either excusable or justifiable. If innovating ideologists produce and disseminate new ways

of seeing (petty and occasional) crime as normal, this can conceivably help would-be offenders in their pursuit to explain their offences. The creators of neutralization theory, Gresham Sykes and David Matza, observed that 'delinquents seem to show a surprising awareness of sociological and psychological explanations of their behavior', and to use such conceptual resources in making sense of their own behaviour (Sykes and Matza, 1957: 667). Not only high prevalence of offending but other rhetorical innovations such as normality, pathology of conformity, and so on, can be used to redescribe delinquent behaviour. There is reason to believe that ways of thinking are operative as causes of human behaviour. For instance, cognitive-behavioural programmes are known to reduce recidivism. Such programmes often include teaching the offenders that neutralizations are not morally valid.[4]

(2) *Pluralistic ignorance*. The concept of pluralistic ignorance was first coined by the American social psychologist Floyd H. Allport in 1931. Even before, he had used the related concept of illusion of universality (O'Gorman, 1986: 335–6). Pluralistic ignorance refers to socially shared knowledge about other people that is mistakenly believed to be correct. Allport and his colleagues studied cognitive beliefs because they were relevant from the point of view of conformity. Individuals attempt to conform to patterns of behaviour they perceive to be prevalent (O'Gorman, 1986: 336). For example, if young people believe that it is very common to use alcohol, they feel pressure to act accordingly to be 'normal' (Lintonen and Konu, 2004). The same probably applies to delinquent behaviour; there is some evidence that deconstructing illusions of universality among youths may result in reduced delinquency (Balvig, 2002: see also Balvig and Holmberg, 2011). The normality perception does appear to increase delinquency, at least at the level of adolescent peer groups.

(3) *Basic social influence*. Learning theoretical research suggests that people are influenced by other people's behaviour, but systematically underestimate this influence. We are moved by how we perceive others behaving, but we like to think that such perceptions do not influence our behaviour. A recent experimental study of theft in the Arizona Petrified Forest National Park supports this conclusion. The park authorities had chosen to stress to visitors

---

[4] This literature on cognitive-behavioural programmes is vast: see for example Van Voorhis et al, 2004.

that many visitors steal pieces of valuable petrified wood, thus destroying the national heritage. The researchers manipulated this message experimentally in order to study processes of basic social influence. In the experiment, the anti-theft sign was alternated, with one sign showing three people stealing, and the other showing one person stealing. The result was that those visitors who saw the 'three people stealing' sign stole more than visitors seeing the 'one person stealing' sign. The researchers concluded: 'Although it is understandable that park officials would want to instigate corrective action by describing *the dismaying size of the problem*, such a message is far from optimal. Indeed, by *normalizing* the unwanted activity, the message stands a good chance of backfiring.' (Cialdini, 2005: 159, emphases added). The experiment suggests that perceived statistical normality of crime can impact human behaviour. As judged on the basis of these theories and research findings, it no longer sounds entirely preposterous that high prevalence findings could have *some* impact on criminal behaviour. Modern developed societies are *reflective* like no other society has ever been: we are constantly barraged with statistical data on how prevalent specific opinions and behaviours are. In this context, crime survey results may support culturally available high prevalence perceptions that exist irrespective of such findings.

The changing political uses of crime survey

The impact of self-report delinquency survey on criminal policies is a complex question, and the answers may differ in various areas and countries. The basic goal of the creators of the self-report delinquency survey was to make criminal policies and people's attitudes towards crime more humane. In the Nordic area, their moral project was to some extent successful, at least from the 1960s to the 1990s. Elsewhere, the story is much more complex. Garland has argued that since the early 1960s, crime surveys[5] buttressed the new notion that deviance is normal (Garland, 2001: 65–7), and the corollary that crime cannot be influenced by treating individual

---

[5] Garland writes that self-report delinquency surveys began in the US in the late 1950s, and refers to a 1958 article by Short and Nye (Garland, 2001: 65–6, 232). As I have described in this study, there was a much longer history of how the confession-based survey method was discovered and used in policy argumentation. The work of Short and Nye built on earlier work that was much more explicitly morally loaded than theirs.

pathologies and ameliorating social disadvantage. The surveys redescribed crime as normal. The intentions of the surveyors (and labelling theoretical critics) were not punitive, but their actions had unintended consequences that contributed to the punitive turn of the 1970s and 1980s. Later on, the self-report delinquency survey was adopted to serve a new kind of crime governance. In the UK, this turn of events has been attributed to Tony Blair's admiration of Bill Clinton's successful presidential campaign which repoliticized crime in order to win over the electorate (McVie, 2009: 170–2). Following this strategy, New Labour started to use punitive rhetoric in its criminal justice policy. After its rise to power in 1997, the proliferation of self-report delinquency studies was facilitated by support from central government (p. 171). The core concept in the new knowledge demand was *risk factor*, that is predictors that help to identify who is, or will become, a frequent offender.

In the Nordic area as well, the tide of penal currents started to turn during the 1990s. The survey methodology was used again in local political battle, albeit in a very different way compared to the first generation hidden crime survey researchers. Feminist researchers used the victimization survey to measure violence against women by men (VAW). In Finland and Sweden, the first national VAW surveys were conducted in the late 1990s (Heiskanen and Piispa, 1998; Lundgren et al, 2001). These were based on earlier models, such as the Canadian VAW survey, which utilized a broad conception of what constitutes violence. It is instructive to compare the VAW surveys of the 1990s with first generation hidden crime surveys. In this comparison, I use ideal typical constructs of 'moderating survey' and 'aggravating survey'. By moderating survey I refer to the kind of survey use whose history has been described in this study: a survey that aims at normalizing specific types of crime and seeks to de-emotionalize the crime problem. By aggravating survey I refer to the kind of survey that seeks to raise the public consciousness about the seriousness of specific types of crime and to re-emotionalize the crime question. The earlier crime normalization movement was trying to shut the genie of 'untutored public emotion towards crime and punishment' (Loader, 2006: 582) into the bottle, while in the 1990s a new generation of survey researchers tried to unleash that genie.

A recent book on the 'deafening silence' about violence against women and children exemplifies the new kind of use to which statistical data were put: 'Having figures about violence in your hand is crucial. In fact, only by examining the extent and frequency of male violence can we appreciate the scale, determination and lack of scruples involved in covering up the violence. Only in this way does the importance of figures and statistics also become clear [. . .].' (Romito, 2008: 11.) This kind of rhetoric would have been strange to the discoverers of the self-report crime survey. The contrast highlights an important aspect and shortcoming of the 'moderating' type of survey use: it focussed on relatively non-serious types of crime, such as sexual deviance and theft. In retrospect, one of the most intriguing design features of the Nordic Draftee Research programme was that it omitted violence from the basic self-report questionnaire. In contrast, the new surge of policy-motivated surveys in the 1990s focussed on violence, especially violence against women. Arguably, the new aggravating survey thus *balanced* an omission made by the early Nordic hidden crime surveyors, who largely *ignored violence* in their quest to change the sensibility of society towards crime. The new focus on violence, spearheaded by feminist researchers, was thus a genuine contribution that may have broken some of the 'gag rules' of the liberal policy elites (Loader, 2006: 582). However, the distinction between what is non-serious and what is serious does not 'cut nature at its joints'; rather, it is the very bone of contention in local policy battles, increasingly fought as fights about the correct numbers.

With respect to using numbers, there is a fundamental similarity between moderating and aggravating surveys. Both seek political impact by exposing high prevalence. The hidden crime researchers of the discovery phase exposed the high prevalence of occasional and petty delinquency. In studies conducted in late 1990s, Finnish and Swedish VAW researchers revealed the high lifetime prevalence of violence or violent threats against women (Heiskanen and Piispa, 1998; Lundgren et al, 2001). Like early self-report delinquency researchers, they produced the high prevalence effect by including questions about relatively lenient and non-serious types of violence, and then calculating and using composite multi-item measures. In the Nordic area, this manoeuvre was adapted from international predecessors. An important model was the Canadian VAW survey, which was conducted in the early 1990s. That survey subsumed under the concept of violence behaviours that many people would describe as relatively trivial acts (Haggerty, 2001: 132–3). Acts such as unwanted kissing and fondling can thus be construed as violence alongside serious behaviours. In Finland, the less serious items of VAW scales were about 'obstruction of movement' and 'threats'. Separate scales tapped into the dimension of 'controlling behaviour'. As in Canada, the purpose of this inclusion was to increase public concern by associating non-serious behaviours with clearly serious incidents (Haggerty, 2001: 131–2). When violence measures were based on lifetime recall periods and included a broad range of behaviours, the victim survey researchers were able to report shocking prevalence levels. The percentage of women victimized at least once after the age of 15 was 40 in Finland and 46 in Sweden (Heiskanen and Piispa, 1998; Lundgren et al, 2001). The logic of the classic hidden offender survey was reversed by the new victim survey: now, the idea was to increase the number of persons who were publicly defined as criminals, or worse.

Both moderating and aggravating survey researchers understood that if you want to talk to power, you have to talk in numbers. Their aims were different, however. The first generation hidden crime survey researchers had aimed at reducing the overall level of punitivity. They called for penal moderation and tried to reduce the emotionality of social reaction to crime. In contrast, the feminists used the high prevalence argument to call for more efficient measures against the offenders. They wanted to expand the conceptual umbrella of violence, so that more types of behaviour would be seen as criminal. For instance, they argued for the seriousness of threats and suggested that verbal controlling behaviours should be seen in the context of violence and crime framework. Indeed, they explicitly called for the cultural denormalization of male violence and controlling behaviours (Lundgren et al, 2001: 18, 79). Just like the discoverers of the hidden crime survey before, the feminists of the 1990s functioned as innovating ideologists who wanted to redescribe specific behaviours.

It is instructive to compare the commanding imagery of these two movements. The early hidden crime survey researchers underscored the normality of the criminal offender, using metaphors like *shades of grey* and even invoking religious rhetoric of mercy. In the rhetoric of the feminist movement, repeat offenders were called *patriarchal terrorists* (Johnson, 1995), a choice of word hardly designed to de-emotionalize the crime problem. The concept of *intimate terrorism* is used as an analytic concept in the Finnish government working papers on intimate partner violence.[6] A related conceptual innovation has been to describe specific crimes as *human rights violations*. It is difficult to avoid the conclusion that these rhetorical redescriptions are meant to re-emotionalize the problem at hand. In the Nordic area, the feminist movement has successfully campaigned for the rhetorical redescription of violence against women as crime, terrorism and human rights violation. Traditions of moderation and diversion in criminal justice response are increasingly, and with some success, critiqued on grounds of just deserts and incapacitation.[7] The VAW surveys have played a prominent role in this process. From a policy perspective, the crime survey is a tool that can be harnessed to serve all kinds of goals.

The expanding circle

The moral philosopher Peter Singer (1981) has suggested that human morality has historically developed by including more and more groups within the sphere of moral consideration. Originally, morality developed within kin and tribal groups. Later on in the historical period, morality was extended to white males. More recently, the whole of humanity has been included. Singer argues that in the future, this trend will continue as animals will be fully included in the sphere of moral consideration.

The quest to normalize crime was always intimately connected to humanize the offender. People who used to be labelled monsters, degenerates, deviants and criminals were drawn to the magic circle of full humanity just like women, coloured people and children earlier. In this respect, it is interesting to note that some of the scholars who contributed to the empirical discovery of hidden crime came from downtrodden minorities. Hirschfeld was a champion of sexual minorities, Du Bois was an African American, and Sophia Moses Robison was Jewish. All three were social activists

---

[6] See, for instance, *Naisiin kohdistuvan väkivallan vähentämisohjelma* (2010). The concept of terrorism appears to be seldom used in other repeat victimization phenomena involving children or men as victims. The *terrorism* concept can be profitably compared with the nineteenth century concept of *monster* and the more recent concept of the *super-predator* that has been used within the US conservative law and order platform.

[7] Incapacitation arguments are used to support measures such as barring orders.

defending the weak. This may be a coincidence, or not. Perhaps these scientists understood the normalcy of people labelled as deviant, and were in some sense inspired by the vision of the expanding circle. Others like Thorsten Sellin were moved to critique official statistics because they were biased against minorities.

From this perspective, the normalization of crime is another wave in the expanding circle that includes new groups to the full status of humanity. Indeed, one might argue that in some sense the attempted normalization of crime took this logic to a new level because the group that was being proposed for human and moral consideration was defined by its own moral action, not by some stable feature such as gender or skin colour. At the same time, the logic of normalization was sometimes drawn to a hyperbole that omitted the all too humane experiences of the crime victim. Be that as it may, it seems clear that the criminal policy developments have not followed the trajectory anticipated by the normalization movement. The ripple waves of the expanding circle no longer move on the surface of the social fabric. Instead, the circle may be contracting. Today, the heyday of the normalization movement seems like a strange and distant reality: a mirage whose remembrance serves the goal of showing that humans can arrange their social relations in multiple and different ways.

Bibliography

Adorno, T., Frenkel-Brunswik, E., Levinson, D. and Sanford, R. (1982 [1950]) *The Authoritarian Personality*. New York: W. W. Norton & Company.
Aebi, M. (2009) 'Self-Reported Delinquency Surveys in Europe' in R. Zauberman (ed.) *Self-Reported Crime and Deviance Studies in Europe. Current State of Knowledge and Review of Use*. Brussels: Brussels University Press.
Alapuro, R. (2000) 'Kolme esimerkkiä vaikuttavuudesta sosiologiassa' in M. Linko, T. Saresma, and E. Vainikkala (eds) *Otteita kulttuurista. Kirjoituksia nykyajasta, tutkimuksesta ja elämäkerrallisuudesta*. Nykykulttuurin tutkimusyksikön julkaisuja 65. Jyväskylä: Jyväskylän yliopisto.
Allen, A. (1984) *Satire and society in Wilhelmine Germany: Kladderadatsch and Simplicissimus, 1890–1914*. Lexington: University Press of Kentucky.
Andenaes, J., Sveri, K. and Hauge, R. (1960) 'Kriminalitetshyppigheten hos ustraffede I. Norsk undersøkelse', *Nordisk Tidskrift for Kriminalvidenskab*, 48: 97–112.
Andersson, L. (2009) 'Self-Reported Delinquency in Sweden' in R. Zauberman (ed.) *Self-Reported Crime and Deviance Studies in Europe. Current State of Knowledge and Review of Use*. Brussels: Brussels University Press.
Anttila, I. (1966) 'Recorded and Unrecorded Criminality' in I. Anttila and R. Jaakkola *Unrecorded Criminality in Finland*. Helsinki: Kriminologinen tutkimuslaitos.
—— (1967) 'Konservativ och radikal kriminalpolitik i Norden', *Nordisk Tidsskrift for Kriminalvidenskab*, 55: 237–51.
—— (2001 [1971]) 'Conservative and Radical Criminal Policy in the Nordic Countries' in R. Lahti and P. Törnudd (eds) *Ad Ius Criminale Humanius. Essays in Criminology, Criminal Justice and Criminal Policy*. Publications of the Finnish Lawyers' Association, D:7. Helsinki: Finnish Lawyers' Association.
—— (2001 [1976]) 'A New Trend in Criminal Law in Finland' in R. Lahti and P. Törnudd (eds) *Ad Ius Criminale Humanius. Essays in Criminology, Criminal Justice and Criminal Policy*. Publications of the Finnish Lawyers' Association, D:7. Helsinki: Finnish Lawyers' Association.

—— (2001 [1979]) 'The Young Offender and the Tug-of-War between Ideologies on Crime Prevention' in R. Lahti and P. Törnudd (eds) *Ad Ius Criminale Humanius. Essays in Criminology, Criminal Justice and Criminal Policy*. Publications of the Finnish Lawyers' Association, D:7. Helsinki: Finnish Lawyers' Association.

—— (1986) *Rikollisuus ja kriminaalipolitiikka*. Helsinki: Lakimiesliiton kustannus.

—— and Törnudd, P. (1973) *Kriminologi i kriminalpolitiskt perspektiv*. Stockholm: P.A. Nordstedt & Söners Förlag.

Aschaffenburg, G. (1903) *Das Verbrechen und seine Bekämpfung. Kriminalpsychologie für Mediziner, Juristen und Soziologen, ein Beitrag zur Reform der Strafgesetzgebung*. Heidelberg: Carl Winter's Universitätsbuchhandlung.

Aubert, V. (1952) 'White-Collar Crime and Social Structure', *American Journal of Sociology*, 58(3): 263–71.

—— (1972 [1954]) *Om straffens sosiale funksjon*. Oslo: Universitetsforlaget.

Baguley, D. (1990) *Naturalistic Fiction. The Entropic Vision*. Cambridge: Cambridge University Press.

Balvig, F. (2002) *Stop Smoking! – Stop Crime? Report of the European Crime Prevention Network Conference*. Aalborg, Denmark 7–8 October 2002. Glostrup: The Danish Crime Prevention Council.

—— (2006) *Den ungdom! Om den stadigt mere omsiggribende lovlydighed blandt unge i Danmark*. Glostrup: Det Kriminalpraeventive råd.

Balvig, F. and Holmberg, L. (2011) 'The Ripple Effect: A Randomized Trial of a Social Norms Intervention in a Danish Middle School Setting. *Journal of Scandinavian Studies in Criminology and Crime Prevention* 12(1): 3–19.

Beaver, K. and Wright, J. (2007) 'A Child Effects Explanation for the Association Between Family Risk and Involvement in an Antisocial Lifestyle', *Journal of Adolescent Research*, 22(6): 640–64.

Becker, P. and Wetzell, R. (2006) 'Introduction' in P. Becker & R. Wetzell (eds) *Criminals and Their Scientists. The History of Criminology in International Perspective*. Cambridge: Cambridge University Press.

Beirne, P. (1988) 'Heredity versus environment. A reconsideration of Charles Goring's "The English Convict"', *British Journal of Criminology*, 28(3): 315–39.

—— (1993) *Inventing Criminology. Essays on the Rise of Homo Criminalis*. New York: State University of New York Press.

Belson, W. (1975) *Juvenile Theft: The Causal Factors*. London: Harper & Row.

Berlin, I. (2000 [1965]) *The Roots of Romanticism*. Edited by H. Hardy. London: Pimlico.

Berntsen, K. (1967) 'Forekomsten af ikke-registreret kriminalitet i to kriminelle grupper' in *Conference publication of the 8th annual seminar of the Nordic Research Council for Criminology*. Espoo, Finland 31 May–3 June, 1965.

Biderman, A. and Reiss, A. (1967) 'On Exploring the "Dark Figure" of Crime', *Annals of the American Academy of Political and Social Sciences*, 374: 1–15.

Boudon, R. (1989) *The Analysis of Ideology*. Translated by M. Slater. Cambridge: Polity Press.

—— (2003) 'The Social Sciences and the Two Types of Relativism', *Contemporary Sociology*, 2(3): 423–40.

Bullough, V. (2003) 'Magnus Hirschfeld, an Often Overlooked Pioneer', *Sexuality and Culture*, 7(1): 62–72.

Bulmer, M., Bales, K. and Sklar, K. (1991) 'The social survey in historical perspective' in M. Bulmer, K. Bales and K. Sklar (eds) *The Social Survey in Historical Perspective 1880-1940*. Cambridge: Cambridge University Press.

Braithwaite, J. (1981) 'The Myth of Social Class and Criminality Reconsidered', *American Sociological Review*, 46(1): 36–57.

Bratholm, A. (1966) 'Kriminalitetsutviklingen I Norge I de senere år' in J. Andenaes, A. Bratholm and N. Christie (eds) *Kriminalitet og samfunn*. Bergen: J. W. Eides Boktrykkeri.

Brown, L. (1947) 'Review of Austin L. Porterfield: Youth in Trouble', *American Journal of Sociology*, 53(1): 77.

Bruun, K. (1967) 'Yhteiskunnan valvojat ja vapaudenriistot' in L. D. Eriksson (ed.) *Pakkoauttajat*. Helsinki: Tammi.

Cabot, P. (1940) 'A Long-Term Study of Children: The Cambridge-Somerville Youth Study', *Child Development*, 11(2): 143–51.

Cain, L. (2005) *A Man's Grasp Should Exceed His Reach. A Biography of Sociologist Austin Larimore Porterfield*. New York: University Press of America.

Camic, C. (1992) 'Reputation and Predecessor Selection: Parsons and the Institutionalists', *American Sociological Review*, 57: 421–45.

—— (2007) 'On Edge: Sociology during the Great Depression and the New Deal' in C. Calhoun (ed.) *Sociology in America. A History*. Chicago: University of Chicago Press.

Canguilhem, G. (1978) *On the Normal and the Pathological*. Boston: D. Reidel Publishing Company.

Cernkovich, S., Giordano, P. and Pugh, M. (1985) 'Chronic Offenders: The Missing Cases in Self-Report Delinquency Research', *Journal of Criminal Law & Criminology*, 76(3): 705–32.

Chaput, D. (1972) 'Generals, Indian Agents, Politicians: The Doolittle Survey of 1865', *Western Historical Review*, 3(3): 269–82.

Christie, N. (1958) 'Synspunkter på kriminologien', *Nordisk Tidskrift for Kriminalvidenskab*, 46: 120–40.

—— (1966 [1964]) 'Hvorfor blif unge mennesker forbrytere?' in J. Andenaes, A. Bratholm and N. Christie (eds) *Kriminalitet og samfunn*. Bergen: J. W. Eides Boktrykkeri.

—— (1967) 'Discussion comment' in *Conference publication of the 8th annual seminar of the Nordic Research Council for Criminology*. Espoo, Finland, 31 May – 3 June, 1965.

—— (1975) *Hvor tett ett samfunn?* Oslo: Christian Ejler's forlag.

—— (1995 [1992]) 'På leting etter det alminnelige' in W. Pedersen, N. Christie, C. Høigård and B. Kyvsgaard (eds) *En debatt om ungdomskriminalitet*. Institutt for kriminologi, Stensilserie nr. 78. Oslo: Institutt for Kriminologi.

——, Andenaes, J. and Skirbekk, S. (1965) 'A Study of Self-Reported Crime' in *Scandinavian Studies in Criminology, Volume 1*. Oslo: Universitetsforlaget.

Churchill, W. (1910) 'The Prison Vote Speech', *Hansard*, 20 July.

Cialdini, R. (2005) 'Basic Social Influence is Underestimated', *Psychological Inquiry*, 16(4): 158–61.

Clarke, R. and Mayhew, P. (1988) 'The British Gas Suicide Story and Its Criminological Implications' in M. Tonry and N. Morris (eds) *Crime and Justice. A Review of Research, Volume 10*. Chicago: University of Chicago Press.

Collins, R. (1998) *The Sociology of Philosophies*. Cambridge: Harvard University Press.

Converse, J. (2009) *Survey Research in the United States. Roots and Emergence 1890-1960*. New Brunswick: Transaction Publishers.

Coser, L. (1971) *Masters of Sociological Thought. Ideas in Historical and Social Context*. San Diego: Harcourt Brace Jovanovich.

Cullen, F. and Messner, S. (2007) 'The making of criminology revisited: An oral history of Merton's anomie paradigm', *Theoretical Criminology*, 11(1): 5–37.

Degler, C. (1991) *In Search of Human Nature. The Decline and Revival of Darwinism in American Social Thought*. New York: Oxford University Press.

Dinerman, M. (2009) 'Sophia Moses Robison' in *Jewish Women: A Comprehensive Historical Encyclopedia*. 1 March 2009. Jewish Women's Archive. [Online] Available at: <http://jwa.org/encyclopedia/article/robison-sophia-moses>.

Dinitz, S., Kay, B. and Reckless, W. (1957) 'Delinquency Proneness and School Achievement', *Educational Research Bulletin*, 26(4): 131–6.

Du Bois, W. (1904) *Notes on Negro Crime Particularly in Georgia*. Atlanta University Publication No. 9. Atlanta: Atlanta University Press.

—— and Dill, A. (1914) *Morals and Manners among Negro Americans*. Atlanta University Publication No. 19. Atlanta: Atlanta University Press.

Durkheim, E. (1982 [1895]) *The Rules of Sociological Method*. Edited by S. Lukes. Translated by H. Wells. New York: Free Press.
—— (1983 [1895]) 'Crime and Social Health' in S. Lukes and A. Scull (eds) *Durkheim and the Law*. Oxford: Basil Blackwell.
Ekelund, E. (1932) 'Om kriminalstatistikens möjligheter att mäta den faktiska brottsligheten', *Nordisk Tidsskrift for Strafferett*, 28: 270–86.
Elliott, M. (1947) 'Review of Austin L. Porterfield: Youth in Trouble', *The Annals of the American Academy of Political and Social Science*, 250: 170–1.
—— (1949) 'Delinquent Behavior of People', *Phylon*, 10(3): 242–51.
—— (1952) *Crime in Modern Society*. New York: Harper & Brothers.
Elliott, D. and Ageton, S. (1980) 'Reconciling Race and Class Differences in Self-Reported and Official Estimates of Delinquency', *American Sociological Review*, 45(1): 95–110.
Elmhorn, K. (1969) *Faktisk brottslighet bland skolbarn*. Statens offentliga utredningar 1969:1. Stockholm: Justitiedepartementet.
Elwin, G., Heckscher, S. and Nelson, A. (1975 [1971]) *Den första stenen. Studiebok i kriminalpolitik*. Stockholm: Tidens Förlag.
Enzmann, D., Haen Marshall, I., Killias, M., Junger-Tas, J., Steketee, M. and Gruszczynska, B. (2010) 'Self-reported youth delinquency in Europe and beyond: First results of the Second International Self-Report Delinquency Study in the context of police and victimization data', *European Journal of Criminology*, 7(2): 159–83.
Eskola, A. (2009) *Mikä henki meitä kantaa. Katselen työni jälkiä*. Helsinki: Tammi.
Estrada, F. (1999) 'Juvenile Crime Trends in Post-War Europe', *European Journal on Criminal Policy and Research*, 7(1): 23–42.
Fischer, G. (1929) 'The Juries, in Felony Cases, in Cook County' in *The Illinois Crime Survey*. Illinois Association for Criminal Justice. [Online] Available at: <http://www.archive.org/details/illinoiscrimesur00illi>.
Forssman, H. and Gentz, C. (1962) 'Kriminalitetsförekomsten hos presumptiv ostraffade. En enkätsundersökning', *Nordisk Tidskrift for Kriminalvidenskab*, 50: 318–24.
Foucault, M. (1990 [1976]) *The History of Sexuality. Volume 1. An Introduction*. Victoria: Penguin Books.
—— (2009 [1976]) 'Alternatives to the Prison. Dissemination or Decline of Social Control?' *Theory, Culture and Society*, 26(6): 12–24.
Fritzsche, P. (1994) 'Vagabond in the Fugitive City: Hans Ostwald, Imperial Berlin and the Gross-Stadt-Dokumente', *Journal of Contemporary History*, 29(3): 385–402.
Galassi, S. (2004) *Kriminologie im Deutschen Kaiserreich. Geschichte einer gebrochenen Verwissenschaftlichung*. Stuttgart: Franz Steiner Verlag.

Galliher, J. and Tyree, C. (1985) 'Edwin Sutherland's Research on the Origins of Sexual Psychopath Laws: An Early Case Study of the Medicalization of Deviance', *Social Problems*, 33(2): 100–13.

Garland, D. (1985) *Punishment and Welfare. A History of Penal Strategies*. Aldershot: Gower.

—— (2001) *The Culture of Control. Crime and Social Order in Contemporary Society*. Chicago: University of Chicago Press.

Gaylord, M. and Galliher, J. (1988) *The Criminology of Edwin Sutherland*. New Brunswick: Transaction Books.

Gehlke, C. (1937) 'Review of Sophia Moses Robison: Can Delinquency Be Measured?', *Journal of the American Statistical Association*, 32: 814–7.

Geis, G. and Goff, C. (1983) 'Introduction' in E. Sutherland, *White Collar Crime. The Uncut Version*. New Haven: Yale University Press.

—— (1986) 'Edwin H. Sutherland's White-Collar Crime in America: An Essay in Historical Criminology', *Criminal Justice History*, 7: 1–31.

Gelsthorpe, L. (2007) 'The Jack-Roller Telling a Story?', *Theoretical Criminology*, 11(4): 515–42.

Gibson, M. (2006) 'Cesare Lombroso and Italian Criminology. Theory and Politics' in P. Becker and R. Wetzell (eds) *Criminals and Their Scientists. The History of Criminology in International Perspective*. Cambridge: Cambridge University Press.

Glueck, S. and Glueck, E. (1968 [1950]) *Unraveling Juvenile Delinquency*. Cambridge: Harvard University Press.

Goff, C. and Geis, G. (2008) 'The Michael-Adler report (1933): Criminology under the microscope', *Journal of the History of the Behavioral Sciences*, 44(4): 350–63.

Goring, C. (1913) *The English convict: A statistical study*. London: His Majesty's Stationery Office [Online] Available at: <http://www.archive.org/stream/englishconvictst00goriuoft#page/n3/mode/2up>.

Gough, H. (1948) 'A Sociological Theory of Psychopathy', *American Journal of Sociology*, 53(5): 359–66.

—— (1954) 'Systematic validation of a test for delinquency', *American Psychologist*, 9(8): 381.

—— (1960) 'Theory and Measurement of Socialization', *Journal of Consulting Psychology*, 24(1): 23–30.

—— and Peterson, D. (1952) 'The Identification and Measurement of Predispositional Factors in Crime and Delinquency', *Journal of Consulting Psychology*, 16(3): 207–12.

Gouldner, A. (1973) 'Foreword' in I. Taylor, P. Walton and J. Young (eds) *The New Criminology: For a Social Theory of Deviance*. London: Routledge and Kegan Paul.

Greve, V. (1972) *Kriminalitet som normalitet*. København: Juristforbundets Forlag.

Guo, G., Roettger, M. E. and Cai, T. (2008) 'The Integration of Genetic Propensities into Social-Control Models of Delinquency and Violence among Male Youths', *American Sociological Review*, 73(4): 543–68.

Guttmacher, M. (1958) 'The Psychiatric Approach to Crime and Correction', *Law and Contemporary Problems*, 23: 633–49.

Hacking, I. (2002) *The Taming of Chance*. Cambridge: Cambridge University Press.

Hagan, J. and McCarthy, J. (1999) *Mean Streets. Youth Crime and Homelessness*. New York: Cambridge University Press.

Haggerty, K. (2001) *Making Crime Count*. Toronto: University of Toronto Press.

Haney, D. (2009) *The Americanization of Social Science. Intellectuals and Public Responsibility in the Postwar United States*. Philadelphia: Temple University Press.

Hartshorne, H. and May, M. (1930) *Studies in the Nature of Character I: Studies in Deceit. Books One and Two*. New York: Macmillan.

Hartung, F. (1953) 'White Collar Crime: Its Significance for Theory and Practice', *Federal Probation*, 31: 31–6.

Healy, W. (1915) *The individual delinquent: a text-book of diagnosis and prognosis for all concerned in understanding offenders*. Boston: Little, Brown and Company. [Online] Available at: <http://www.archive.org/stream/individualdelinq00heal#page/n5/mode/2up>.

—— (1937) 'Review of Sophia Moses Robison: Can Delinquency Be Measured?', *American Journal of Psychiatry*, 93: 236–7.

Heindl, R. (1927) *Der Berufsverbrecher. Ein Beitrag zur Strafrechtsreform*. Berlin: Pan-Verlag Rolf Heise.

Heiskanen, M. and Piispa, M. (1998) *Usko, toivo, hakkaus. Kyselytutkimus miesten naisille tekemästä väkivallasta*. Helsinki: Statistics Finland.

von Hentig, H. (1964) *Die Unbekannte Straftat*. Berlin: Springer Verlag.

Heritage, J. (1989) *Garfinkel and Ethnomethodology*. Cambridge: Polity Press.

Hindelang, M., Hirschi, T. and Weis, J. (1979) 'Correlates of Delinquency: The Illusion of Discrepancy between Self-Report and Official Measures', *American Sociological Review*, 44(6): 995–1014.

—— (1981) *Measuring Delinquency*. Beverly Hills: Sage.

Hirschfeld, M. (1914) *Die Homosexualität des Mannes und des Weibes*. Berlin: Louis Marcus Verlagsbuchhandlung.

Hirschi, T. (1969) *Causes of Delinquency*. Berkeley: University of California Press.

—— and Hindelang, M. (2002 [1977]) 'Intelligence and Delinquency: A Revisionist Review' in J. Laub (ed.) *Travis Hirschi. The Craft of Criminology. Selected Papers*. New Brunswick: Transaction Publishers.

Høigård, C. (1995 [1993]) 'Alminnelig og forskjellig' in W. Pedersen, N. Christie, C. Høigård and B. Kyvsgaard (eds) *En debatt om ungdomskriminalitet.* Institutt for kriminologi, Stensilserie No. 78. Oslo: Institutt for Kriminologi.

—— and Christie, N. (1995) 'Hva er god kriminologi? Sluttreplikk til Willy Pedersen' in W. Pedersen, N. Christie, C. Høigård and B. Kyvsgaard (eds) *En debatt om ungdomskriminalitet.* Institutt for kriminologi, Stensilserie No. 78. Oslo: Institutt for Kriminologi.

Hofstadter, R. (1977 [1955]) *The Age of Reform. From Bryan to F.D.R.* New York: Albert A Knopf.

Hoyningen-Huene, P. (2006) 'Context of Discovery Versus Context of Justification and Thomas Kuhn' in J. Schickore and F. Steinle (eds) *Revisiting Discovery and Justification. Historical and philosophical perspectives on the context distinction.* Dordrecht: Springer.

Jaakkola, R. (1966) 'Social background and criminality' in I. Anttila and R. Jaakkola, *Unrecorded criminality in Finland.* Kriminologinen tutkimuslaitos, A:2. Helsinki: Kriminologinen tutkimuslaitos.

—— (2010) Risto Jaakkola's interview. Interviewed by J. Kivivuori. 4 February 2010.

Jamison, W. (1929) 'Crime Record Systems' in *The Illinois Crime Survey.* Illinois Association for Criminal Justice. [Online] Available at: <http://www.archive.org/details/illinoiscrimesur00illi>.

Jazbinsek, D. (2005) *Kinometerdichter. Karrierepfade im Kaiserreich zwischen Stadtforschung und Stummfilm.* Berlin: Wissenschaftszentrum Berlin für Sozialforschung.

——, Joerges, B. and Thies, R. (2001) *The Berlin 'Grossstadt-Dokumente': A Forgotten Precursor of the Chicago School of Sociology.* Berlin: Wissenschaftszentrum Berling für Sozialforschung.

Johnson, C., Kelly, S. and Bishop, P. (2010) 'Measuring the Mnemonic Advantage of Counter-intuitive and Counter-schematic Concepts', *Journal of Cognition and Culture,* 10(1-2): 109–21.

Johnson, M. (1995) 'Patriarchal Terrorism and Common Couple Violence: Two Forms of Violence against Women', *Journal of Marriage and Family,* 57(2): 283–94.

Junger-Tas, J. and Haen Marshall, I. (1999) 'The Self-Report Methodology in Crime Research' in M. Tonry (ed.) *Crime and Justice. A Review of Research, Volume 25.* Chicago: The University of Chicago Press.

Kinsey, A., Pomeroy, W. and Martin, C. (1948) *Sexual Behavior in the Human Male.* Bloomington: Indiana University Press.

Kivivuori, J. (2000) 'Delinquent Behaviour, Psychosomatic Symptoms and the Idea of "Healthy Delinquency"', *Journal of Scandinavian Studies in Criminology and Crime Prevention,* 1(2): 121–39.

—— (2007) *Delinquent Behaviour in Nordic Capital Cities.* Scandinavian Research Council for Criminology & National Research Institute of Legal Policy, Publication No. 227. Helsinki: National Research Institute of Legal Policy.

—— (2009) 'Self-Reported Delinquency Surveys in Finland' in R. Zauberman (ed.) *Self-Reported Crime and Deviance Studies in Europe. Current State of Knowledge and Review of Use*. Brussels: Brussels University Press.

—— and Bernburg, J. G. (forthcoming). 'Research on Delinquent Behaviour in Nordic Countries: Main Currents and Focal Concerns' in M. Tonry and T. Lappi-Seppälä (eds) *Crime and Justice in Scandinavia. A Review of Research*. Chicago: University of Chicago Press.

—— and Salmi, V. (2009) 'The Challenge of Special Needs Education in School-Based Delinquency Research', *Journal of Scandinavian Studies in Criminology and Crime Prevention*, 10(1): 2–17.

——, Savolainen, J. and Danielsson, P. (forthcoming) 'Theory and Explanation in Contemporary European Homicide Research' in M. Liem and W. Pridemore (eds) *Sourcebook of European Homicide Research*. New York: Springer.

Klein, M. (1989) 'Introduction' in M. Klein (ed) *Cross-National Research in Self-Reported Crime and Delinquency*. NATO ASI Series D, Vol. 50. Dordrecht: Kluwer Academic Publishers.

Krohn, M., Thornberry, T. and Gibson, C. and Baldwin, J. (2010) 'The Development and Impact of Self-Report Measures of Crime and Delinquency', *Journal of Quantitative Criminology*, 26(4): 509–25.

Kyvsgaard, B. (1992) *Ny ungdom? Om familie, skole, fritid, lovlydighet og kriminalitet*. Denmark: Jurist- og Oegonomsforbundets Forlag.

Lång, K. (2004 [1966]) 'Havaintoja sukupuolikäyttäytymisen rangaistavuuden perusteluista' in K. Mäkelä and I. Taipale (eds) *Rikos ja rangaistus, oikeus ja kohtuus*. Acta Poenologica 1/2004. Vantaa: Vankeinhoidon koulutuskeskus.

—— (1967) 'Discussion comment' in *Conference publication of the 8th annual seminar of the Nordic Research Council for Criminology*. Espoo, Finland 31 May – 3 June 1965.

Laub, J. (2004) 'The Life Course of Criminology in the United States: The American Society of Criminology 2003 Presidential Address', *Criminology*, 42(1): 1–26.

—— and Sampson, R. (1991) 'The Sutherland-Glueck Debate: On the Sociology of Criminological Knowledge', *American Journal of Sociology*, 96(6): 1402–40.

Laune, F. (1937) 'Review of Sophia Moses Robison: Can Delinquency Be Measured?', *American Sociological Review*, 2(3): 456–7.

Lindemann, G. (1993) 'Magnus Hirschfeld' in R. Lautmann (ed.) *Homosexualität. Handbuch der Theorie- und Forschungsgeschichte*. Frankfurt am Main: Campus Verlag.

Link, J. (1997) *Versuch über den Normalismus. Wie Normalität produziert wird*. Opladen: Westdeutscher Verlag.

Lintonen, T. and Konu, A. (2004) 'The misperceived social norm of drunkenness among early adolescents in Finland', *Health Education Research*, 19(1): 64–70.

Loader, I. (2006) 'Fall of the "Platonic Guardians": Liberalism, Criminology and Political Responses to Crime in England and Wales', *British Journal of Criminology*, 46(4): 561–86.

—— and Sparks, R. (2004) 'For an Historical Sociology of Crime Policy in England and Wales since 1968', *Critical Review of International Social and Political Philosophy*, 7(2): 5–32.

—— and Sparks, R. (2011) *Public Criminology?* Padstow: Routledge.

Lombroso, C. (1882) 'Über der Ursprung, das Wesen und die Bestrebungen der neuen anthropologisch-kriminalistischen Schule in Italien', *Zeitschrift für die gesamte Strafrechtswissenschaft*, 1(1): 108–29.

Lukes, S. (1985) *Emile Durkheim. His Life and Work. A Historical and Critical Study.* Stanford: Stanford University Press.

Lundgren, E., Heimer, G., Westerstrand, J. and Kalliokoski, A. (2001) *Slagen dam. Mäns våld mot kvinnor i jämställda Sverige. En omfångsundersökning.* Umeå: Brottsoffermyndigheten.

Madge, J. (1963) *The Origins of Scientific Sociology.* London: Tavistock.

Mannheim, H. (1965) *Comparative Criminology: A Text Book.* London: Routledge.

Matza, D. (1969) *Becoming Deviant.* New Jersey: Prentice Hall Inc.

Mayo-Smith, R. (1895). *Statistics and Sociology.* New York: Macmillan.

von Mayr, G. (1917) *Statistik und Gesellschaftslehre. Dritter Band. Moralstatistik mit Einschluss der Kriminalstatistik.* Tübingen: J.C.B. Mohr.

Mays, J. (1963) *Crime and Social Structure.* London: Faber and Faber.

McClintock, F. (1970) 'The Dark Figure', *Collected Studies in Criminological Research*, 5: 7–34.

McGonical, K. and Galliher, J. (2009) *Mabel Agnes Elliott. Pioneering Feminist, Pacifist Sociologist.* Maryland: Lexington Books.

McKenzie, A. (2006) 'The Real Macheath: Social Satire, Appropriation, and Eighteenth-Century Criminal Biography', *Huntington Library Quarterly*, 69(4): 581–605.

McVie, S. (2009) 'Self-Reported Crime and Delinquency Surveys in Great Britain and Ireland' in R. Zauberman (ed.) *Self-Reported Crime and Deviance Studies in Europe. Current State of Knowledge and Review of Use.* Brussels: Brussels University Press.

Measham, F. and Shiner, M. (2009) 'The legacy of "normalisation": The role of classical and contemporary criminological theory in understanding young people's drug use', *International Journal of Drug Policy*, 20(6): 502–8.

Meier, R. (1988) 'Discovering Delinquency', *Sociological Inquiry*, 58(3): 242–51.

Menninger, K. (2007 [1966]) *The Crime of Punishment*. Bloomington: AuthorHouse.
Merton, R. (1938) 'Social Structure and Anomie', *American Sociological Review*, 3(5): 672–82.
—— (1968 [1938]) 'Social Structure and Anomie' in R. Merton, *Social Theory and Social Structure*. New York: Free Press.
—— (1996a [1949]) 'Manifest and Latent Functions' in R. Merton, *On Social Structure and Science*. Chicago: University of Chicago Press.
—— (1996b [1976]) 'Social Dysfunctions' in R. Merton, *On Social Structure and Science*. Chicago: University of Chicago Press.
Meyer, K. (1941) *Die unbestraften Verbrechen. Eine Untersuchung über die sog. Dunkelziffer in der deutschen Kriminalstatistik. Kriminalistische Abhandlungen herausgegeben von Dr. Franz Exner. Heft XLVII*. Leipzig: Dr Ernst Wiegandt Verlagsbuchhandlung.
Michael, J. and Adler, M. (1933) *Crime, Law and Social Science*. New York: Harcourt, Brace and Company.
Michael, R., Gagnon, J., Laumann, E. and Kolata, G. (1994) *Sex in America. A Definitive Survey*. Boston: Little, Brown and Company.
Michel, J. and Cain, L. (1980) 'Austin L. Porterfield (1896–1979)', *ASA Footnotes*, 8(3): 9.
Mills, C. (1943) 'The Professional Ideology of Social Pathologists', *American Journal of Sociology*, 49 (2): 165-80.
—— (1958) 'Psychology and Social Science', *Monthly Review*, 10 (5): 204–9.
Monroe, W. (1897) 'Child Study and School Discipline', *Educational Review*, 14: 451–6.
—— (1904) *De ontwikkeling van het Sociale Bewustzijn der Kinderen. Bijdrage tot de Studie der Psychologie en Paedagogiek van de Kinderjaren*. Amsterdam: G. P. Tierie.
Morgan, J. (1969) 'The Development of Sociology and the Social Gospel in America', *Sociological Analysis*, 30(1): 42–53.
Moynihan, D. (1993) 'Defining Deviancy Down', *American Scholar*, 62(1): 17–30.
Murphy, F., Shirley, M. and Witmer, H. (1946) 'The Incidence of Hidden Delinquency', *American Journal of Orthopsychiatry*, 16(4): 686–96.
Naisiin kohistuvan vakivallan vähentämisohjelma (2010) Sosiaali-ja terveysministeriön julkaisuja 2010:5. Helsinki: Sosiaali- ja terveysministeriö. [English summary: Action Plan to Reduce Violence Against Women.]
Nickles, T. (2006) 'Heuristic Appraisal: Context of Discovery or Justification' in J. Schickore and F. Steinle (eds) *Revisiting Discovery and Justification. Historical and philosophical perspectives on the context distinction*. Dordrecht: Springer.

Nugent, W. (2010) *Progressivism. A Very Short Introduction*. Oxford: Oxford University Press.
Nye, F. (1956a) 'The Rejected Parent and Delinquency', *Marriage and Family Living*, 18(4): 291–300.
—— (1956b) 'Parent-Adolescent Relationships and Delinquent Behavior in a Non-Institutional Population: Frame of Reference and Method', *Research Studies of the State College of Washington*, 24: 160–9.
—— and Short, J. (1957) 'Scaling Delinquent Behavior', *American Sociological Review*, 22(3): 326–31.
Nyquist, O. and Strahl, I. (1960) 'II. Svensk undersökning', *Nordisk Tidskrift for Kriminalvidenskab*, 48: 113–7.
Oba, S. (1908) *Unverbesserliche Verbrecher und ihre Behandlung. Inaugural-Dissertation der juristischen Fakultät der Friedrich-Alexanders-Universität zu Erlangen*. Borna-Leipzig: Buchdruckerei Robert Noske.
O'Gorman, H. (1986) 'The Discovery of Pluralistic Ignorance: An Ironic Lesson', *Journal of the History of Behavioural Sciences*, 22(4): 333–47.
Ohlsson, A. (2008) *Myt och manipulation. Radikal psykiatrikritik i svensk offentlig idédebatt 1968–1973*. Stockholm: Acta Universitas Stockholmiensis. [English Summary: Radical critique of psychiatry in the Swedish public debate 1968–1973.]
Papendorf, K (2006) '"The Unfinished": Reflections on the Norwegian Prison Movement', *Acta Sociologica*, 49(2): 127–37.
Parker, H., Williams, L. and Aldridge, J. (2002) 'The Normalization of "Sensible" Drug Use: Further Evidence, from the North West England Longitudinal Study', *Sociology*, 36(4): 941–64.
Pedersen, W. (1995 [1992]) 'Ungdomskriminalitet: Nyanser I grått?' in W. Pedersen, N. Christie, C. Høigård and B. Kyvsgaard (eds) *En debatt om ungdomskriminalitet*. Institutt for kriminologi, Stensilserie 78. Oslo: Institutt for kriminologi.
—— (1995 [1993]) 'Strange Fruits' in W. Pedersen, N. Christie, C. Høigård and B. Kyvsgaard (eds) *En debatt om ungdomskriminalitet*. Institutt for kriminologi, Stensilserie 78. Oslo: Institutt for kriminologi.
Perlman, I. (1959) 'Delinquency Prevention: The Size of the Problem', *Annals of the American Academy of Political and Social Science*, 322(1): 1–9.
Petersen, T., Voss, P., Sabel, P. and Grube, N. (2004) 'Der Fragebogen Karls des Grossen', *Kölner Zeitschrift für Soziologie und Sozialpsychologie*, 56(4): 736–45.
Pfiffner, J. (1929) 'Notes on Judicial Organization and Structure: The Activities and Results of Crime Surveys', *American Political Science Review*, 23(4): 930–55.

Pfuhl, E. (1956) 'The Relationship of Crime and Horror Comics to Juvenile Delinquency', *Research Studies of the State College of Washington*, 24: 170–7.

Pietikäinen, P. (2004) 'Truth hurts: the sociobiology debate, moral reading and the idea of "dangerous knowledge"', *Social Epistemology* 18(2-3): 165–79.

Pikulik, L. (1979) *Romantik als Ungenügen an der Normalität. Am Beispiel Tiecks, Hoffmanns, Eichendorffs*. Frankfurt am Main: Suhrkamp.

Pilarczyk, I. (1997) 'The Terrible Haystack Murder: The Moral Paradox of Hypocrisy, Prudery and Piety in Antebellum America', *American Journal of Legal History*, 41(1): 25–60.

Platt, J. (1998) *A History of Sociological Research Methods in America*. Cambridge: Cambridge University Press.

Popitz, H. (1968) *Über die Präventivwirkung des Nichtwissens*. Tübingen: J.C.B. Mohr.

Porter, T. (2004) 'Statistics and Statistical Methods' in T. Porter and D. Ross (eds) *The Cambridge History of Science. Volume 7: The Modern Social Sciences*. Cambridge: Cambridge University Press.

Porterfield, A. (1941) *Creative Factors in Scientific Research*. Durham: Duke University Press.

—— (1943) 'Delinquency and Its Outcome in Court and College', *American Journal of Sociology*, 49(3): 199–208.

—— (1946) *Youth in Trouble*. Fort Worth: Leo Potishman Foundation.

—— (1947) 'Current Notes', *Journal of Criminal Law, Criminology and Police Science*, 37(5): 425–6.

—— (1957) 'The "We-They" Fallacy in Thinking About Delinquents and Criminals', *Federal Probation*, 21(4): 44–7.

—— and Gibbs, J. (1953) 'Law and the Mores', *Sociology and Social Research*, 37: 223–9.

—— and Salley, E. (1946) 'Current Folkways of Sexual Behavior', *American Journal of Sociology*, 52(3): 209–16.

Powers, E. (1949) 'An Experiment in Prevention of Delinquency', *Annals of the American Academy of Political and Social Science*, 261(1): 77–88.

Quetelet, A. (2009 [1835]) 'Criminal Statistics and What They Show' in N. Rafter (ed.) *The Origins of Criminology. A Reader*. Translated by N. Rafter. London: Routledge.

Rafter, N. (1997) 'Psychopathy and the evolution of criminological knowledge', *Theoretical Criminology*, 1(2): 235–59.

—— (2006) 'H. J. Eysenck in Fagin's kitchen: the return to biological theory in 20th century', *History of the Human Sciences*, 19(4): 37–56.

—— (2009) 'Introduction to part IX' in N. Rafter (ed.) *The Origins of Criminology. A Reader*. London: Routledge.

—— (2010) 'Science and Memory in Criminology—The American Society of Criminology 2009 Sutherland Address', *Criminology*, 48(2): 339–55.
Rauschenbusch, W. (1922 [1917]) *A Theology for the Social Gospel*. New York: Macmillan Co.
Reckless, W., Dinitz, S. and Kay, B. (1957a) 'The self component in potential delinquency and potential non-delinquency', *American Sociological Review*, 22(5): 566–70.
——, Dinitz, S. and Murray, E. (1957b) 'The "Good" Boy in a High Delinquency Area', *Journal of Criminal Law, Criminology and Police Science*, 48(1): 18–25.
Robison, S. (1936) *Can Delinquency Be Measured?* New York: Columbia University Press.
—— (1960) *Juvenile Delinquency. Its Nature and Control*. New York: Holt, Rhinehart and Winston.
Roe, S. and Ashe, J. (2008) *Young people and crime: Findings from the 2006 Offending, Crime and Justice Survey*. Home Office Statistical Bulletin 08/09. [Online] Available at: <http://rds.homeoffice.gov.uk/rds/pdfs08/hosb0908.pdf>.
von Römer, L. (1905) *Het uranisch gezin. Wetenschappelijk onderzoek en conclusien over homosexualiteit*. Amsterdam: Uitgave G. P. Tierie.
Romito, P. (2008) *A Deafening Silence. Hidden violence against women and children*. New York: Polity Press.
Ross, E. (2009 [1901]) *Social Control. A Survey of the Foundations of Order*. New Brunswick: Transaction Publishers.
—— (1973 [1907]) *Sin and Society. An Analysis of Latter-Day Iniquity*. New York: Harper & Row.
—— (1977 [1936]) *Seventy Years of It. Autobiography*. New York: Arno Press.
Rozin, P. (1999) 'The Process of Moralization', *Psychological Science*, 10(3): 218–21.
Salerno, R. (2007) *Sociology Noir. Studies at the University of Chicago in Loneliness, Marginality and Deviance, 1915–1935*. Jefferson, North Carolina: McFarland.
Salmi, V. (2008) *Nuorten miesten rikoskäyttäytyminen 1962 ja 2006*. Oikeuspoliittisen tutkimuslaitoksen julkaisuja 235. Helsinki: Oikeuspoliittinen tutkimuslaitos. [English Summary: Self-Reported Delinquent Behaviour of Young Males in Finland, 1962 and 2006.]
Sanders, W. (1937) 'New Light on Delinquency', *Social Forces*, 15(4): 575–9.
Saul, S. (1981) *Sophia Moses Robison. Woman of the Twentieth Century*. New York: Adelphi University Press.
Savelsberg, J. (2004) 'Religion, Historical Contingencies, and Institutional Conditions of Criminal Punishment: The German Case and Beyond', *Law & Social Inquiry*, 2(2): 373–401.

—— and Flood, S. (2004) 'Criminological knowledge: Period and cohort effects in scholarship', *Criminology*, 42(4): 101–33.

—— and Flood, S. (2010) 'American Criminology meets Collins: Global Theory of Intellectual Change and a Policy-oriented Field', *Sociological Forum*, forthcoming.

Scheff, T. (1995) 'Academic gangs', *Crime, Law & Social Change*, 23: 157–62.

Schiemann, G. (2006) 'Inductive Justification and Discovery. On Hans Reichenbach's Foundation of the Autonomy of the Philosophy of Science' in J. Schickore and F. Steinle (eds) *Revisiting Discovery and Justification. Historical and philosophical perspectives on the context distinction*. Dordrecht: Springer.

Schneider, H. (1987) *Kriminologie*. Berlin: Walter de Gruyter.

Schön, D. (1980) 'Generative Metaphor: A Perspective on Problem-Setting in Social Policy' in A. Ortony (ed.) *Metaphor and Thought*. Cambridge: Cambridge University Press.

Schwartz, H. (1997) 'On the Origin of the Phrase "Social Problems"', *Social Problems*, 44(2): 276–96.

SDP (Suomen Sosialidemokraattinen Puolue) (1969) *Kriminaalipolitiikka muuttuvassa yhteiskunnassa*. Hyväksytty SDP:n XXVIII puoluekokouksessa. Turku, Finland, 6–9 June 1969. [Online] Available at: <http://www.fsd.uta.fi/pohtiva/ohjelma?tunniste=sdpkriminaali1969>.

Sellin, T. (1928) 'The Negro Criminal. A Statistical Note', *The Annals of the American Academy of Political and Social Science*, 140(1): 52–64.

—— (1931–32) 'The Basis of a Crime Index', *American Institute of Criminal Law and Criminology*, 335: 335–56.

—— (1937) *Research Memorandum on Crime in the Depression*. New York: Social Science Research Council.

—— (1938) *Culture Conflict and Crime*. New York: Social Science Research Council.

—— and Wolfgang, M. (1964) *The Measurement of Delinquency*. New York: John Wiley & Sons.

Selling, L. (1947) 'Review of Austin L. Porterfield: Youth in Trouble', *American Sociological Review*, 12(3): 378.

Shaw, C. R. (1930) *The Jack-Roller: A Delinquent Boy's Own Story*. Chicago: University of Chicago Press.

—— and Myers, E. (1929) 'The Juvenile Delinquent' in *The Illinois Crime Survey*. Illinois Association for Criminal Justice. [Online] Available at: <http://www.archive.org/details/illinoiscrimesur00illi>.

——, McKay, H., McDonald, J., Hanson, H. and Burgess, E. (1938) *Brothers in Crime*. Chicago: University of Chicago Press.

Short, J. and Nye, F. (1957–58) 'Reported Behavior as a Criterion of Deviant Behavior', *Social Problems*, 5(3): 207–13.

—— and Hughes, L. (2007) 'Criminology, Criminologists and the Sociological Enterprise' in C. Calhoun (ed.) *Sociology in America. A History*. Chicago: University of Chicago Press.

Shover, N. and Cullen, F. (2008) 'Studying and Teaching White-Collar Crime: Populist and Patrician Perspectives', *Journal of Criminal Justice Education*, 19(2): 155–74.

Singer, P. (1981) *The Expanding Circle. Ethics and Sociobiology*. Oxford: Clarendon Press.

Skinner, Q. (2002) *Visions of Politics. Volume 1: Regarding Method*. Cambridge: Cambridge University Press.

Smith, M. (1994) *Social Science in the Crucible: The American Debate Over Objectivity and Purpose, 1918–1941*. Durham: Duke University Press.

Snodgrass, J. (1972) *The American Criminological Tradition: Portraits of the Men and Ideology in a Discipline*. A Dissertation in Sociology, University of Pennsylvania.

—— (1982) *The Jack-Roller at Seventy*. Lanham: Lexington Books.

Spencer, D. (1938) 'The frankness of subjects on personality measures', *Journal of Educational Psychology*, 29(1): 26–35.

Stangeland, P. and Hauge, R. (1974) *Nyanser i grått. En undersøkelse av selfrapportert kriminalitet blant norsk ungdom*. Oslo: Universitetsforlaget.

Steinmetz, G. (2007) 'American Sociology before and after World War II: The (Temporary) Settling of a Disciplinary Field' in C. Calhoun (ed.) *Sociology in America. A History*. Chicago: University of Chicago Press.

Stouffer, S. (1937) 'Review of Sophia Moses Robison: Can Delinquency Be Measured?', *American Journal of Sociology*, 42(4): 586–90.

Sumner, F. (1947) 'Review of Austin L. Porterfield: Youth in Trouble', *Journal of Abnormal and Social Psychology*, 42(3): 377.

Sutherland, E. (1924) *Criminology*. Philadelphia: J. B. Lippincott Company.

—— (1927) 'Review of the Missouri Crime Survey', *American Journal of Sociology*, 33(3): 480–3.

—— (1931) 'Mental Deficiency and Crime' in K. Young (ed.) *Social Attitudes*. New York: Henry Holt.

—— (1973 [1933]) 'The Michael-Adler Report' in K. Schuessler (ed.) *Edwin H. Sutherland: On Analyzing Crime*. Chicago: University of Chicago Press.

—— (1973 [1936]) 'Juvenile Delinquency and Community Organization' in K. Schuessler (ed.) *Edwin H. Sutherland: On Analyzing Crime*. Chicago: University of Chicago Press.

—— (1972 [1937]) *The Professional Thief, by a Professional Thief. Annotated and Interpreted by E. H. Sutherland*. Chicago: University of Chicago Press.

—— (1940) 'White-Collar Criminality', *American Sociological Review*, 5(1): 1–12.
—— (1945) 'Social Pathology', *American Journal of Sociology*, 50(6): 429–35.
—— (1983 [1949]) *White-Collar Crime. The Uncut Version*. New Haven: Yale University Press.
—— and Cressey, D. (1955) *Principles of Criminology*. 5th ed. Chicago: J. B. Lippincott Company.
—— and Gehlke, C. (1933) 'Crime and Punishment' in *Recent Social Trends in the United States*. Report of the President's Research Committee on Social Trends. Volume II. New York: McGraw-Hill Book Company.
Svendsen, B. (1977) 'Is the existence of forensic psychiatry justified? On forensic psychiatry in the Scandinavian countries', *Acta psychiatrica scandinavica*, 55(3): 161–4.
Sveri, K. (1967) 'Konsekvenserna av våra ökade kunskaper om "dold" brottslighet', in *Conference publication of the 8th annual seminar of the Nordic Research Council for Criminology*. Espoo, Finland 31 May – 3 June, 1965.
Swatos, W. (1983) 'The Faith of the Fathers: on the Christianity of Early American Sociology', *Sociological Analysis*, 44(1): 33–52.
Sykes, G. and Matza, D. (1957) 'Techniques of Neutralization: A Theory of Juvenile Delinquency', *American Sociological Review*, 22(6): 664–73.
Tarde, G. (1983 [1895]) 'Criminality and Social Health' in S. Lukes and A. Scull (eds) *Durkheim and the Law*. Oxford: Basil Blackwell.
Taylor, C. (1991) *The Ethics of Authenticity*. Cambridge: Harvard University Press.
Thornberry, T. and Krohn, M. (2003) 'Comparison of Self-Report and Official Data for Measuring Crime' in J. Pepper and C. Petrie (eds) *Measurement Problems in Criminal Justice Research. Workshop summary. National Research Council of the National Academies.* Washington DC: The National Academies Press.
Thue, F. (2009) 'Americanised social science as anti-communist containment? The case of the Oslo Institute of Social Research, 1945–1965', *Ideas in History*, 4(1): 93–129.
Tilman, R. (1984) *C. Wright Mills. A Native Radical and His American Intellectual Roots*. University Park: Pennsylvania State University Press.
Törnudd, P. (1960) 'Nonkonformisten—vår tids hjälte?', *Nya Argus* 53(4): 47–8.
—— (1967) 'Discussion comment' in *Conference publication of the 8th annual seminar of the Nordic Research Council for Criminology*. Espoo, Finland 31 May – 3 June 1965.
—— (1996a [1969]) 'In Defence of General Prevention' in I. Anttila, K. Aromaa, R. Jaakkola, T. Lappi-Seppälä and H. Takala (eds) *Facts,*

Values and Visions. Essays in Criminology and Crime Policy. National Research Institute of Legal Policy, Publication No. 138. Helsinki: National Research Institute of Legal Policy.

—— (1996b [1969]) 'The Futility of Searching for Causes of Crime' in I. Anttila, K. Aromaa, R. Jaakkola, T. Lappi-Seppälä and H. Takala (eds) *Facts, Values and Visions. Essays in Criminology and Crime Policy*. National Research Institute of Legal Policy, Publication No. 138. Helsinki: National Research Institute of Legal Policy.

—— (1996c [1975]) 'Towards a Statistics Based on Damages' in I. Anttila, K. Aromaa, R. Jaakkola, T. Lappi-Seppälä and H. Takala (eds) *Facts, Values and Visions. Essays in Criminology and Crime Policy*. National Research Institute of Legal Policy, Publication No. 138. Helsinki: National Research Institute of Legal Policy.

—— (1996d [1975]) 'Deterrence Research and the Needs of Legislative Planning' in I. Anttila, K. Aromaa, R. Jaakkola, T. Lappi-Seppälä and H. Takala (eds) *Facts, Values and Visions. Essays in Criminology and Crime Policy*. National Research Institute of Legal Policy, Publication No. 138. Helsinki: National Research Institute of Legal Policy.

Tschlenoff [first name unknown] (1908) 'Die Sexualenquete unter der Moskauer Studentenschaft', *Zeitschrift für Bekämpfung der Geschlechtskrankheiten*, 8: 211–24 and 245–55. Translated into German by M. Feldhusen.

Turner, S. (2007) 'A Life in the First Half-Century of American Sociology: Charles Ellwood and the Division of Sociology' in C. Calhoun (ed.) *Sociology in America. A History*. Chicago: University of Chicago Press.

—— and Turner, J. (1990) *The Impossible Science. An Institutional Analysis of American Sociology*. Newbury Park: Sage.

United States Strategic Bombing Survey (1947) *The Effects of Strategic Bombing on German Morale. Volume 1*. Washington DC: US Government Printing Office.

van Lieshout, M. (1993) 'Lucien von Römer' in R. Lautmann (ed.) *Homosexualität. Handbuch der Theorie- und Forschungsgeschichte*. Frankfurt am Main: Campus Verlag.

van Voorhis, P., Spruance, L., Ritchey, P., Johnson Listwan, S. and Seabrook, R. (2004) 'The Georgia Cognitive Skills Experiment. A Replication of Reasoning and Rehabilitation', *Criminal Justice and Behavior*, 31(3): 282–305.

Verkko, V. (1930) 'Kriminalstatistiken och den verkliga brottsligheten', *Nordisk tidsskrift for strafferett*, 18: 95–127.

Wallerstein, J.S. (1947) 'Roots of Delinquency', *The Nervous Child*, 6(4): 399–412.

—— (1951) *The Demon's Mirror*. New York: Harbinger House.

Bibliography 195

—— and Wyle, C. (1947b) '"Biological Inferiority" as a Cause for Delinquency. E. A. Hooton's Findings Reviewed and Analysed', *The Nervous Child*, 6(4): 467–72.

—— and Wyle, C. (1953 [1947a]) 'Our Law-abiding Law-breakers' in C. Vedder, S. Konig, and R. Clark (eds) *Criminology. A Book of Readings*. New York: Dryden Press.

Werner, B. (1969) 'Nyare undersökningar av "dold brottslighet" och konsekvenserna härav för kriminologisk teori' in *Det 5. Nordiske Kontaktseminar 1969. Rapport fra et kontaktseminar mellem kriminologer, anklagere og forsvarere*. København: Nordisk Samarbejdsråd for kriminologi.

—— (1971) 'Den faktiska brottsligheten', *Nordisk Tidskrift for kriminalvidenskab*, 59: 106–41.

West, D. (1970 [1967]) *The Young Offender*. London: Penguin Books.

—— (1969) *Present Conduct and Future Delinquency. First Report of the Cambridge Study in Delinquent Development*. New York: International Universities Press.

—— (1982) *Delinquency. Its Roots, Careers and Prospects*. London: Heinemann.

—— and Farrington, D. (1973) *Who Becomes Delinquent? Second Report of the Cambridge Study in Delinquent Development*. London: Heinemann.

White, R. and Hopkins, H. (1976) *The Social Gospel. Religion and Reform in Changing America*. Philadelphia: Temple University Press.

Willcock, H. (1949) *Report on Juvenile Delinquency. Mass Observation*. London: The Falcon Press.

—— (1974) *Deterrents and Incentives to Crime among Boys and Young Men aged 15-21 years. An inquiry undertaken for the Home Office in 1963*. Office of Population Censuses and Surveys, Social Survey Division, Publication No. 352. London: Office of Population Censuses and Surveys.

Williams, J. and Gold, M. (1972) 'From Delinquent Behavior to Official Delinquency', *Social Problems*, 202: 209–29.

Witmer, H. and Kotinsky, R. (eds) (1956) *New perspectives for research on juvenile delinquency*. US Children's Bureau, Publication No. 356. Washington, DC: US Government Printing Office.

Wolf, P. (1994) 'Thorsten Sellin in Memoriam', *Nordisk Tidsskrift in Memoriam*, 81(4): 361–2.

Wolfensberger, W. and Tullman, S. (1982) 'A Brief Outline of the Principle of Normalization', *Rehabilation Psychology*, 27(3): 131–45.

Wolfgang, M., Figlio, R. and Sellin, T. (1972) *Delinquency in a Birth Cohort*. Chicago: University of Chicago Press.

Yeo, E. (2004) 'Social Surveys in the Eighteenth and Nineteenth Centuries' in T. Porter and D. Ross (eds) *The Cambridge History of Science. Volume 7: The Modern Social Sciences.* Cambridge: Cambridge University Press.

Zauberman, R. (ed.) (2009) *Self-Reported Crime and Deviance Studies in Europe. Current State of Knowledge and Review of Use.* Brussels: Brussels University Press.

Index

References are to page number and notes indicated by 'n'.

abnormality paradigm 22, 23, 24
  born criminals 24–5
  degeneration 25–6
  dichotomies versus continuum 114, 115n
  Goring 70
  law-abiding law-breakers and Freudian cultural impact 95–7
  Merton 97–101
  Wallerstein 94–5
  psychologization of abnormality 25, 26–8
  refuted by white-collar crime 61, 80
Adorno, T. 147
African Americans 44, 64, 74
Alapuro, Risto 144, 145
alcohol, prohibition of 44–5, 168
Allport, Floyd H. 170
Andenaes, J. 131, 133, 142, 143
anecdotal evidence 45, 46
animal intercourse 106
anomie 36, 98
anonymity 52, 161
anti-psychiatry movement and ideology 122, 136, 166–7
Anttila, Inkeri 133, 137, 144, 157
Aubert, Vilhelm 61, 130–1, 148
Authoritarian Personality, The 147
authoritarianism 147

Balance doctrine in criminal policy 146, 146n, 158
Balvig, Flemming 155
basic social influence 170–1
Baudelaire, Charles 30
Beggar's Opera, The 55
Benedict, Ruth 91
Berlin humanitarian-scientific circle 71, 72, Figure 4.1, 121
bias 74, 112, 139
biased control hypothesis 138–9, 143
biological causation 37, 50, 94, 124

biological psychiatry 96, 100n
Blair, Tony 172
Boas, Franz 90–1
Booth, Charles 7, 63
born criminals 24–5
Brown, L. Guy 84
Burgess, Ernest 57

Cain, Leonard 87
California Personality Inventory (CPI) 114, 115, 116
Cambridge-Somerville Youth Study 101–3, 117
Cambridge Study in Delinquent Development 2, 124–5
canonical tradition 117–22
capitalism 14
  robber barons 55, 56, 57–8
Catholicism 10, 52
causal analysis 112–13
causal explanations 18–19, 24–5, 37, 42
Central Registers 76–8
Character Education Inquiry (CEI) 67–8
Charlemagne 1
Chicago School of Sociology 71–2
Christie, Nils 131, 138, 142, 149–50, 152, 153, 154, 155, 169
Churchill, Winston 8–9
Clarke, Ron 33n
class phenomena 8–9, 14–15, 34, 112
  biased control 139
  class-delinquency link 122–3, 124–5, 164
  Nordic studies 139, 143–4
  sexual attitudes 106
  social gradient 116, 117
  see also white-collar criminals
Cleveland crime survey 65
Clinton, Bill 172
confessions 5–6, 52, 161

conformity 23, 30, 35, 45, 91, 147–8, 154–5
  defined as problem by criminologists 145, 154–5
  defined as problem in the Romantic tradition 30
constant ratio doctrine 4, 31, 40–1, 43, 45, 73, 75, 76
context distinction 11–13
Converse, J. 162
corporate crime 88
counter-intuitive statements 144n, 159n
Cressey, Paul 57
crime-related irritability 40, 41
crime surveys
  aggravating and moderating types of 172–5
  Cambridge-Somerville Youth Study 101–3, 117
  Cleveland crime survey 65
  Illinois crime survey 65, 66
  Missouri crime survey 65–6
  official statistics 3, 4, 11, 40, 43–4
    alternative sources 60–1, 98–9
    Can Delinquency Be Measured? (Robison) 73–5
  Political use of 171–5
  qualitative methods 71–2
  self-report *see* self-report delinquency surveys
  victimization surveys 172–5
criminaloids 59, 89
criminology 19
  abnormality *see* abnormality paradigm
  Michael-Adler Report 69–71
  normality *see* normality paradigm
  sociology's 'coup' of 81, 166–7
cross-sectional survey designs 2
cultural movements 19
cultural relativity 90–1

decriminalization 8, 16, 156
degeneration theory 25–6
delinquency continuum 113–17
Denmark 2, 128, 129, 131, 135, 143, 152, 156n
deviance 16, 19
  artificiality of 60
  humanizing offenders 175–6
  innovation and 34
  latent function of 35

pathology paradigm 37
pluralism and the modern metropolis 72
psychologization 26–8
Romanticism 30
sexual 50–4, 105
Dewey, John 37, 57
differential association 70
Dinitz, S. 116
disease metaphors 20
  functionalist theory of disease 29–30
Doolittle survey 62, 63
drugs normalization 17
Du Bois, W.E.B. 63–4, 161, 175
Dunkelziffer 41–2
Durkheim, Émile 29, 31–3, 135, 146, 159, 166

Eichendorff, Joseph von 30, 36
Elias, Norbert 36n
Elliott, Mabel A. 85–6, 118, 119
Ellwood, Charles A. 88, 89
Elmhorn, K. 135
empiricism 21, 109, 116, 161
environmental factors 25, 26, 42, 59, 98
Erikson, Erik 97–8
Eskola, Antti 145
ethnography of urban underworlds 71–2
evolutionary criminology 25

facade normality 46–8, 105
Farrington, David 124, 151
fascism 147
  see also Nazi Germany
Finland 2, 5, 126–7, 128, 129, 131–2, 133, 137, 139, 140, 143, 144–5, 150n, 151
  development of rational and humane criminal policy 156–8, 159
  prohibition of alcohol 44–5
  victimization surveys 172, 173, 174
Foucault, M. 5, 6, 8, 15–16
frequent offenders 100, 117, 122, 140–1, 164
  risk factors 172
Freud, Sigmund 6, 34, 94, 95–7
  theories of conformity 147–8
functionalism 35, 99
functionalist theory of disease 29–30

Garland, D. 22–4, 126, 171
Gehlke, C.E. 76
German Reich 48, 50–3
 see also Nazi Germany
Glueck, S. and E. 118
Goring, Charles 27, 70
Gough, Harrison 113–17
Greve, Vagn 131, 134, 135, 141, 142n, 143n, 144, 149, 156n
Guerry, André-Michel 31
Guttmacher, Manfred 96, 119
Guttman scale 111, 115n

Haney, D. 109
Harrison, Tom 90
Hartung, F. 61
Hauge, R. 131, 134, 135, 140, 143
Healy, William 27, 76
Henderson, Charles 57, 58
hidden crime 4, 7
 crime-related irritability 40–1
 intelligence and detection 81, 124
 luck and detection 88, 93
 measurement 7, 11, 119–20, 121
 Can Delinquency Be Measured? (Robison) 73–5
 non-survey responses 45–6
 normalization *see* normalization
 unfair punishment of detected minority 134–5
Hirschfeld, Magnus 5, 48, 49, 50–4, 71, 163, 175
historiography 13
Hofstadter, R. 56
Høigård, C. 153, 154
homeostasis 146
homosexuality
 Kinsey Report 106
 normalization 48–53
Hooton, E.A. 94
Hull House Maps and Papers 63
human rights violations 175
humane criminal policy 156–8, 159, 160, 168–9, 175–6
hydraulic notion of motivation 36
hypocrisy 9, 30, 46–7, 52, 55, 93, 120, 148, 155, 167, 169
 Porterfield's social satire 86–7, 106–7, 147, 154
 Social Gospel and 88, 89

Illinois crime survey 65, 66
incidence 99
indeterminate sentencing 97n
individual differences 123–4
innovating ideologists 13–14, 32, 155, 169
innovation, crime as 33–7
Institute of Social and Religious Research (ISSR) 67, 68, 69
intelligence 81, 94, 116, 124
International Self-Report Delinquency Study (ISRD) 3, 125, 152

Jaakkola, Risto 131–3, 139, 140, 144, 153, 157
Jamison, W.C. 66
Jensen, Howard 88
Jesus of Nazareth 91, 149
Jung, Carl 48
Junger-Tas, Josine 3, 125
juridical systems 6–7
jurors 65
juvenile populations 2, 45–6, 66
 Cambridge-Somerville Youth Study 101–3, 117
 class-delinquency link 122–3, 124–5
 delinquency continuum 116
 'lying to win approval' scale 67–9
 qualitative studies 72
 school discipline 50

Kinsey, Alfred 54, 103–8, 118–19, 147, 162
Kinsey Report 103–4
 object of Kinsey's attack 104–5, 147
 tolerance and understanding 105–8
Ku Klux Klan 168

labelling theory 2, 122, 123
Lander, Bernard 99
Lång, Karl J. 156
latent function 35
Laune, Ferris F. 75
law-abiding law-breakers 91–2
 abnormality paradigm and Freudian cultural impact 95–7
 Merton 97–101
 Wallerstein 94–5
 Randen Foundation crime survey 92–3
Lazarsfeld, Paul 109
learning theory 170

left radicalism 151
legislative activism 44–5, 60
liberalization 16, 23
  see also normalization
Link, Jürgen 164–5
literacy 163
Loader, I. 135
Lombroso, Cesare 24–5, 59
longitudinal research programmes 2
loophole theory 65
Lundberg, Charles 108
'lying to win approval' scale 67–9, 120

Madge, John 106, 107
Marxism 151
Mass Observation method
  45–6, 125
masturbation 105
Matza, David 18, 170
Mayhew, Pat 33n
Mayr, G. von 41
Mays, John Barron 90
McKay, Henry 72, 75, 90
Mead, George Herbert 57, 114
Mead, Margaret 91
medical model 28, 97
Menninger, Carl 97
Merton, Robert K. 33–7, 97–101, 109,
  159, 166, 167
metaphors
  disease 20
  functionalist theory of
    disease 29–30
  war and combat 22
methods history 3
Meyer, Kurt 53
Michael-Adler Report 69–71
Mills, C. Wright 37, 38, 88, 89, 91
Missouri crime survey 65–6
Monroe, W.S. 50
moral panic 135
moral statistics 4, 40–1
  dark figure of crime 41–2
  institutionalists and realists 43
  non-survey responses 45–6
  Oba 41–2
  replaced by criminology 161–2
  Sellin 41, 43–5
motivation 36
Murphy, F. 118
Myers, Earl 66

naturalist fiction 47
Nazi Germany 53, 109, 147, 153
necessity doctrine of crime 146
Neubauer, Peter 99
neutralization theory 18–19, 169–70
nonconformity 91, 147–8, 154–5
Nordic countries 2–3, 20–1, 122, 124,
  125, 126–7
  anomalous findings 139
  accuracy of police control 142–4
  frequency of offending 140–1
  early self-report studies 127, 167
  Nordic Draftee Research (NDR)
    programme 128–9, 131, 132,
    134, 137, 138, 140, 141, 144,
    145, 149, 152, 153
  Oslo, Uppsala and Gothenburg
    127–8
  reframing of the crime issue
    156–9
  effects of the hidden crime survey
    155–6
  decriminalization proposals 156
  victimization surveys 172–5
  later developments in hidden crime
    data interpretation
  Norwegian debate 152–4
  pathology of conformity 154–5
  phases of Nordic hidden crime
    research 150–2
  normality of crime as a policy frame
    Aubert 130–1
  biased control hypothesis
    138–9, 143
  Jaakkola 131–3
  opposition to psychiatric and
    psychological
    explanations 135–7, 167
  pathology of conformity
    147–8
  post-war social scientists
    129–30, 147
  random control hypothesis 138,
    143, 144–5
  relevance for criminal
    policy 133–4
  religious influences 148–50
  sociological theory 145–6
  unfair punishments 134–5
*normal-because-prevalent
  argument* 8, 10, 16, 85, 120

normality paradigm 28–9
  attack against social
    pathologists 37–8
  'black and white' versus 'shades of
    grey' 130–1, 133–4, 149–50,
    152, 153
  crime as innovation 33–7
  Durkheim 29, 31–3, 146, 159
  functionalist theory of disease
    29–30
  individualization and 123–4
  Merton 33–7, 159
  necessity doctrine of crime 146
  Romanticism 30, 36
  statistical fatalism 31
normalization 8, 10, 15–17
  drugs use 17
  flexible normalization 165–6
  homosexuality 48–53
  humanizing offenders 175–6
  impact on crime levels 169–71
  Nordic countries *see* Nordic
    countries: normality of crime
    as a policy frame
  penal-welfare complex 23
  pre-normalization 164, 165
  proto-normalization 165
  sex *see* sexology
normative regulation 4, 5, 15–16
  based on descriptions instead of
    normative rules 16, 166, 171
  conformity 147–8
  facade normality 46–8, 105
  reflective society 171
Norway 127–8, 129, 130, 131, 133,
    134, 135, 137, 140, 141, 142,
    143, 150, 152–4
  decriminalization 156
Nye, James F. 108–14

Oba, Shigema 41–2
official control barrier 3, 11, 22, 40–1,
    43, 44, 121, 161, 163
official statistics 3, 4, 11, 40,
    43–4
  alternative sources 60–1, 98–9
  Can Delinquency Be Measured?
    (Robison) 73–5
Ogburn, William F. 108
opportunity structure 74
Ostwald, Hans 71

Panopticon 6, 7, 77
Parsons, Talcott 109
pathology paradigm *see also*
  abnormality paradigm 37–8,
  80–1, 91
patterns of crime 2, 3
Pedersen, Willy 152, 153, 154
penal-welfare complex 22–3, 42, 126
personality measurement scales 68–9
  California Personality Inventory
    (CPI) 114, 115, 116
Pfuhl, Edwin 113
pluralistic ignorance 170
police folklore 45
populism 56, 66, 87–90, 109, 167–9
Porterfield, Austin Larimore 4, 9, 39,
    57, 72
  Boasian relativity 90–1
  canonization 118
  influence of Social Gospel and
    Midwestern populism 87–90
  self-report survey (1940–41) 82–3
  prevalence of delinquency 83–4
  reception by contemporaries
    84–6
  sex normalization 103
  social satire 86–7, 106–7, 147, 154
  Youth in Trouble (1946) 83
positivism 108–9, 151
power relations 6–7, 8, 15–16
Powers, Edwin 102
prevalence 2, 3, 17, 84, 98
  frequent offending 117, 122, 140–1
  incidence and 99
  versatility and 99, 139
prisons 6–7, 15–16, 132
Progressivism 56, 66, 109, 168
prohibition of alcohol 44–5, 168
Protestantism 10, 56–7, 58n, 150
psychiatry 65, 66, 80, 81, 118–19
  biological and Freudian 96–7, 100n
  disciplinary warfare 119, 120, 122,
    135–7, 160, 166–7
psychoanalysis 6, 94–7
psychologization of deviance 25, 26–8
psychology 68–9, 80, 81, 118–19
  disciplinary warfare 119, 120, 122,
    135–7, 160, 166–7
psychopathy 28
public criminology 19–20, 109, 112
  demise of during the 1950s 109, 112

punitive sanctions 65, 88, 95, 132, 146, 157–8, 168–9, 172

qualitative methods 71–2
quantitative methods 109
questionnaires 9, 162
Quetelet, Adolphe 31, 40

racism 87n
 as a source of bias in official control based statistics 44
Rafter, N. 151
Randen Foundation crime survey 92–3, 166
random control hypothesis 120, 138, 143, 144–5
Rauschenbusch, Walter 87–8
Reckless, W. 116
register-based studies 123
Reichenbach, Hans 11
religion 10, 14, 52–3
 influence on sociology 57, 58n
 Nordic countries 148–50
 regulation of sex 105
 Social Gospel 56–7, 87–90, 109, 168
reporting propensity studies 46, 74, 161
rhetorical redescription 13–15, 18, 19, 34, 35, 126
risk factors 172
robber barons 55, 56, 57–8
Robison, Sophia Moses 108, 175, 119–20
 Can Delinquency Be Measured? 73–5
 Central Register 76–8
 reception of Robison's work 75–6
Romanticism 9, 30
Römer, Lucien von 48–50, 54
Ross, Edward Alsworth 47, 58–60, 89, 135
Rowntree, Seebohm 63

Salley, Ellison 103
sample surveys 4
Sanders, Wiley 76
satire 9, 30, 46–7, 52, 55, 93, 120, 148, 155, 167, 169
 Porterfield's social satire 86–7, 106–7, 147, 154
 Social Gospel and 88, 89

Savelsberg, J. 159
scale development 111–12
Scandinavia *see* Nordic countries
scapegoats 148
school board visitors 63, 163
school discipline 50
scientific discovery 11–12
 explained by external reality versus socially constructed paradigms 163–4
 explanation of 160–1
 Porterfield's views on 39
self-regulation 146
self-report delinquency studies 1–2
 advantages over other types of hidden crime estimation 78
 'Americanization' 21, 108–10, 116, 121, 122, 126, 129–30
 canonization and predecessor selection 117–22
 central developments after 1960 122–5
 classical studies 20–1, 118
 confessions 5–6, 161
 disciplinary warfare 119, 120, 122, 135–7, 160
 empiricism 21, 109, 116, 161
 Gough and the delinquency continuum 113–17
 impact on crime levels 169–71
 impact on criminal policy 171–5
 impact on criminology 122–4
 international comparisons 2–3, 125
 invention 39, 161–2
 moral context 21
 neutrality 4
 Nordics *see* Nordic countries
 preconditions of survey penetration 163–4
 Randen Foundation crime survey 92–3, 166
 reliability 3, 111
 Shaw and McKay 72, 75
 Short-Nye papers 110–11
  causal analysis 112–13
  scale development 111–12
Sellin, Thorsten 41, 43–5, 60, 70, 161, 176
Selling, Lowell S. 84
sex, adolescent 156

sexology 4, 5–6, 7
  class phenomena 106
  homosexuality and normalization 48–53, 106
  Kinsey Report 103–4
    object of Kinsey's attack 104–5
    tolerance and understanding 105–8
Shaw, Clifford 57, 66, 72, 75, 90, 108
Shirley, M. 118
Short, F. Ivan 108–14
Singer, Peter 175
Skinner, Quentin 8, 10, 12, 13–14, 18
Small, Albion W. 57
social constructs 83, 118, 154, 164
  crime statistics as 83
  intellectual traditions as 118
  politically useful 154
  scientific findings not merely 164
social control 4, 15–16, 32, 47
  normalization and 165
  random operation 83, 93
social desirability measures 67, 111, 120
Social Gospel 56–7, 87–90, 109, 168
social gradient 116, 117
social influence 170–1
social interactionism 114
social pathology 37–8, 80–1, 91
social satire 9, 30, 46–7, 52, 55, 93, 120, 148, 155, 167, 169
  Porterfield's social satire 86–7, 106–7, 147, 154
  Social Gospel and 88, 89
social structures 98, 123
social surveys 62–3, 162
social vocabulary 19
socio-economic groups *see* class phenomena; white-collar criminals
sociology 3
  'Americanization' 109, 126, 129–30
  Chicago School 71–2
  disciplinary warfare 119, 120, 122, 160, 166–7
  influence of religion 57, 58n
sociopathy 136
Socrates 32, 53, 91
Stangeland, P. 131, 134, 135, 140, 143
state crime 88
state institutions 7, 163

statistical fatalism 31
statistics 3, 4, 11, 40, 43–4
  alternative sources 60–1, 98–9
  Can Delinquency Be Measured? (Robison) 73–5
  see also moral statistics; offical control barrier
Stouffer, Samuel 75, 79
suicide 33n
Sumner, F.C. 84–5
surveys
  diffusion of the survey method to new topics 161–2
  Du Bois survey in Atlanta 63–4
  preconditions of survey penetration 163–4
  social surveys 62–3, 162
  United States Strategic Bombing Survey 109–10
  victimization surveys 1, 172–5
  see also crime surveys
Sutherland, Edwin 4, 9, 37, 38, 44, 54, 65, 66, 70, 91
  analysis of white-collar crime 60–2, 81–2, 89, 90, 147, 166
  experiments in the 1930s 78–9
    context 80–2
    self-reports 79–80
  opposition to psychiatric and psychological explanations 135
  place in the hidden crime survey canon 118, 119, 159
Sveri, Knut 133, 141, 143
Sweden 2, 128, 129, 133, 135, 136, 143, 151
  victimization surveys 172, 173, 174
Sykes, Gresham 18, 170

Tarde, Gabriel 32–3
Taylor, Charles 160
theft 1
Thomas, William I. 57
Thorndike, Edward Lee 68
Thue, Fredrik 147
Törnudd, Patrik 141, 145–6, 148, 150, 158
treatment ideology 42, 66, 97n, 132, 136
Tschlenoff (first name unknown) 49

underclass 15
United State Strategic Bombing Survey 109–10
unrecorded crime *see* hidden crime

Verkko, Veli 44–5
versatility 99, 139
victimization surveys 1, 172–5
violence against women 172–5

Wallerstein, James S. 91–2
 canonization 118, 119
 critique of abnormality paradigm 94–5
 Randen Foundation crime survey 92–3, 166
Ward, Lester 38
Weber, Max 14
Werner, Birgit 133, 138, 143
West, Donald J. 124, 151

white-collar criminals 9, 14–15, 55–6
 analysis
  progressive and religious critiques in American sociology 56–8, 66
 Randen Foundation crime survey 93
 Ross 58–60, 89
 Sutherland 60–2, 81–2, 89
 covert offenders 59
 criminaloids 59, 89
 evasion of detection 58
Willcock, H.D. 45–6, 125
Witmer, Helen 102, 118
Wyle, Clement J. 92, 94
 canonization 118, 119

zero-tolerance 74
Zola, Émile 47

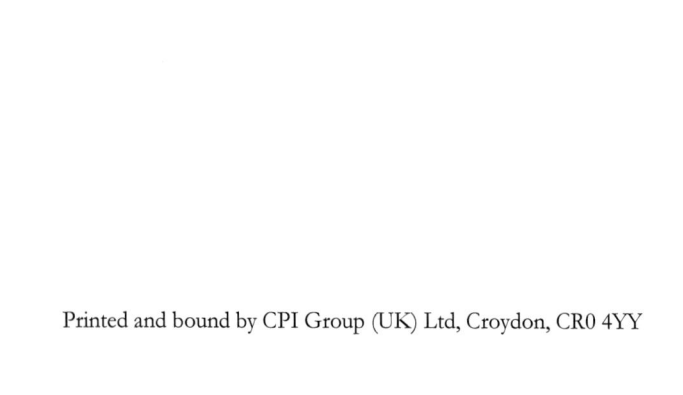

Printed and bound by CPI Group (UK) Ltd, Croydon, CR0 4YY